Unity 2022 Mobile Game Development

Third Edition

Build and publish engaging games for Android and iOS

John P. Doran

BIRMINGHAM—MUMBAI

Unity 2022 Mobile Game Development
Third Edition

Group Product Manager: Rohit Rajkumar
Publishing Product Manager: Nitin Nainani
Senior Editor: Mark D'Souza
Senior Content Development Editor: Feza Shaikh
Technical Editor: Simran Ali
Copy Editor: Safis Editing
Project Coordinator: Sonam Pandey
Proofreader: Safis Editing
Indexer: Manju Arasan
Production Designer: Vijay Kamble
Marketing Coordinator: Anamika Singh, Namita Velgekar, and Nivedita Pandey

First published: November 2017
Second edition: August 2020
Third edition: July 2023

Production reference:160623

Published by Packt Publishing Ltd.
Livery Place
35 Livery Street
Birmingham
B3 2PB, UK.

ISBN 978-1-80461-372-6

www.packtpub.com

To my wife, Hien, who, has always believed in me and has supported me every step of the way as we've traveled all around the world. And to my precious daughter, Johanna, who's inspired me with her boundless imagination and sense of wonder. This book is dedicated to you both with all my love and gratitude.

– John P. Doran

Contributors

About the author

John P. Doran is a passionate and seasoned technical game designer, software engineer, and author who is based in Songdo, South Korea. His passion for game development began at an early age. He later graduated from DigiPen Institute of Technology with a bachelor of science in game design and a master of science in computer science from Bradley University.

For over a decade, John has gained extensive hands-on expertise in game development, working in various roles ranging from game designer to lead user interface (UI) programmer, working in teams consisting of just himself to over 70 people in student, mod, and professional game projects, including working at LucasArts on *Star Wars: 1313*. Additionally, John has worked in game development education, teaching in Singapore, South Korea, and the US. To date, he has authored 17 books pertaining to game development and is a 2023 Unity Education Ambassador.

John is currently an instructor at George Mason University Korea. Prior to his present ventures, he was an award-winning videographer.

Learn more about John at `http://johnpdoran.com`.

I extend my deepest gratitude to the Packt Publishing team, including Mark D'Souza, Feza Shaikh, Sonam Pandey, and Nitin Nainani, for their invaluable support, expertise, and guidance in bringing this new edition of the book to life.

About the reviewers

Shubham Thakur is a full stack developer at Ceryx Digital in Pune. Proficient in JavaScript, PHP, and Flutter, he has worked on cutting-edge projects involving the **Internet of Things** (**IoT**), metaverse, **augmented reality** (**AR**), **virtual reality** (**VR**), and cloud computing using AWS. Shubham volunteers with Google Developer Groups Pune, has won various hackathons, and is learning Solidity for Web3. He's a team player, collaborator, and effective communicator who is committed to delivering high-quality solutions on time and within budget.

I am deeply grateful to Priya for the unwavering support, boundless love, and endless inspiration she brings daily. Yash, thank you for always being there. Amit Jain, thank you for your exceptional mentorship. Thanks to Packt Publishing for the reviewer opportunity. Special thanks to Urvi Sambhav Shah for onboarding me and to Sonam Pandey for her invaluable assistance and guidance during the reviewing process.

David Cantón Nadales is a software engineer from Seville, Spain, with more than 20 years of experience. He is currently a technical leader at Grupo Viajes El Corte Inglés, a leading travel company in Europe. He has done a multitude of projects and games with Unity, VR with Oculus/Meta Quest 2, Hololens, HTC Vive, DayDream, and LeapMotion. He was an ambassador of the Samsung community "Samsung Dev Spain," and organizer of "Google Developers Group Sevilla." He has led more than 100 projects throughout his career. As a social entrepreneur he created the app "Grita", a social network that emerged during the confinement of COVID-19 that allowed people to talk to other people and help each other psychologically. In 2022, he won the Top Developer Award organized by Samsung.

Table of Contents

Part 2: Mobile-Specific Features

3

Mobile Input/Touch Controls   91

4

Resolution-Independent UI   141

5

Advanced Mobile UI   181

6

Implementing In-App Purchases   201

7

Advertising Using Unity Ads   219

8

Integrating Social Media into Our Project   249

Part 3: Game Feel/Polish

9

Keeping Players Involved with Notifications   287

14

15

Preface

As a game developer, your goal is to reach your customers where they are, and with more and more people purchasing mobile devices every year, mobile is a crucial platform to consider. Luckily, Unity offers cross-platform capabilities, allowing you to write your game once and then port it to other consoles with minimal changes. However, developing for mobile devices also requires specific considerations and features, which is where *Unity 2022 Mobile Game Development* comes in.

In this book, we'll guide you through the process of using Unity to create and deploy a mobile game to both iOS and Android. We'll cover essential topics such as adding input for mobile devices, designing interfaces that adapt to various screen sizes, and exploring ways to monetize your game with Unity's **In-App Purchase (IAP)** and advertisement systems. We'll also discuss the importance of using notifications to retain users and share your game with the world using Twitter and Facebook's SDKs.

Additionally, we'll delve into Unity's analytics system to optimize your game's performance and provide insights into user behavior. You'll also learn how to polish your game in various ways before publishing it on the Google Play and iOS app stores.

Lastly, we'll cover the use of Unity's AR Foundation framework, which enables you to create **Augmented Reality (AR)** apps that are future-proof and compatible with multiple devices.

By the end of this book, you'll have a solid understanding of how to use Unity for mobile game development, including crucial features unique to mobile devices.

Who this book is for

If you're a Unity game developer interested in building mobile games for iOS and Android, then this book is an ideal resource for you. Although prior knowledge of C# is helpful, it is not required. Whether you're a seasoned developer or just starting out, the step-by-step guidance provided in this book will help you understand the unique features and considerations necessary for mobile game development using Unity.

What this book covers

Chapter 1, Building Your Game, introduces the basics of Unity game development by creating a simple project that will be modified throughout the book to incorporate mobile-specific features.

Chapter 2, Project Setup for Android and iOS Development, explains the process of configuring your development environment for deploying your game to both Android and iOS mobile devices.

Chapter 3, Mobile Input/Touch Controls, teaches you the fundamentals of mobile input, covering touch and gesture recognition, using the accelerometer, and accessing device information through the Touch class.

Chapter 4, Resolution-Independent UI, focuses on how to build resolution-independent UI elements, which are useful for all game projects that utilize different aspect ratios and resolutions.

Chapter 5, Advanced Mobile UI, builds upon the knowledge from the previous chapter, expanding to include mobile-specific aspects of working on a UI, such as requiring on-screen controls and adapting the UI to fit devices with notches.

Chapter 6, Implementing In-App Purchases, explains how to integrate Unity's IAP system into our project, including the creation of both consumable and non-consumable IAPs.

Chapter 7, Advertising Using Unity Ads, covers the integration of Unity's ad framework into our project and explores the creation of both simple and complex advertisements.

Chapter 8, Integrating Social Media into Our Project, shows how to integrate social media into your game by incorporating features such as sharing high scores on Twitter and using the Facebook SDK to log in and display a player's name and profile picture.

Chapter 9, Keeping Players Involved with Notifications, demonstrates the integration of notifications into your game, including their setup, creating basic notifications, and customizing how they are presented.

Chapter 10, Using Unity Analytics, covers integrating Unity's analytics tools into your game, including tracking custom events and using remote settings to modify gameplay without requiring players to redownload the game.

Chapter 11, Remote Config, will show just how easy it is to set up Unity's Remote Config system, and how we can utilize it for a simple example by changing the difficulty of our game by changing the speed at which the player moves.

Chapter 12, Improving Game Feel, introduces the concept of "game feel" in game design and explores how to integrate tweening animations, materials, postprocessing effects, and particle effects to enhance the player experience.

Chapter 13, Building a Release Copy of Our Game, walks you through the steps required to build a release copy of your game for both iOS and Android devices.

Chapter 14, Submitting Games to App Stores, provides tips and tricks for submitting your game to the Google Play and iOS app stores.

Chapter 15, Augmented Reality, covers the process of adding AR to your game, including the setup, installation, and configuration of ARCore, ARKit, and AR Foundation, detecting surfaces in the real world, and interacting with the environment through spawning objects.

To get the most out of this book

Throughout this book, we will work within the Unity 3D game engine, which you can download from `https://unity.com/download`. The projects were created using Unity 2022.1.0b16, but minimal changes should be required if you're using future versions of the engine. If there is a new version out and you would like to download the exact version used in this book, you can visit Unity's download archive at `https://unity3d.com/get-unity/download/archive`. You can also find the system requirements for Unity at `https://docs.unity3d.com/2022.1/Documentation/Manual/system-requirements.html` in the Unity Editor system requirements section. To deploy your project, you will need an Android or iOS device.

For the sake of simplicity, we will assume that you are working on a Windows-powered computer when developing for Android and a Macintosh computer when developing for iOS.

Software/hardware covered in the book	Operating system requirements
Unity 2022.1.0b16	Windows, macOS, or Linux
Unity Hub 3.3.1	Windows, macOS, or Linux

If you are using the digital version of this book, we advise you to type the code yourself or access the code from the book's GitHub repository (a link is available in the next section). Doing so will help you avoid any potential errors related to the copying and pasting of code.

Download the example code files

You can download the example code files for this book from GitHub at `https://github.com/PacktPublishing/Unity-2022-Mobile-Game-Development-3rd-Edition`. If there's an update to the code, it will be updated in the GitHub repository.

We also have other code bundles from our rich catalog of books and videos available at `https://github.com/PacktPublishing/`. Check them out!

Download the color images

We also provide a PDF file that has color images of the screenshots and diagrams used in this book. You can download it here: `https://packt.link/6M4wR`.

Conventions used

There are a number of text conventions used throughout this book.

`Code in text`: Indicates code words in text, database table names, folder names, filenames, file extensions, pathnames, dummy URLs, user input, and Twitter handles. Here is an example: "This gives us the code needed – in particular, the `GameNotificationManager` class – to be added to our script."

A block of code is set as follows:

```
public void ShowNotification(string title, string body,
                             DateTime deliveryTime)
{
    IGameNotification notification =
    notificationsManager.CreateNotification();

    if (notification != null)
    {
        notification.Title = title;
        notification.Body = body;
        notification.DeliveryTime = deliveryTime;
        notification.SmallIcon = "icon_0";
        notification.LargeIcon = "icon_1";


        notificationsManager.ScheduleNotification(notification);
    }
}
```

When we wish to draw your attention to a particular part of a code block, the relevant lines or items are set in bold:

```
ShowNotification("Endless Runner", notifText, notifTime);

        // Example of cancelling a notification
        var id = ShowNotification("Test", "Should Not Happen",
            notifTime);

        if(id.HasValue)
        {
            notificationsManager.CancelNotification(id.Value);
        }
```

```
        /* Cannot be added again until the user quits game */
        addedReminder = true;
    }

}
```

Any command-line input or output is written as follows:

```
$ mkdir css
$ cd css
```

Bold: Indicates a new term, an important word, or words that you see onscreen. For instance, words in menus or dialog boxes appear in **bold**. Here is an example: "Open the **Project Settings** menu by going to **Edit | Project Settings**."

Tips or important notes
Appear like this.

Get in touch

Feedback from our readers is always welcome.

General feedback: If you have questions about any aspect of this book, email us at customercare@ packtpub.com and mention the book title in the subject of your message.

Errata: Although we have taken every care to ensure the accuracy of our content, mistakes do happen. If you have found a mistake in this book, we would be grateful if you would report this to us. Please visit www.packtpub.com/support/errata and fill in the form.

Piracy: If you come across any illegal copies of our works in any form on the internet, we would be grateful if you would provide us with the location address or website name. Please contact us at copyright@packt.com with a link to the material.

If you are interested in becoming an author: If there is a topic that you have expertise in and you are interested in either writing or contributing to a book, please visit authors.packtpub.com.

Share Your Thoughts

Once you've read, we'd love to hear your thoughts! Scan the QR code below to go straight to the Amazon review page for this book and share your feedback.

https://packt.link/r/180461372X

Your review is important to us and the tech community and will help us make sure we're delivering excellent quality content.

Download a free PDF copy of this book

Thanks for purchasing this book!

Do you like to read on the go but are unable to carry your print books everywhere?

Is your eBook purchase not compatible with the device of your choice?

Don't worry, now with every Packt book you get a DRM-free PDF version of that book at no cost.

Read anywhere, any place, on any device. Search, copy, and paste code from your favorite technical books directly into your application.

The perks don't stop there, you can get exclusive access to discounts, newsletters, and great free content in your inbox daily

Follow these simple steps to get the benefits:

1. Scan the QR code or visit the link below

https://packt.link/free-ebook/9781804613726

2. Submit your proof of purchase
3. That's it! We'll send your free PDF and other benefits to your email directly

Part 1: Gameplay/Development Setup

In this part of the book, we will be exploring the foundational elements of Unity game development, specifically with a focus on preparation for creating mobile games. The chapters in this part will provide you with the necessary knowledge and skills to set up your development environment, as well as guide you through the process of building a game project and deploying it to a mobile device.

By the end of this part, you will have a solid foundation of knowledge about Unity game development and will be ready to move on to the more advanced topics covered in subsequent parts of the book.

This part has the following chapters:

- *Chapter 1, Building Your Game*
- *Chapter 2, Project Setup for Android and iOS Development*

1

Building Your Game

As we start on our journey of building mobile games using the Unity game engine, it's important that you are familiar with the engine itself before we dive into the specifics of building things for mobile platforms. Although there is a chance that you've already built a game and want to transition it to mobile, there will also be those of you who haven't touched **Unity** before or may not have used it in a long time. This chapter will act as an introduction to newcomers and a refresher for those coming back, and it will provide some best practices for those who are already familiar with Unity. While you may skip this chapter if you're already familiar with Unity, I think it's also a good idea to go through the project so that you know the thought processes behind why the project is made in the way that it is, so that you can keep it in mind for your own future titles.

In this chapter, we will build a 3D endless runner game in the same vein as *Imangi Studios LLC's Temple Run* series. In our case, we will have a player who will run continuously in a certain direction and dodge the obstacles that are in their way. We can also add additional features to the game easily, as the game will endlessly have new things added to it.

This chapter will be split into several topics. It will contain simple, step-by-step processes for you to follow. Here is an outline of our tasks:

- Setting up the project
- Creating the player
- Moving the player through a C# script
- Improving scripts using attributes and XML comments
- Update function versus FixedUpdate function
- Having the camera follow our player
- Creating a basic tile
- Making the game endless
- Creating obstacles

Technical requirements

This book utilizes *Unity 2022.1.0b14* and *Unity Hub 3.3.1*, but the steps should work with minimal changes in future versions of the editor. If you would like to download the exact version used in this book, and there is a new version out, you can visit Unity's download archive at https://unity3d.com/get-unity/download/archive.

You can also find the system requirements for Unity at https://docs.unity3d.com/2022.1/Documentation/Manual/system-requirements.html in the *Unity Editor system requirements* section.

You can find the code files for this chapter on GitHub at https://github.com/PacktPublishing/Unity-2022-Mobile-Game-Development-3rd-Edition/tree/main/Chapter01.

Setting up the project

Now that we have our goals in mind, let's start building our project:

1. To get started, open Unity Hub on your computer.

2. From startup, we'll opt to create a new project by clicking on the **New** button.

3. Next, under **Project Name**, put in a name (I have chosen MobileDev), and under **Templates**, make sure that **3D** is selected. Afterward, click on **CREATE** and wait for Unity to load up:

Figure 1.1 – Creating a 3D project

4. After it's finished, you'll see the Unity Editor pop up for the first time:

Figure 1.2 – The Unity Editor

5. If your layout doesn't look the same as in the preceding screenshot, go to the top-right section of the toolbar and select the drop-down menu there that reads **Layout**. From there, select **Default** from the options presented:

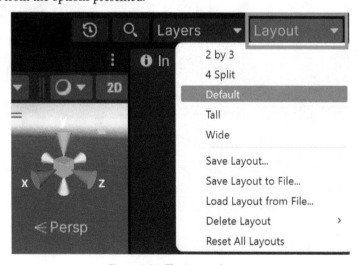

Figure 1.3 – The Layout button

We now have opened Unity for the first time and have the default layout displayed!

> **Tip**
> If this is your first time working with Unity, then I highly recommend that you read the *Unity's interface* section of the *Unity Manual*, which you can access at https://docs.unity3d.com/Manual/UsingTheEditor.html.

Now that we have Unity open, we can actually start building our project.

Creating the player

To get started, we'll build a player that will always move forward. Let's start with that now:

1. To get started, we will create some ground for our player to walk on. To do that, go to the top menu and select **GameObject | 3D Object | Cube**.

2. From there, we'll move over to the **Inspector** window and change the name of the object to Floor. Then, for the **Transform** component, set **Position** to (0, 0, 0). This can be done by either typing the values in or right-clicking on the **Transform** component and then selecting the **Reset Position** option.

3. Then, we will set the **Scale** values of the object to (7, 0.1, 10):

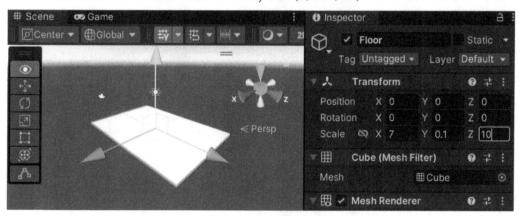

Figure 1.4 – Creating the ground

In Unity, by default, 1 unit of space is representative of 1 meter in real life. So, our **Scale** values will make the floor longer than it is wide (**X** and **Z**), and we have some size on the ground (**Y**), so the player will collide and land on it because we have a **Box Collider** component attached to it by default.

> **Note**
>
> The **Box Collider** component is added automatically when creating a **Cube** object and is required to have objects collide with it. For more information on the **Box Collider** component, check out `https://docs.unity3d.com/Manual/class-BoxCollider.html`.

4. Next, we will create our player, which will be a sphere. To do this, we will go to **GameObject | 3D Object | Sphere**.

5. Rename the sphere to `Player` and set the **Transform** component's **Position** values to (0, 1, -4):

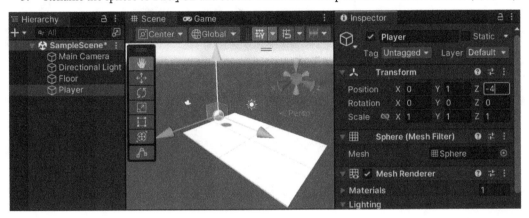

Figure 1.5 – Positioning the player

This places the ball slightly above the ground and shifts it back to near the starting point. Note that the camera object (see the camera icon) is pointing toward the ball by default because it is positioned at (0, 1, -10).

6. We want the ball to move, so we will need to tell the physics engine that we want to have this object react to forces, so we will need to add a **Rigidbody** component. To do so, with the **Player** object selected, go to the menu and select **Component | Physics | Rigidbody**. To see what happens now, let's click on the **Play** button, which can be seen in the middle of the first toolbar:

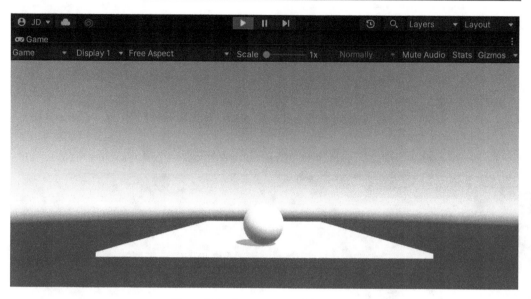

Figure 1.6 – Current state of the game

As in the preceding screenshot, you should see the ball fall down onto the ground when we play the game.

> **Tip**
>
> You can disable/enable having the **Game** tab take up the entire screen when being played by clicking on the **Maximize On Play** button at the top, or by right-clicking on the **Game** tab and then selecting **Maximize**.

7. Click on the **Play** button again to turn the game off and go back to the **Scene** tab, if it doesn't happen automatically.

We now have the objects for both the floor and the player in the game and have told the player to react to physics! Next, we will add interactivity to the player through the use of code.

Moving the player through a C# script

We want the player to move, so in order to do that, we will create our own piece of functionality in a script, effectively creating our own custom component in the process:

1. To create a script, we will go to the **Project** window and select the **Create** button in the top-left corner of the menu by clicking on the + icon, and then we will select **Folder**:

Figure 1.7 – Location of the + icon

> **Tip**
>
> You can also access the **Create** menu by right-clicking on the right-hand side of the **Project** window. With this method, you can right-click and then select **Create | Folder**.

2. From there, we'll name this folder `Scripts`. It's always a good idea to organize our projects, so this will help with that.

> **Tip**
>
> If you happen to misspell the name of an item in the **Project** window, you can rename it by either right-clicking and selecting the **Rename** option or selecting the object and then single-clicking on the name.

3. Double-click on the folder to enter it, create a script by going to **Create | C# Script**, and rename the newly created item to `PlayerBehaviour` (no spaces).

> **Note**
>
> The reason I'm using the *behaviour* spelling instead of *behavior* is that all components in Unity are children of another class called `MonoBehaviour`, and I'm following Unity's lead in that regard.

4. Double-click on the script to open up the script editor (IDE) of your choice and add the following code to it:

```csharp
using UnityEngine;

public class PlayerBehaviour : MonoBehaviour
{
```

```csharp
// A reference to the Rigidbody component
private Rigidbody rb;

// How fast the ball moves left/right
public float dodgeSpeed = 5;

// How fast the ball moves forward  automatically
public float rollSpeed = 5;

// Start is called before the first frame update
void Start()
{
    // Get access to our Rigidbody component
    rb = GetComponent<Rigidbody>();
}

// Update is called once per frame
void Update()
{
    // Check if we're moving to the side
    var horizontalSpeed =
        Input.GetAxis("Horizontal") * dodgeSpeed;

    rb.AddForce(horizontalSpeed, 0, rollSpeed);

}
}
```

In the preceding code, we have a couple of variables that we will be working with. The rb variable is a reference to the GameObject's Rigidbody component that we added previously. It gives us the ability to make the object move, which we will use in the Update function. We also have two variables, dodgeSpeed and rollSpeed, which dictate how quickly the player will move when moving left/right or when moving forward, respectively.

Since our object has only one Rigidbody component, we assign rb once in the Start function, which is called when the GameObject is loaded into the scene at the beginning of the game.

Then, we use the Update function to check whether our player is pressing keys to move left or right based on Unity's **Input Manager** system. By default, the Input.GetAxis function will return to us a negative value, moving to -1 if we press *A* or the left arrow. If we press the right arrow or *D*, we will get a positive value up to 1 returned to us, and the input will move toward 0 if nothing is pressed. We then multiply this by dodgeSpeed in order to increase the speed so that the movement of the object is easier to see.

> **Note**
>
> For more information on the Input Manager, check out `https://docs.unity3d.com/Manual/class-InputManager.html`.

Finally, once we have that value, we will apply a force to our ball's `horizontalSpeed` units on the *X* axis and `rollSpeed` on the *Z* axis.

5. Save your script and return to the Unity Editor.

6. We will now need to assign this script to our player by selecting the `Player` object in the **Hierarchy** window, and then in the **Inspector** window, we will drag and drop the `PlayerBehaviour` script from the **Project** window to be on top of the `Player` object.

> **Note**
>
> Note that when writing scripts, if we declare a variable as `public`, it will show up in the **Inspector** window for us to be able to set it. We typically set a variable as `public` when we want designers to tweak the values for gameplay purposes, but it also allows other scripts to access the property in code. By default, variables and methods are `private`, which means they can only be used within the class. For more information on access modifiers, check out `https://docs.microsoft.com/en-us/dotnet/csharp/language-reference/keywords/access-modifiers`.

If all goes well, we should see the script appear on our object, as follows:

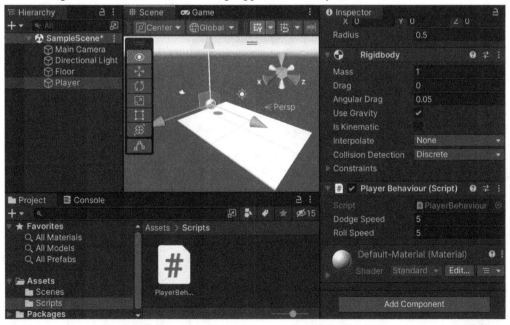

Figure 1.8 – The PlayerBehaviour component added

7. Save your scene by going to **File | Save**. Afterward, play the game and use the left and right arrows to see the player moving according to your input, but no matter what, moving forward by default:

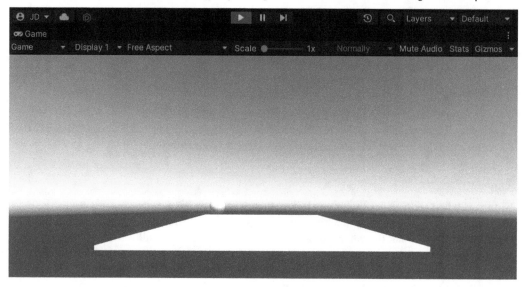

Figure 1.9 – The current state of the game

Now you can see that the ball moves automatically, and our input is received correctly!

Improving our scripts with attributes and XML comments

We could stop working with the `PlayerBehaviour` class script here, but I want to touch on a couple of things that we can use in order to improve the quality and style of our code. This becomes especially useful when you start building projects in teams. As you'll be working with other people, some of them will be working on code with you. Then, there will be designers and artists who will not be working on code with you but will still need to use the things that you've programmed.

When writing scripts, we want them to be as error-proof as possible. Making the `rb` variable `private` starts that process, as now the user will not be able to modify that anywhere outside of this class. We want our teammates to modify `dodgeSpeed` and `rollSpeed`, but we may want to give them some advice as to what it is and/or how it will be used. To do this in the **Inspector** window, we can make use of something called an **attribute**.

Using attributes

Attributes are things we can add to the beginning of a variable, class, or function declaration, which allow us to attach additional functionality to them. There are many of them that exist inside Unity, and you can write your very own attributes as well, but right now, we'll talk about the ones that I use most often.

The Tooltip attribute

If you've used Unity for a period of time, you may have noted that some components in the **Inspector** window, such as `Rigidbody`, have a nice feature—if you move your mouse over a variable name, you'll see a description of what the variables are and/or how to use them. The first thing you'll learn is how we can get the same effect in our own components by making use of the `Tooltip` attribute. If we do this for the `dodgeSpeed` and `rollSpeed` variables, it will look something like this:

```
[Tooltip("How fast the ball moves left/right")]
public float dodgeSpeed = 5;

[Tooltip("How fast the ball moves forward  automatically")]
public float rollSpeed = 5;
```

Save the preceding script and return to the editor:

Figure 1.10 – Tooltip attribute example

Now, when we highlight the variable using the mouse and leave it there, the text we placed will be displayed. This is a great habit to get into, as your teammates can always tell what it is that your variables are being used for without having to actually look at the script itself.

> **Note**
> For more information on the `Tooltip` attribute, check out `https://docs.unity3d.com/ScriptReference/TooltipAttribute.html`.

The Range attribute

Another thing that we can use to protect our code is the `Range` attribute. This will allow us to specify a minimum and maximum value for a variable. Since we want the player to always be moving forward, we may want to restrict the player from moving backward. To do that, we can add the following highlighted line of code:

```
[Tooltip("How fast the ball moves forward  automatically")]
[Range(0, 10)]
public float rollSpeed = 5;
```

Save your script, and return to the editor:

Figure 1.11 – Range attribute example

We have now added a slider beside our value, and we can drag it to adjust between our minimum and maximum values. Not only does this protect our variable from being changed to an invalid state but also makes it so that our designers can tweak things easily by just dragging them around.

The RequireComponent attribute

Currently, we are using the Rigidbody component in order to create our script. When working as a team member, others may not be reading your scripts but are still expected to use them when creating gameplay. Unfortunately, this means that they may do things that have unintended results, such as removing the Rigidbody component, which will cause errors when our script is run. Thankfully, we also have the RequireComponent attribute, which we can use to fix this.

It looks something like this:

```
using UnityEngine;

[RequireComponent(typeof(Rigidbody))]
public class PlayerBehaviour : MonoBehaviour
```

By adding this attribute, we state that when we include this component in a GameObject and it doesn't have a Rigidbody component attached to its GameObject, the component will be added automatically. It also makes it so that if we were to try to remove the Rigidbody component from this object, the editor will warn us that we can't, unless we remove the PlayerBehaviour component first. Note that this works for any class extended from MonoBehaviour; just replace Rigidbody with whatever it is that you wish to keep.

Now, if we go into the Unity Editor and try to remove the Rigidbody component by right-clicking on it in **Inspector** and selecting **Remove Component**, the following message will be seen:

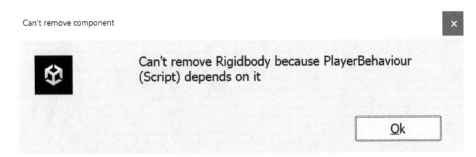

Figure 1.12 – Can't remove component window

This is exactly what we want, and this ensures that the component will be there, allowing us not to have to include `if` checks every time we want to use a component.

Note that, previously, we did not use a `Tooltip` attribute on the private `rb` variable. Since it's not being displayed in the editor, it's not really needed. However, there is a way that we can enhance that as well: using XML comments.

XML comments

We can achieve a couple of nice things with XML comments that we otherwise couldn't with traditional comments, which we were using previously. When using variables/functions instead of code in Visual Studio, we will now see a comment about it. This will help other coders on your team with additional information and details to ensure that they are using your code correctly.

XML comments look something like this:

```
/// <summary>
/// A reference to the Rigidbody component
/// </summary>
private Rigidbody rb;
```

It may appear that a lot more writing is needed to use this format, but I did not actually type the entire thing out. XML comments are a fairly standard C# feature, so if you are using MonoDevelop or Visual Studio and type `///`, the action will automatically generate the summary blocks for you (and the `param` tags needed, if there are parameters needed for something such as a function).

Now, why would we want to do this? Well, if you select the variable in IntelliSense, it will display the following information to us:

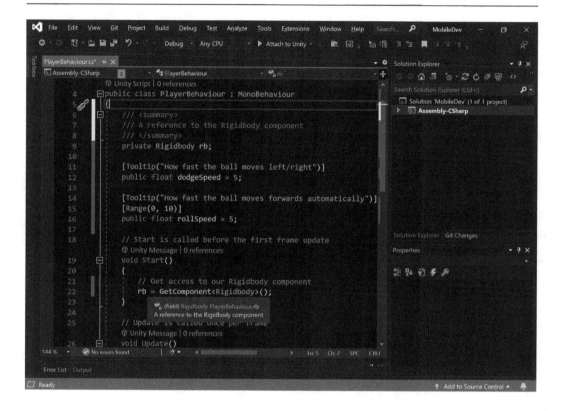

Figure 1.13 – An example of tooltips from XML comments

This is a great help when other people are trying to use your code and it is how Unity's staff write their code. We can also extend this to functions and classes to ensure that our code is more self-documented.

Unfortunately, XML comments do not show up in the Inspector, and the `Tooltip` attribute can't be used for some aspects of projects such as functions. With that in mind, I use `Tooltip` for public instructions and/or things that will show up in the **Inspector** window and XML comments for everything else.

> **Note**
>
> If you're interested in looking into XML comments more, feel free to check out `https://msdn.microsoft.com/en-us/library/b2s063f7.aspx`.

Now that we have looked at ways of improving the formatting of our code; let's look at how we can improve the performance by looking at some of the different `Update` functions Unity provides.

Update function versus FixedUpdate function

The next thing to look at is our movement code. You may have noticed that we are currently using the Update function in order to move our player. As the comment above it states, the Update function is called once per frame that the game is running. One thing to consider is that the frequency of Update being called is variable, meaning that it can change over time. This is dependent on a number of factors, including the hardware that is being used. This means that the more times the Update function is called, the better the computer is. We want a consistent experience for all of our players, and one of the ways that we can do that is by using the FixedUpdate function.

FixedUpdate is similar to Update with some key differences. The first is that it is called at fixed timesteps, meaning the same time between calls. It's also important to note that physics calculations are done after FixedUpdate is called. This means code-modifying physics-based objects should be executed within the FixedUpdate function generally, apart from one-off events such as jumping:

```
/// <summary>
/// FixedUpdate is a prime place to put physics
/// calculations happening over a period of time.
/// </summary>

void FixedUpdate()
{
    // Check if we're moving to the side
    var horizontalSpeed = Input.GetAxis("Horizontal") *
                            dodgeSpeed;

    rb.AddForce(horizontalSpeed, 0, rollSpeed);

}
```

By adjusting the code to use FixedUpdate, the ball should be much more consistent in its movement speed.

Note

For more information on FixedUpdate, check out https://docs.unity3d.com/ScriptReference/MonoBehaviour.FixedUpdate.html.

Putting it all together

With all of the stuff we've been talking about, we can now have the final version of the script, which looks like the following:

```csharp
using UnityEngine;

/// <summary>
/// Responsible for moving the player automatically and
/// receiving input.
/// </summary>
[RequireComponent(typeof(Rigidbody))]
public class PlayerBehaviour : MonoBehaviour
{
    /// <summary>
    /// A reference to the Rigidbody component
    /// </summary>
    private Rigidbody rb;

    [Tooltip("How fast the ball moves left/right")]
    public float dodgeSpeed = 5;

    [Tooltip("How fast the ball moves
        forward  automatically")]
    [Range(0, 10)]
    public float rollSpeed = 5;

    // Start is called before the first frame update
    public void Start()
    {
        // Get access to our Rigidbody component
        rb = GetComponent<Rigidbody>();
    }

    /// <summary>
    /// FixedUpdate is a prime place to put physics
    /// calculations happening over a period of time.
    /// </summary>

    void FixedUpdate()
    {
        // Check if we're moving to the side
        var horizontalSpeed = Input.GetAxis("Horizontal") *
                            dodgeSpeed;
```

```
        rb.AddForce(horizontalSpeed, 0, rollSpeed);

    }
}
```

I hope that you also agree that this makes the code easier to understand and better to work with. Now, we can move on to additional features in the game!

Having the camera following our player

Currently, our camera stays in the same spot while the game is going on. This does not work very well for this game, as the player will be moving while the game is going on. There are two main ways that we can move our camera. We can just move the camera and make it a child of the player, but that will not work due to the fact that the camera would have the same rotation as the ball, which would cause the camera to spin around constantly and likely cause dizziness and disorientation for the players. Due to that, we will likely want to use a script to move it instead. Thankfully, we can modify how our camera looks at things fairly easily, so let's go ahead and fix that next:

1. Go to the Project window and create a new C# script called CameraBehaviour. From there, use the following code:

```
using UnityEngine;

/// <summary>
/// Will adjust the camera to follow and face a target
/// </summary>
public class CameraBehaviour : MonoBehaviour
{
    [Tooltip("What object should the camera be looking
        at")]
    public Transform target;

    [Tooltip("How offset will the camera be to the
        target")]
    public Vector3 offset = new Vector3(0, 3, -6);

    /// <summary>
    /// Update is called once per frame
    /// </summary>
    private void Update()
    {
        // Check if target is a valid object
        if (target != null)
```

```
        {
            // Set our position to an offset of our
            // target
            transform.position = target.position +
                offset;

            // Change the rotation to face target
            transform.LookAt(target);
        }
    }
}
```

This script will set the position of the object it is attached to to the position of a target with an offset. Afterward, it will change the rotation of the object to face the target. Both of the parameters are marked as `public`, so they can be tweaked in the **Inspector** window.

2. Save the script and dive back into the Unity Editor. Select the **Main Camera** object in the **Hierarchy** window. Then, go to the **Inspector** window and add the `CameraBehaviour` component to it. You may do this by dragging and dropping the script from the **Project** window onto the GameObject or by clicking on the **Add Component** button at the bottom of the **Inspector** window, typing in the name of our component, and then hitting *Enter* to confirm once it is highlighted.

3. Afterward, drag and drop the `Player` object from the **Hierarchy** window into the **Target** property of the script in the **Inspector** window:

Figure 1.14 – CameraBehaviour component setup

4.   Save the scene and play the game:

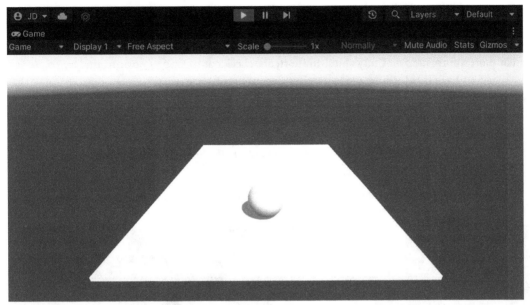

Figure 1.15 – The current state of the game

The camera now follows the player as it moves. Feel free to tweak the variables and see how it affects the look of the camera to get the feeling you'd like best for the project. After this, we can have a place for the ball to move toward, which we will be covering in the next section.

Creating a basic tile

We want our game to be endless, but in order to achieve that, we will need to have pieces that we can spawn to build our environment; let's do that now:

1.   To get started, we will first need to create a single repeatable piece for our runner game. To do that, we'll add some walls to the floor we already have. From the **Hierarchy** window, select the **Floor** object and duplicate it by pressing *Ctrl + D* in Windows or *Command + D* on macOS. Rename this new object Left Wall.

2.   Change the **Left Wall** object's **Transform** component by adjusting the **Scale** values to (1, 2, 10). From there, select the **Move** tool by clicking on the button with arrows on the tools overlay or by pressing the *W* key.

> **Note**
>
> A recent addition to Unity is the concept of **Overlays**, which have replaced the original toolbar. For more information about them and how to use them, check out `https://docs.unity3d.com/2022.1/Documentation/Manual/overlays.html`.
>
> For more information on Unity's built-in shortcuts, check out `https://docs.unity3d.com/Manual/UnityHotkeys.html`.

3.   We want this wall to match up with the floor, so hold down the *V* key to enter *Vertex Snap* mode. In Vertex Snap mode, we can select any of the vertices on a mesh and move them to the same position as another vertex on a different object. This is really useful for making sure that objects don't have holes between them.

4.   With Vertex Snap mode on, select the inner edge and drag it until it hits the edge of the floor. Alternatively, you can set the **Position** values to (3, 0.95, 0):

Figure 1.16 – Left Wall setup

> **Note**
>
> For more information on moving objects through the scene, including more details on Vertex Snap mode, check out `https://docs.unity3d.com/Manual/PositioningGameObjects.html`.

5.   Then, duplicate this wall and put the other object on the other side (-3, 0.95, 0), naming it `Right Wall`:

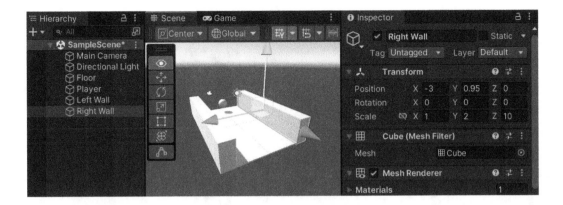

Figure 1.17 – Right Wall setup

As you can see in the preceding screenshot, we now protect the player from falling off the left and right edges of the play area. Due to how the walls are set up, if we move the Floor object, the walls will move as well.

> **Note**
>
> For information on moving Unity's camera or navigating to the **Scene** view, check out https://docs.unity3d.com/Manual/SceneViewNavigation.html.

The way this game is designed, after the ball rolls past a single tile, we will no longer need it to be there anymore. If we just leave it there, the game will get slower over time due to us having so many things in the game environment using memory, so it's a good idea to remove assets we are no longer using. We also need to have some way to figure out when we should spawn new tiles to continue the path the player can take.

6. Now, we also want to know where this piece ends, so we'll add an object with a trigger collider in it. Select **GameObject | Create Empty** and name this object Tile End.

7. Then, we will add a **Box Collider** component to our **Tile End** object. Under **Box Collider** in the **Inspector** window, set the **Scale** values to (7, 2, 1) to fit the size of the space the player can walk in. Note that there is a green box around that space showing where collisions can take place. Set the **Position** property to (0, 1, 10) to reach past the end of our tile. Finally, check the **Is Trigger** property so that the collision engine will turn the collider into a trigger, which will be able to run code events when it is hit, but will not prevent the player from moving through it:

Figure 1.18 – Caption

As I mentioned briefly before, this trigger will be used to tell the game that our player has finished walking over this tile. This is positioned past the tile due to the fact that we want to still see tiles until they pass what the camera can see. We'll tell the engine to remove this tile from the game, but we will dive more into that later on in the chapter.

8. Now that we have all of the objects created, we want to group our objects together as one piece that we can create duplicates of. To do this, let's create an empty GameObject instance by going to **GameObject | Create Empty** and naming the newly created object `Basic Tile`. Set the **Position** values of this new object to (0, 0, 0).

9. Then, go to the **Hierarchy** window and drag and drop the **Floor**, **Tile End**, **Left Wall**, and **Right Wall** objects on top of it to make them children of the **Basic Tile** object.

10. Currently, the camera can see the start of the tiles, so to fix that, let's set the **Basic Tile Position** values to (0, 0, -5). As you can see in the following screenshot, now the entire tile will shift back:

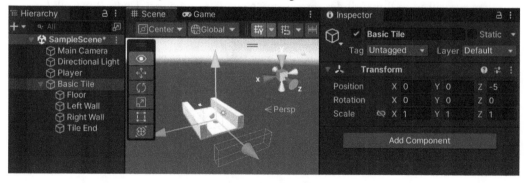

Figure 1.19 – Shifting the tile back

11. Finally, we will need to know at what position we should spawn the next piece, so create another empty GameObject by going to **GameObject | Create Empty** or by pressing *Ctrl + Shift + N*. Make the new object a child of **Basic Tile** as well, give it the name `Next Spawn Point`, and set its **Position** values to (0, 0, 5).

> **Note**
>
> Note that when we modify an object that has a parent, the position is relative to the parent, not its world position.

As you can see, the spawn point position will now be on the edge of our current title:

Figure 1.20 – Next Spawn Point position

12. Now we have a single tile that is fully completed. Instead of duplicating this a number of times by hand, we will make use of Unity's concept of **Prefabs**. Prefabs, or prefabricated objects, are blueprints of GameObjects and components that we can turn into files, which can be duplicated. There are other interesting features that Prefabs have, but we will discuss them as we make use of them.

From the **Project** window, go to the **Assets** folder and then create a new folder called `Prefabs`. Then, drag and drop the **Basic Tile** object from the **Hierarchy** window to the **Project** window inside the **Prefabs** folder. If the text for the **Basic Tile** name in the **Hierarchy** window becomes blue, we will know that it was made correctly:

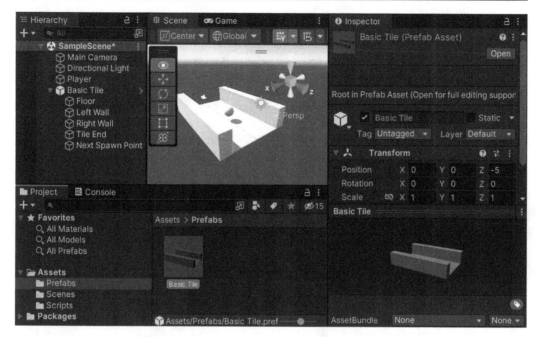

Figure 1.21 – Basic Tile Prefab created

We now have a tile prefab that we can create duplicates of through code to extend our environment.

Making it endless

Now that we have a foundation, let's make it so that we can continue running instead of stopping after a short time by spawning copies of this basic tile in front of each other:

1. To start off with, we have our prefab, so we can delete the original **Basic Tile** in the **Hierarchy** window by selecting it and then pressing the *Delete* key.

2. We need to have a place to create all of these tiles and potentially manage information for the game, such as the player's score. In Unity, this is typically referred to as a GameManager. From the **Project** window, go to the **Scripts** folder and create a new C# script called GameManager.

3. Open the script in your IDE and use the following code:

```
using UnityEngine;

/// <summary>
/// Manages the main gameplay of the game
/// </summary>
public class GameManager : MonoBehaviour
{
```

```csharp
[Tooltip("A reference to the tile we want to
    spawn")]
public Transform tile;

[Tooltip("Where the first tile should be placed
    at")]
public Vector3 startPoint = new Vector3(0, 0, -5);

[Tooltip("How many tiles should we create in
    advance")]
[Range(1, 15)]
public int initSpawnNum = 10;

/// <summary>
/// Where the next tile should be spawned at.
/// </summary>
private Vector3 nextTileLocation;

/// <summary>
/// How should the next tile be rotated?
/// </summary>
private Quaternion nextTileRotation;

/// <summary>
/// Start is called before the first frame update
/// </summary>
private void Start()
{
    // Set our starting point
    nextTileLocation = startPoint;
    nextTileRotation = Quaternion.identity;

    for (int i = 0; i < initSpawnNum; ++i)
    {
        SpawnNextTile();
    }
}


/// <summary>
/// Will spawn a tile at a certain location and
/// setup the next position
/// </summary>
```

```
public void SpawnNextTile()
{
    var newTile = Instantiate(tile,
        nextTileLocation, nextTileRotation);

    // Figure out where and at what rotation we
    /// should spawn the next item
    var nextTile = newTile.Find("Next Spawn
        Point");
    nextTileLocation = nextTile.position;
    nextTileRotation = nextTile.rotation;
}
}
```

This script will spawn a number of tiles, one after another, based on the `tile` and `initSpawnNum` properties.

4. Save your script and dive back into Unity. From there, create a new `empty GameObject` and name it `Game Controller`, optionally resetting the position if wanted for organizational purposes. Drag and drop it at the top of the **Hierarchy** window. For clarity's sake, go ahead and reset the position if you want to. Then, attach the **Game Manager** script to the object and then set the **Tile** property by dragging and dropping the **Basic Tile** prefab from the **Project** window into the **Tile** slot:

Figure 1.22 – Assigning the Tile property

5. Save your scene and run the project:

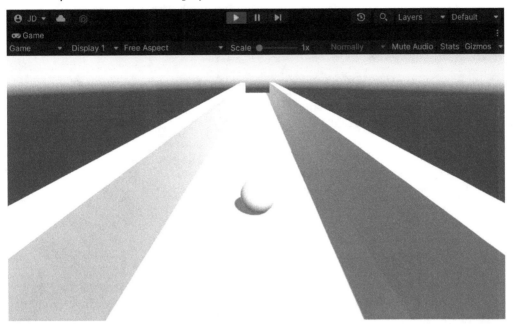

Figure 1.23 – The current state of the game

Great, but now we will need to create new objects after these, and we don't want to spawn a crazy number of these at once. It's better that once we reach the end of a tile, we create a new tile and remove it. We'll work on optimizing this more later, but that way, we always have about the same number of tiles in the game at any given time.

6. Go into the **Project** window and from the **Scripts** folder, create a new script called `TileEndBehaviour`, using the following code:

```
using UnityEngine;

/// <summary>
/// Handles spawning a new tile and destroying this
/// one upon the player reaching the end
/// </summary>
public class TileEndBehaviour : MonoBehaviour
{
    [Tooltip("How much time to wait before destroying
        " + "the tile after reaching the end")]
    public float destroyTime = 1.5f;

    private void OnTriggerEnter(Collider other)
```

```
        {
            // First check if we collided with the player
            if(other.gameObject.GetComponent
            <PlayerBehaviour>())
            {
                // If we did, spawn a new tile
                var gm = GameObject.FindObjectOfType
                    <GameManager>();
                gm.SpawnNextTile();

                // And destroy this entire tile after a
                // short delay
                Destroy(transform.parent.gameObject,
                    destroyTime);
            }
        }
    }
```

7. Now, to assign it to the prefab, we can go to the **Project** window and then go into the **Prefabs** folder. From there, double-click on the **Basic Tile** object to open up its editor. From the **Hierarchy** tab, select the **Tile End** object and then add a **Tile End Behaviour** component to it:

Figure 1.24 – Adding the Tile End Behaviour

8. Click on the left arrow next to the prefab name to return to the basic scene:

Figure 1.25 – Left Arrow location

> **Tip**
> You can also open the prefab editor by selecting a prefab object from the **Project** window, going
> to the **Inspector** tab, and clicking the **Open Prefab** button.

9. Save your scene and play. You'll now note that as the player continues to move, new tiles will
    spawn as you go; if you switch to the **Scene** tab while playing, you'll see that as the ball passes
    the tiles, they will destroy themselves:

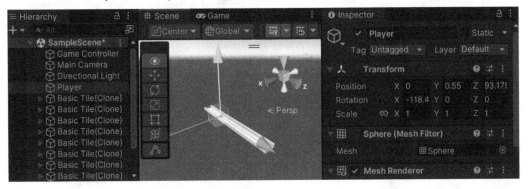

Figure 1.26 – Tiles automatically being destroyed

This will ensure that there will be tiles in front of the player to visit! But of course, this is just an
endless straight line. In the next section, we will see how to make the game much more interesting.

Creating obstacles

It's great that we have some basic tiles, but it's a good idea to give the player something to do, or in our case, something to avoid. This will provide the player with some kind of challenge and a basic gameplay goal, which is avoiding obstacles here. In this section, you'll learn how to customize your tiles to add obstacles for your player to avoid. So, let's look at the steps:

1. Just like we created a prefab for our basic tile, we will create a single obstacle through code. I want to make it easy to see what the obstacle will look like in the world and make sure that it's not too large, so I'll drag and drop a **Basic Tile** prefab back into the world.

2. Next, we will create a cube by going to **GameObject | 3D Object | Cube**. We will name this object Obstacle. Change the **Scale** value of **Y** to 2 and position it above the platform at (0, 1, 0.25):

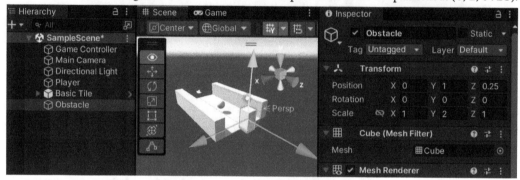

Figure 1.27 – Adding obstacles

3. We can then play the game to see how that'll work:

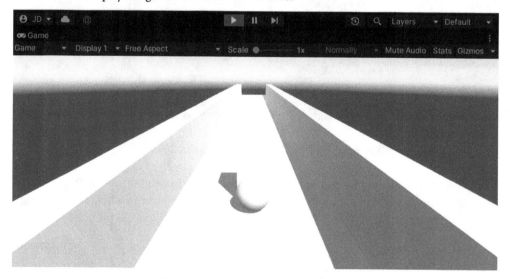

Figure 1.28 – Obstacles stop the player

4. As you can see in the preceding screenshot, the player gets stopped, but nothing really happens. In this instance, we want the player to lose when they hit this obstacle and then restart the game; to do that, we'll need to write a script. From the **Project** window, go to the **Scripts** folder and create a new script called `ObstacleBehaviour`. We'll use the following code:

```
using UnityEngine;
using UnityEngine.SceneManagement; // LoadScene

public class ObstacleBehaviour : MonoBehaviour
{
    [Tooltip("How long to wait before restarting the
        game")]
    public float waitTime = 2.0f;

    private void OnCollisionEnter(Collision collision)
    {
        // First check if we collided with the player
        if (collision.gameObject.GetComponent
        <PlayerBehaviour>())
        {
            // Destroy the player
            Destroy(collision.gameObject);

            // Call the function ResetGame after
            // waitTime has passed
            Invoke("ResetGame", waitTime);
        }
    }


    /// <summary>
    /// Will restart the currently loaded level
    /// </summary>
    private void ResetGame()
    {
        // Get the current level's name
        string sceneName =
            SceneManager.GetActiveScene().name;

        // Restarts the current level
        SceneManager.LoadScene(sceneName);
    }
}
```

5. Save the script and return to the editor, attaching the script to the `Obstacle` GameObject we just created.

6. Save your scene and try the game:

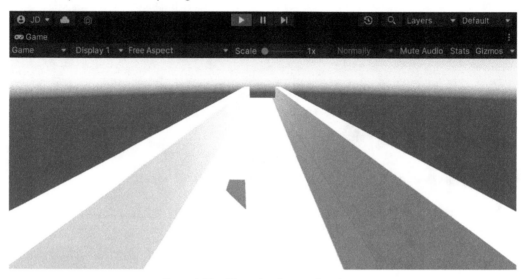

Figure 1.29 – Obstacles destroy the player

As you can see in the preceding screenshot, once we hit the obstacle, the player gets destroyed, and then after a few seconds, the game starts up again. You'll learn how to use particle systems and other things to polish this up, but at this point, it's functional, which is what we want.

7. Now that we know it works correctly, we can make it a prefab. Just as we did with the original tile, go ahead and drag and drop the **Obstacle** object from **Hierarchy** into the **Project** tab and into the **Prefabs** folder:

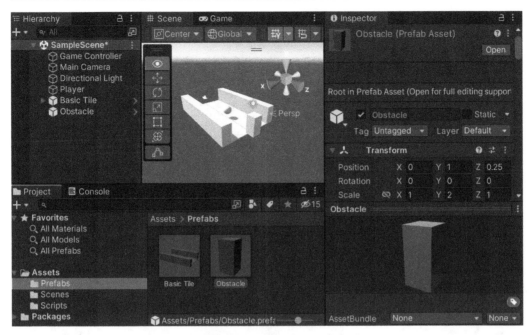

Figure 1.30 – Creating the Obstacle prefab

8. Next, we will remove the **Obstacle** object, as we'll spawn it upon creating the tile. To do so, select the **Obstacle** object in the **Hierarchy** window and then press the *Delete* key.

9. We will make markers to indicate where we would possibly like to spawn our obstacles. Expand the **Basic Tile** object to show its children and then duplicate the Next Spawn Point object and move the new one's **Position** to (0, 1, 4). We will then rename the object Center.

10. Afterward, to help see the objects within the **Scene** window, go to the **Inspector** window and click on the *gray cube* icon, and then on the **Select Icon** menu, select whichever of the color options you'd like (I went with blue). Upon doing this, you'll see that we can see the text inside the editor if we are close to the object (but it won't show up in the **Game** tab by default):

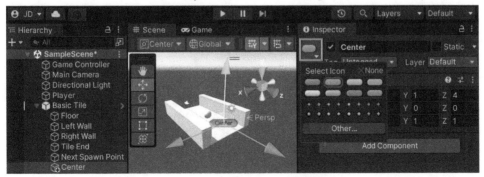

Figure 1.31 – Creating a Center marker

11. We want a way to get all of the potential spawn points we will want in case we decide to extend the project in the future, so we will assign a tag as a reference to make those objects easier to find. To do that, at the top of the **Inspector** window, click on the **Tags** dropdown and select **Add Tag...**. From the menu that pops up, press the + button and then name it `ObstacleSpawn`:

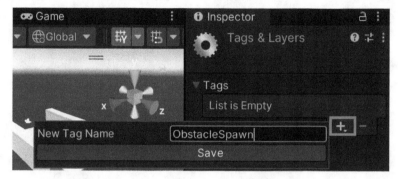

Figure 1.32 – Creating the ObstacleSpawn tag

12. Go back and select the **Center** object and assign the **Tag** property to **ObstacleSpawn**:

Figure 1.33 – Assigning the tag to the Center object

> **Note**
>
> For more information on tags and why we'd want to use them, check out `https://docs.unity3d.com/Manual/Tags.html`.

13. Go ahead and duplicate this twice and name the others `Left` and `Right`, moving them two units to the left and right of the center to become other possible obstacle points:

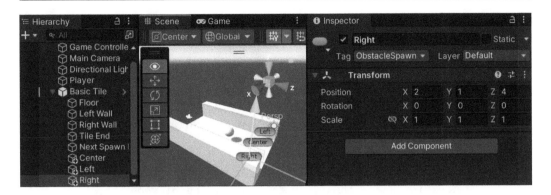

Figure 1.34 – Creating the Left and Right markers

14. Note that these changes don't affect the original prefab, by default; that's why the objects are currently black text. To make this happen, select **Basic Tile**, and then in the **Inspector** window under the **Prefab** section, click on **Overrides** and select **Apply All**:

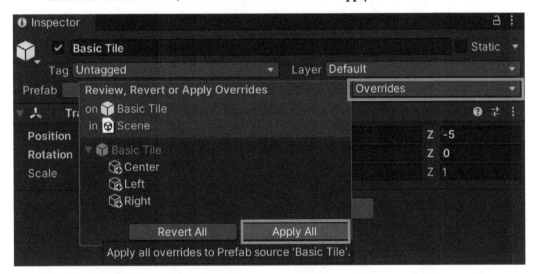

Figure 1.35 – Applying changes to the prefab

15. Now that the prefab is set up correctly, we can go ahead and remove it by selecting it in the **Hierarchy** window and pressing *Delete*.

16. We then need to go into the GameManager script and make some modifications. To start with, we will need to introduce some new variables:

```
/// <summary>
/// Manages the main gameplay of the game
/// </summary>
```

```
public class GameManager : MonoBehaviour
{
    [Tooltip("A reference to the tile we want to
        spawn")]
    public Transform tile;

    [Tooltip("A reference to the obstacle we want to
        spawn")]
    public Transform obstacle;

    [Tooltip("Where the first tile should be placed
        at")]
    public Vector3 startPoint = new Vector3(0, 0, -5);

    [Tooltip("How many tiles should we create in
        advance")]
    [Range(1, 15)]
    public int initSpawnNum = 10;

    [Tooltip("How many tiles to spawn with no
        obstacles")]
    public int initNoObstacles = 4;
```

The first of these variables is a reference to the obstacle that we will be creating copies of. The second is a parameter of how many tiles should be spawned before spawning obstacles. This is to ensure that the player can see the obstacles before they need to avoid them.

17. Then, we need to modify the SpawnNextTile function in order to spawn obstacles as well:

```
/// <summary>
/// Will spawn a tile at a certain location and setup
/// the next position
/// </summary>
/// <param name="spawnObstacles">If we should spawn an
/// obstacle</param>
public void SpawnNextTile(bool spawnObstacles = true)
{
    var newTile = Instantiate(tile, nextTileLocation,
                              nextTileRotation);

    // Figure out where and at what rotation we should
    // spawn the next item
    var nextTile = newTile.Find("Next Spawn Point");
    nextTileLocation = nextTile.position;
    nextTileRotation = nextTile.rotation;
```

```
    if (spawnObstacles)
    {
        SpawnObstacle(newTile);
    }

}
```

Note that we modified the `SpawnNextTile` function to now have a default parameter set to `true`, which will tell us whether we want to spawn obstacles or not. At the beginning of the game, we may not want the player to have to start dodging immediately, but we can tweak the value to increase or decrease the number we are using. Because it has a default value of `true`, the original version of calling this in the `Start` function will still work without an error, but we will be modifying it later on.

18. Here, we ask whether the value is `true` to call a function called `SpawnObstacle`, but that isn't written yet. We will add that next, but first, we will be making use of the `List` class and we want to make sure that the compiler knows which `List` class we are referring to, so we need to add a `using` statement at the top of the file:

```
using UnityEngine;
using System.Collections.Generic; // List
```

19. Now we can write the `SpawnObstacle` function. Add the following function to the script:

```
private void SpawnObstacle(Transform newTile)
{
    // Now we need to get all of the possible places
    // to spawn the obstacle
    var obstacleSpawnPoints = new List<GameObject>();

    // Go through each of the child game objects in
    // our tile
    foreach (Transform child in newTile)
    {
        // If it has the ObstacleSpawn tag
        if (child.CompareTag("ObstacleSpawn"))
        {
            // We add it as a possibility
            obstacleSpawnPoints.Add(child.gameObject);

        }

    }
```

```
    // Make sure there is at least one
    if (obstacleSpawnPoints.Count > 0)
    {
        // Get a random spawn point from the ones we
        // have
        int index = Random.Range(0,
            obstacleSpawnPoints.Count);
        var spawnPoint = obstacleSpawnPoints[index];

        // Store its position for us to use
        var spawnPos = spawnPoint.transform.position;

        // Create our obstacle
        var newObstacle = Instantiate(obstacle,
            spawnPos, Quaternion.identity);

        // Have it parented to the tile
        newObstacle.SetParent(spawnPoint.transform);
    }
}
```

20. Lastly, let's update the `Start` function:

```
/// <summary>
/// Start is called before the first frame update
/// </summary>
private void Start()
{
    // Set our starting point
    nextTileLocation = startPoint;
    nextTileRotation = Quaternion.identity;

    for (int i = 0; i < initSpawnNum; ++i)
    {
        SpawnNextTile(i >= initNoObstacles);
    }
}
```

Now, as long as `i` is less than the value of `initNoObstacles`, it will not spawn a variable, effectively giving us a buffer of four tiles that can be adjusted by changing the `initNoObstacles` variable.

21. Save the script and go back to the Unity Editor. Then, assign the `Obstacle` variable of the **Game Manager (Script)** component in the **Inspector** window with the **Obstacle** prefab we created previously:

Figure 1.36 – Assigning the Obstacle property

22. It's a bit hard to see things currently due to the default light settings, so let's go to the **Hierarchy** window and select the **Directional Light** object. A directional light acts similar to how the Sun works on Earth, shining everywhere from a certain position.

23. With the default settings, the light is a bit too bright and the shadows are too dark by default, so in the **Inspector** window, I changed **Intensity** to 0.5 and then the **Realtime Shadows | Strength** property to 0.5:

Figure 1.37 – Adjusting the Directional Light

24. Save your scene and play the game:

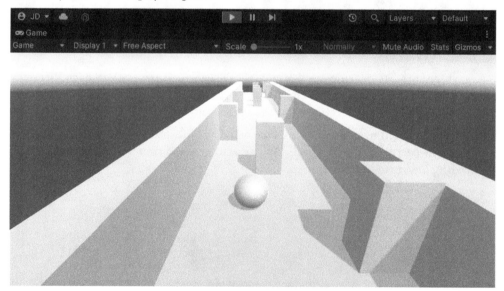

Figure 1.38 – The current state of the game

As you can see in the preceding screenshot, we now have a number of obstacles for our player to avoid!

> **Note**
>
> For more information on directional lights and the other lighting types that Unity has, check out `https://unity3d.com/learn/tutorials/topics/graphics/light-types?playlist=17102`.

Summary

There you have it! A solid foundation – but just that, a foundation. However, that being said, we covered a lot of content in this chapter. We discussed how to create a new project in Unity, and we built a player that will move continuously, as well as take inputs to move horizontally. We then discussed how we can use Unity's attributes and XML comments to improve our code quality and help us when working in teams. We also covered how to have a moving camera. We created a tile-based level design system where we created new tiles as the game continued, randomly spawning obstacles for the player to avoid.

Throughout this book, we will explore more that we can do to improve this project and polish it while changing it to make for the best experience possible on mobile platforms. However, before we get to that, we'll actually need to figure out how to deploy our projects, which is what we will be working on in the next chapter.

2
Project Setup for Android and iOS Development

We now have a project to start with, but currently, it's built with playing on a PC in mind. However, since this book is about mobile development, it's very important to have the game working on the device itself before we get much further.

In this chapter, we will go through all of the setups we need to perform to deploy the project in its current state to our mobile devices. At the time of writing this book, mobile development is typically done either for Android or iOS, so we will cover those two platforms.

This chapter will be split into a number of topics. The chapter itself will be a simple step-by-step process from beginning to end. The following is a list of the tasks we will perform:

- Introducing the **Build Settings** menu
- Building a project for a PC
- Exporting your project to Android
- Running the Android APK with an emulator
- Putting the project on your Android device
- Unity iOS installation and Xcode setup
- Building a project for iOS
- Running the project via the iOS simulator

Technical requirements

This book utilizes Unity 2022.1.0b16 and Unity Hub 3.3.1, but the steps should work with minimal changes in future versions of the editor. If you would like to download the exact version used in this book, and there is a new version out, you can visit Unity's download archive at `https://unity3d.com/get-unity/download/archive`. You can also find the system requirements for Unity at `https://docs.unity3d.com/2022.1/Documentation/Manual/system-requirements.html` in the *Unity Editor system requirements* section.

If you wish to deploy to an Android device, you can use macOS, Linux, or Windows, and depending on the features you wish to use, it is possible to export your game in such a way as to run apps on Android 5.1 Lollipop and above.

> **Note**
>
> For more information on the different types of Android versions that are supported, check out `https://docs.unity3d.com/ScriptReference/AndroidSdkVersions.html`.

To develop for an iOS device, in addition to the device itself running iOS 12 or later, you'll need to do some work on a Macintosh computer that runs OS X 10.13 High Sierra or a later version for an Intel-based Macintosh and Big Sur 11.0 for a Macintosh using Apple silicon. I'll be using 12.3.1 macOS Monterey. If you do not have one, it is possible to develop your game using Windows and, when you want to publish the game, bring your project to a Macintosh to do the final export.

> **Note**
>
> There are some other potential ways to build iOS apps using Windows, but they are not within the scope of this book. One possible option is to use Unity's CI/CD Cloud Build Automation & Deployment Tools service, which automatically creates versions of your game. For more information, check out `https://unity.com/solutions/ci-cd`.
>
> Another potential option would be to rent a Macintosh via the cloud to do the building yourself. For more information on that and other potential options, check out `https://mindster.com/how-develop-ios-apps-windows/`.

You can find the code files for this chapter on GitHub at `https://github.com/PacktPublishing/Unity-2022-Mobile-Game-Development-3rd-Edition/tree/main/Chapter02`.

Introducing the Build Settings menu

There are times during development when you may want to see what your game looks like outside of the editor. It can give you a sense of accomplishment. I know I felt that way the first time I pushed a build to a console devkit. Whether it's for PC, Macintosh, Linux, web player, mobile, or console, we have to go through the same menu – the **Build Settings** menu:

1. Start off by opening up the project we created in *Chapter 1, Building Your Game*. In addition, open the scene we created (SampleScene.unity, which is inside the Scenes folder):

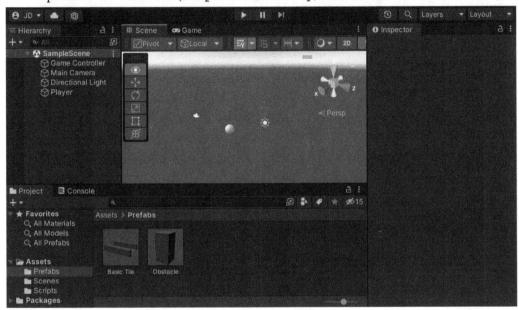

Figure 2.1 –The SampleScene file

2. Since the scene is our gameplay, let's rename the file by first opening the Scenes folder in the **Project** window, right-clicking on the SampleScene object, and selecting **Rename**. Rename the file to Gameplay and then press the *Enter* key to submit the change. Unity will ask whether you want to reload the scene. Do so by clicking **Reload**.

3. From here, we will open the **Build Settings** menu by selecting **File | Build Settings**:

> **Tip**
> You may alternatively press *Ctrl* + Shift + *B* or *Command* + Shift + *B* to bring the menu up as well.

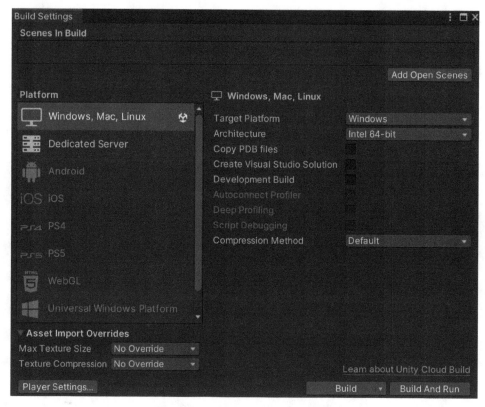

Figure 2.2 – The Build Settings menu

In the preceding screenshot, you will notice that the **Build Settings** menu came up. This menu contains three sections:

- **Scenes In Build** (top): This window contains the scenes in our project that we want to include when we build our project. This ensures that things such as test levels won't be included unless specified.

- **Platform** (bottom left): This is a list of all of the platforms to which you can export your game. The Unity logo shows up on the current platform you're compiling for. To change your platform, you'll need to select it from this list and then click on the **Switch Platform** button, which appears below the list.

- **Options** (bottom right): To the right of the **Platform** section, you'll see some settings that can be tweaked based on how you want the build to work, with certain options that change based on the platform you will work with.

4. By default, we have no scenes in our build, so let's go ahead and change that. Click on the **Add Open Scenes** button; you should see the Scenes/Gameplay level appear in the list at index **0**, which means that when your game is played, this level will be the first one to load:

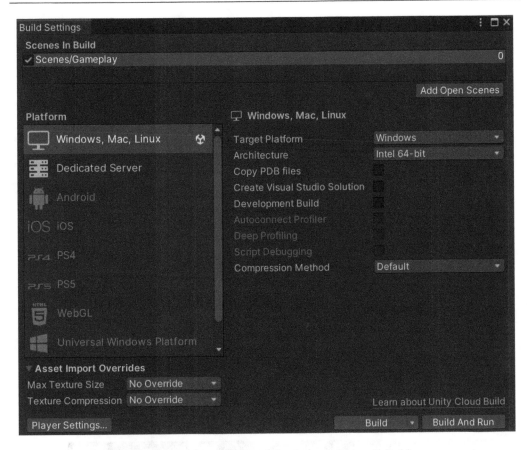

Figure 2.3 – Adding the Gameplay Scene to Scenes In Build

Now that we know how the build settings work, let's see how to build the project for a PC to understand the general case before continuing to build our mobile game.

> **Note**
>
> You may also add scenes to the **Scenes In Build** section by dragging and dropping them from the **Project** window. You may also drag the scenes to reorder them however you wish.

Building a project for a PC

By default, our platform is set to **Windows, Mac, Linux**. Just to verify that everything is working correctly, let's go ahead and get the game working on our own platform before moving to mobile:

1. To get started, we will select the **Build** option. In my case, I'll be exporting the project to Windows, but the process is similar for macOS and Linux.

2. Once this is done, a window will pop up asking for a name and a location to put the game in. I'm going to create a new `Export` folder located in the same folder that contains `Assets` and `Library`, so it won't show up in the **Project** window, but it will be in the same folder as my project:

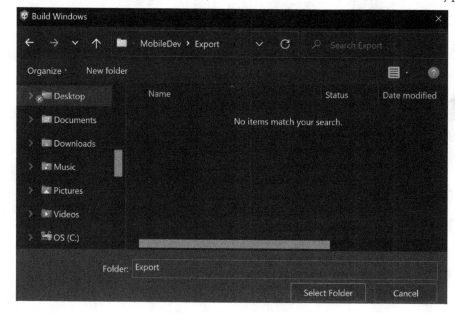

Figure 2.4 – The Export folder

3. Click on **Select Folder** and wait for it to finish. Once it's done, a window should appear as follows:

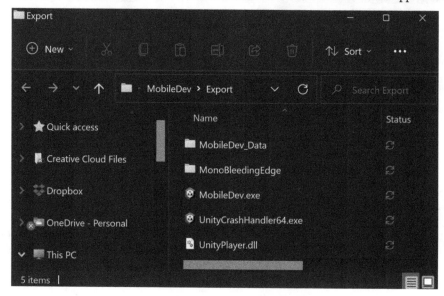

Figure 2.5 – Folder created

We have the executable, but we also have a data folder containing all the assets for our application (right now, it's called `MobileDev_Data`). You must include the data folder and the other files created with your game, or it will not run.

If you build for Mac, it will bundle the app and data altogether, so once you export the game, all you need to provide is the application.

4. If you double-click on the `.exe` file to run the game, you'll be taken to the proper game screen, as shown in the following screenshot:

Figure 2.6 – Running the game

With that, we should be able to control and play the game as we would usually do. This is great!

> **Tip**
> You'll have to use *Alt* + *F4* (*Command* + *Q* on Macintosh) to quit the game, and you can switch to windowed mode by pressing *Alt* + *Enter*.

Now that we have discussed the universal ways of building a project, let's dive into the specifics of different platforms. In the next section, we will discuss getting our project onto an Android device.

Exporting a project for Android

Now that we have all of the setup done, we can open Unity with our project and export it for Android devices. In this section, we will first check whether we have Android Build Support installed, and then we will update the build and player settings to export our project. So, let's get started.

Installing Android Build Support for Unity

First of all, if you haven't done so already, you'll need to select to add **Android Build Support** as an option when you install Unity. If you have installed it, you can skip this section. If you did not install it when doing the initial installation, we will cover the installation in the following steps:

1. Close the Unity Editor and open the Unity Hub and select the **Installs** section.

2. From there, click on the gear icon to the right of your current version of Unity and select the **Add modules** option:

Figure 2.7 – Selecting the Add Modules option

3. Check the **Android Build Support** option, which should also check the **Android SDK and NDK Tools** and **OpenJDK** options. Afterward, click on the **Continue** button:

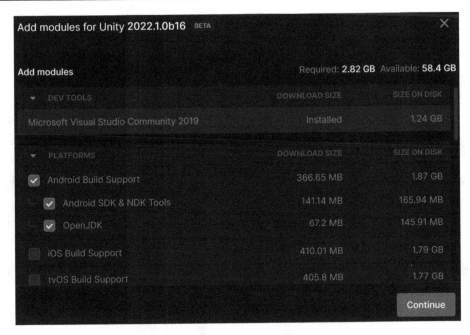

Figure 2.8 – Checking the Android Build Support option

4. You'll be brought to a license terms page. Read it over and if you agree to it, check the agreement box and click on the **Install** button:

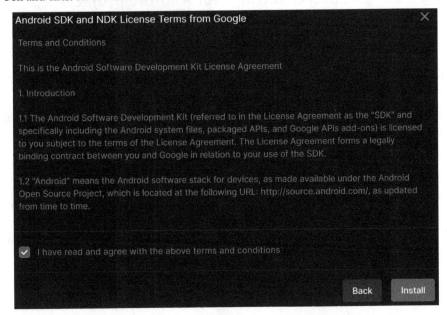

Figure 2.9 –Android SDK and NDK License Terms from Google

Wait for it to finish installing. Once finished, you should see the Android logo at the bottom of your installation:

Figure 2.10 – The newly added platform

This means that Android Build Support has now been added to our version of Unity, and we can build projects there. Next, we will see how to build the project for Android and the required settings.

Updating build and player settings for Android projects

Now that we have Android support, let's open up our project again and change the platform we are developing for:

1. At this point, we will dive into Unity and move into our **Build Settings** menu once again by going to **File | Build Settings**.

2. Click on the **Android** option from the **Platform** list and then click on the **Switch Platform** button to make the change:

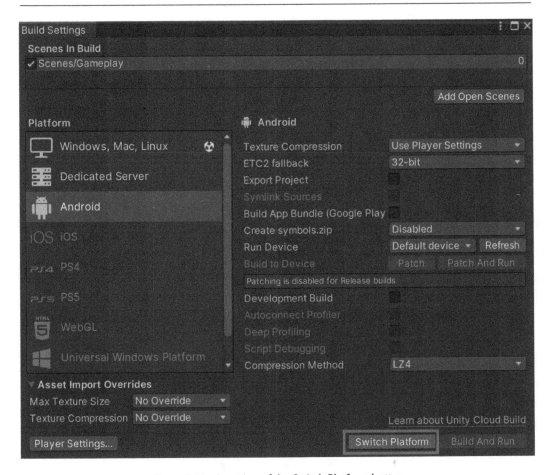

Figure 2.11 – Location of the Switch Platform button

Note that this will make Unity reimport all of the assets in our game, so this may be time-consuming when you start to build larger projects. Once this is complete, you should notice that the Unity logo is now next to the **Android** option, signifying that's the platform to be built for:

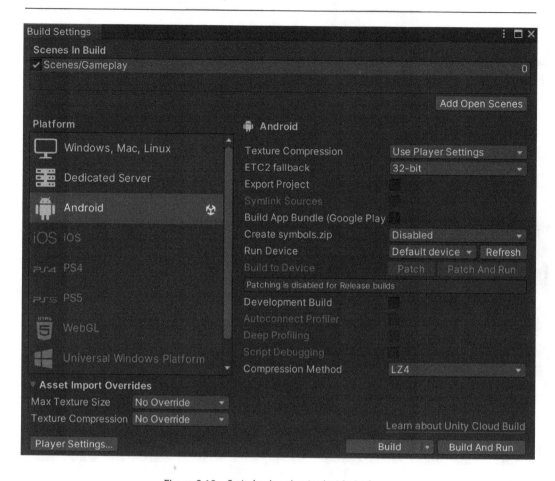

Figure 2.12 – Switched to the Android platform

3.   Now, in order to be able to build our project, we must set the bundle identifier for our game, which is a string that identifies the app. It's written like a URL in reverse, for example, `com.yourCompanyName.yourGameName`. To modify this, we'll need to open up the **Player Settings** menu, which we can access by clicking on the **Player Settings…** button in the bottom-left part of the **Build Settings** menu or by going into **Edit** | **Project Settings** | **Player**. You'll note that the menu appears as a new window:

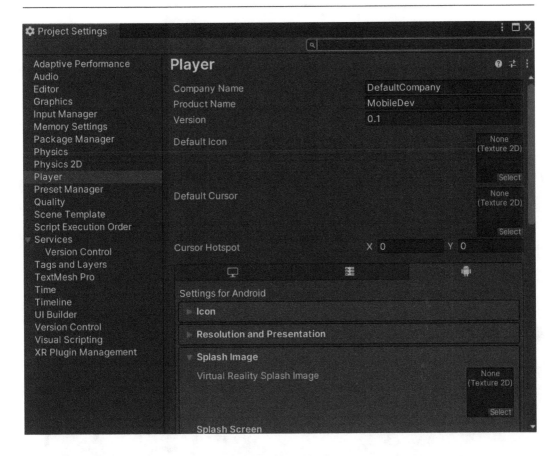

Figure 2. 13 – The Player Settings menu

Now that we're in the **Android** mode (note the text on the title bar of the Unity Editor), we can change these properties:

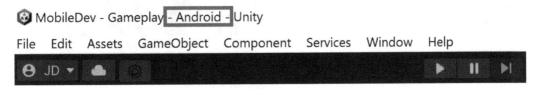

Figure 2.14 – The Android mode

4. We'll discuss more of these in a later chapter, but for now, change your **Company Name** property to either your company name or some type of identifier; I used JohnPDoran.

5. Then scroll down until you get to the **Other Settings** option. From there, you'll see the **Package Name** property is using whatever we set for **our Company Name** and **Product Name** properties, but we can customize it if we'd like by checking the **Override Default Package Name** property; we just have to ensure that it is different than the default value.

    There's also a **Minimum API Level** option; make sure that your option is set to the same version as your phone or earlier, depending on what you want to support. Note that the earlier you go, the fewer things you'll have access to, but your project will be able to support more phones:

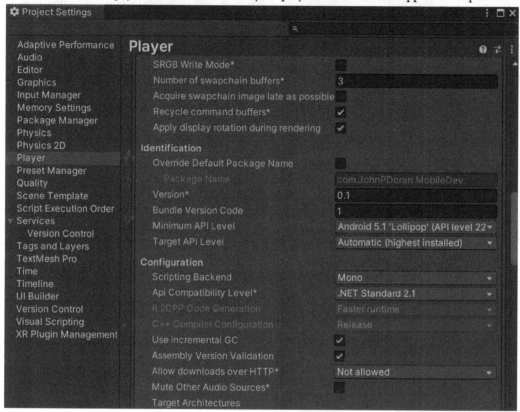

Figure 2.15 – Player settings adjustments

6. Close the **Project Settings** window and open the **Build Settings** menu again if it is not open, by going to **File | Build Settings**. Now, we can try to build the project by clicking on the **Build** button and saving it in the same `Export` folder we created earlier. It will ask for the name you'd like the file to have. I will use `MobileDev` as we did previously because instead of a `.exe` file, it will create a `.apk` file:

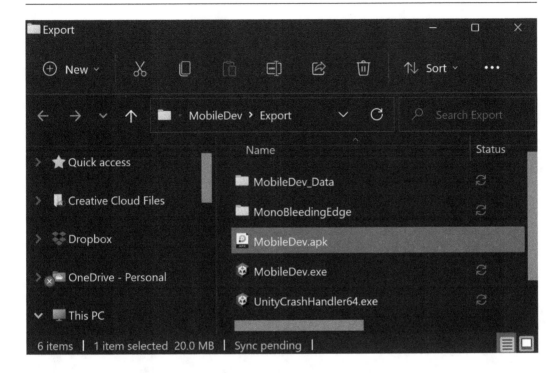

Figure 2.16 – Android APK created

Wait a bit, and once it's finished, you should have a new `.apk` file located in the folder. Of course, just having the APK file doesn't do much if we can't put it on our actual phone, so in the next section, we will enable our phone to test the game on our device.

Running the Android APK with an emulator

While the best way to test an Android game is on an actual Android device, it is also possible to test the game out on an emulator, which is a medium through which we can have our computer run software that was created for Android devices. There are several Android emulators available for Windows at the time of writing, but the one that I've had the most success with is one called *LDPlayer*, a lightweight and fast Android emulator; however, it does contain ads due to it being free. For those on an Intel-powered Macintosh, you can use *BlueStacks* (`https://www.bluestacks.com/download.html`), but at the time of writing, there are no Android emulators available on Apple silicon-powered Macintoshes. This section is completely optional; if you'd rather test on an actual device, skip ahead to the *Putting the project on your Android device* or the *Unity for iOS setup and Xcode installation* section.

To test the game on an emulator, follow these steps:

1. From your web browser, go to `https://www.ldplayer.net/`. From there, click on the **Download LDPlayer 9** button:

Figure 2.17 – The LDPlayer website

2. Once the program is downloaded, open the installer, go through the standard installation process, and click the **Try Now** button once you've finished installation:

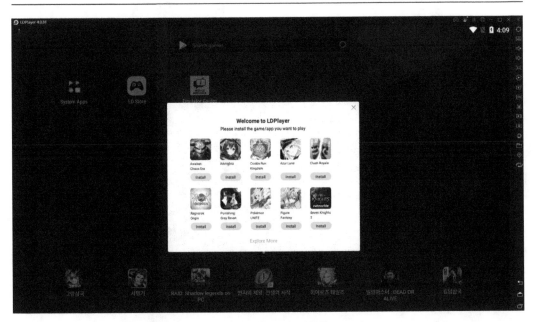

Figure 2.18 – The Welcome to LDPlayer menu

3. From the welcome screen, click on the **X** in the top right of the **Welcome to LDPlayer** menu.

4. Drag and drop the `MobileDev.apk` file from your `Export` folder onto the LDPlayer menu. If all goes well, you should see the **MobileDev** icon show up on the screen:

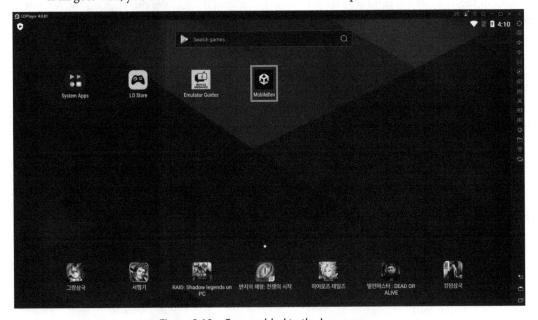

Figure 2.19 – Game added to the home screen

5.   From there, you can click the icon to start the game!

Figure 2.20 – The game is running on the emulated device

As you can see, the game is running perfectly on the emulated device! We can click on the **X** from the **MobileDev** tab whenever we are finished playing. Now that we've seen how easy it is to run the game on an emulator, let's see how to do it on an actual device!

Putting the project on your Android device

The following steps may be different for you depending on your Android version and your specific phone, but here is a general set of steps to be able to sideload our Android app to our device:

1.   On your Android device, you'll need to go to your **Settings** app. From there select the **Apps** section:

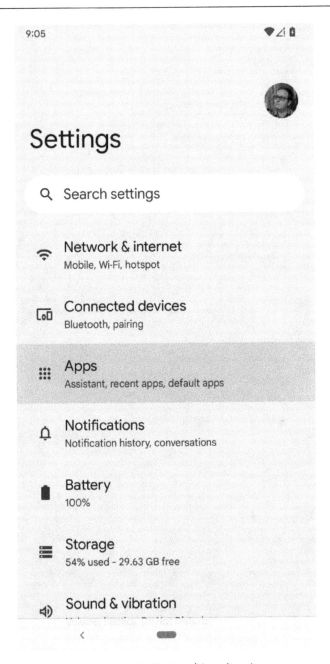

Figure 2.21 – The Settings | Apps location

2. From there, scroll down till you get to the **Special app access** section or similar, and then tap on it to go into the menu:

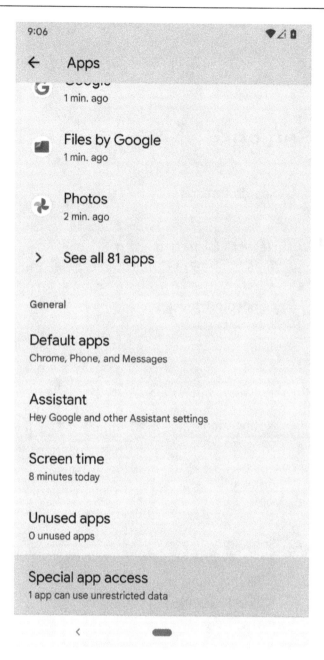

Figure 2.22 – The Special app access option

3.   Inside there, you'll see a section called **Install unknown apps**. Enter this option:

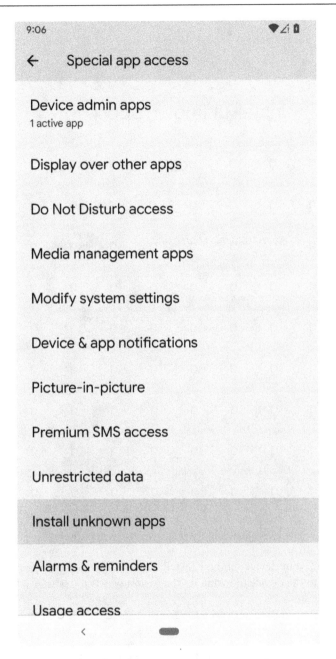

Figure 2.23 – The Install unknown apps option

4.   We will be uploading our app to the device's files, so we will want to enable **Install unknown apps** from the **Files** app. Select it and then enable it from the menu:

Figure 2.24 – Enabling the Install unknown apps option

With this enabled, your device can now install the .apk file, but now you will need to move your game over to the device to install it. The easiest way is to transfer it to your device via USB; we'll do that now.

> **Tip**
>
> For those of you who'd rather not use USB, I would suggest using a cloud storage app, such as Dropbox, to upload the .apk file and then download it from the app and install it that way. There's also another tool called ADB that can send files to your phone via USB or Wi-Fi. For more information on that and the rest of the Android build process, check out https://docs.unity3d.com/Manual/android-BuildProcess.html.

5. Connect your phone to your computer via USB. Upon being connected, your phone will show a notification that it's connected via USB for charging. Click on that notification and change the option to **File Transfer**:

Figure 2. 25 – USB Preferences

6. After that, go back to your computer and go into **Windows Explorer/Finder**, and then go to the **Devices and drives** section; you should see your device appear there:

Figure 2.26 – Selecting our Android device

7. Double-click on your device and access the internal shared storage section. Then, drag the
    .apk file we made before into this folder:

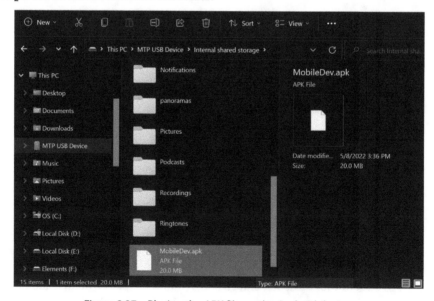

Figure 2.27 – Placing the APK file on the Android device

8. Now, back in your phone, open the **Files/File Explorer** app. From there, scroll down to the bottom of the menu and select the **Internal storage** option:

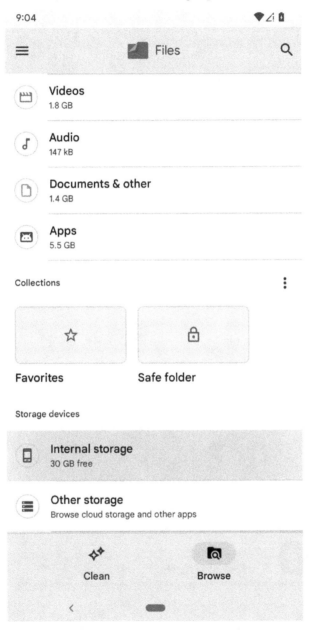

Figure 2.28 – The Internal storage location

9.   From there, select your .apk file from the listed files:

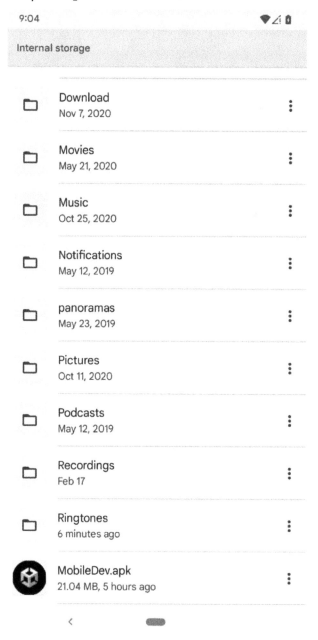

Figure 2.29 – Selecting the application

10. You'll be asked to confirm the installation. Hit the **Install** button:

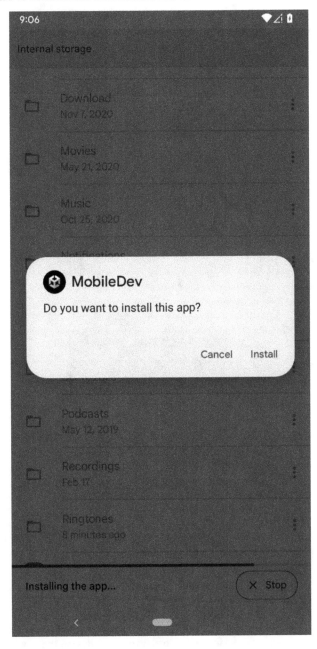

Figure 2.30 – Installing the app

11. You may see a window pop up that mentions that Play Protect doesn't recognize the developer. We will see how to solve this issue later on, in *Chapter14 Submitting Games to App Stores*, but for now, click **INSTALL ANYWAY** and wait for the installation to finish:

Figure 2.31 – INSTALL ANYWAY

Your phone may also ask if you want to send the app for scanning by Play Protect. Since we will be creating several versions of the project while working through this book, it's likely not needed, so I would select **Don't Send**.

> **Tip**
> Of course, I can't note the steps for all devices as some have different drivers that are required or additional steps that need to be performed in order to open files on the device. If these steps do not work and you do not know how to get files onto your device and access them and add new ones to them, go ahead and search on your internet search engine of choice for **phone name file transfer**, replacing the phone name with your phone's name.

12. Once it's finished, go ahead and click on the **Open** button to open our game:

Figure 2.32 – The game running on an Android device

As you can see, the game is on there, and it's working. Granted, you can't control it yet, and there are many new things that you can't do, but this lets you know that you've set up your Android device properly. Of course, now that you have your game on an Android device, you now need to get it working on iOS, which we will cover in the next section.

Unity for iOS setup and Xcode installation

With Android, there's a lot of setup effort required, but building and getting a game onto your device is less work, whereas, with iOS, there's less work to do on the setup and more involvement with getting the game actually onto the device.

Previously, you had to have a paid Apple Developer license to get your game onto an iOS device. Although that's still required to get the game on the App Store, you are no longer required to get it for testing. Note that the free option doesn't have everything available to you, most notably **in-app purchases (IAPs)** and the Game Center; however, the game should work just fine on your device. We will go over how to adjust your project to reflect being in the Apple Developer portal in *Chapter 13, Building a Release Copy of Our Game*, when we cover putting our project on the App Store.

To develop for an iOS device, in addition to the device itself running iOS 12 or later, you'll also need to do some work on a Macintosh computer that runs OS X 10.13 High Sierra or a later version for an Intel-based Macintosh and Big Sur 11.0 for a Macintosh using Apple silicon. I'll be using 12.3.1 macOS Monterey. Just like working with Android, we'll also need to do some setup before we can actually do the exporting. Let's get started on that now:

1. First of all, if you haven't done so already, you'll need to add **iOS Build Support (*)** as an option when you are installing Unity. If you did not install it when doing the initial installation, you can open up the Unity Hub and select the **Installs** section.

2. From there, click on the three dots to the right of your current version of Unity and select the **Add modules** option:

Figure 2.33 – The Unity Hub Installs screen

3. From the menu that pops up, check the **iOS Build Support** option:

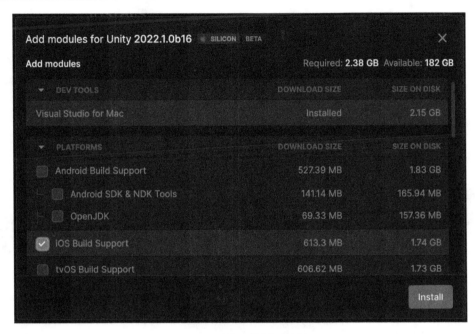

Figure 2.34 – Adding iOS Build Support

4. Click on the **Install** button and wait for the installation to finish. Once it's complete, you should see some text in the platforms list for iOS support appear:

Figure 2.35 – iOS support added

This module allows you to be able to export your projects for iOS. Since I'll mainly use my Windows machine, I'm only adding iOS support, but you can export both iOS and Android apps from your Macintosh computer.

5. You'll also need to have **Xcode**, which is the program used to build iOS apps. To download it, you'll need to open up the App Store application on your computer. In the search bar in the top-left corner, type Xcode and press *Enter*.

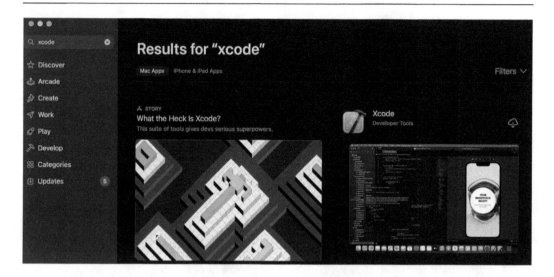

Figure 2.36 – Searching for "xcode"

6. From there, you'll see the **Xcode** program at the top right of the page. Click on it and then on the **Install/Update** button (in my case, a cloud icon) and go through the installation process:

7. You may need to enter your Apple ID information; go ahead and do so and then wait for it to finish.

> **Note**
>
> If you do not have an Apple ID, you can get one from https://appleid.apple.com/.

8. Once Xcode is installed, open it up. There will be a license agreement for Xcode and the iOS SDK; go ahead and click on **Agree**. It'll then begin installing components that are needed for it to work.

9. When you open Xcode, you'll be brought to a welcome screen, but we want to do some setup first. From the top menu bar, go ahead and select **Xcode | Preferences** (or press *Command* + ,). From there, click on the **Accounts** button. This will display all of the Apple IDs that you want to be able to use in Xcode:

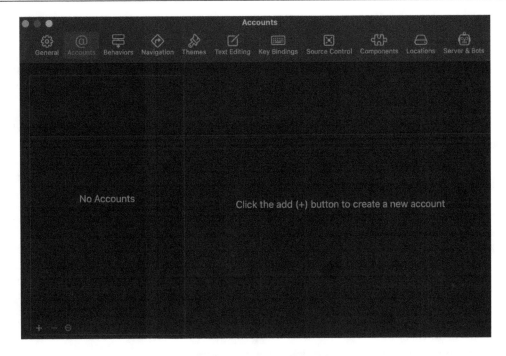

Figure 2.37 – The Accounts window

10. Click on the + icon at the bottom left of the screen and then select **Apple ID** when it asks what kind of account to create:

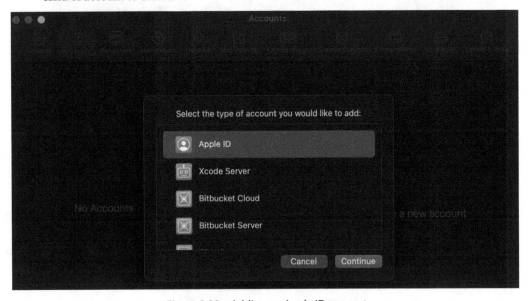

Figure 2.38 – Adding an Apple ID account

11. From the menu that pops up, add your Apple ID information, and you should see it appear on the screen.

If you select the name, you'll see additional information on the right side, such as what teams you are on. If you are not enrolled in the Apple Developer Program, it'll just be a personal team, but if you are paying for it, you should see additional teams there as well.

Now that we have completed the setup and installation of iOS and Xcode, let's continue to build our project.

Building a project for iOS

While there are some similarities to working with Android, some differences are very important to note, so keep that in mind while reading this section. Let's build our project for the iOS device using the following steps:

1. At this point, we will dive into Unity (switching **Target** to **MacStandalone** if needed) and then move into our **Build Settings** menu once again by going to **File | Build Settings**.

2. Click on the **iOS** option from the **Platform** list and then click on the **Switch Platform** button to make the change:

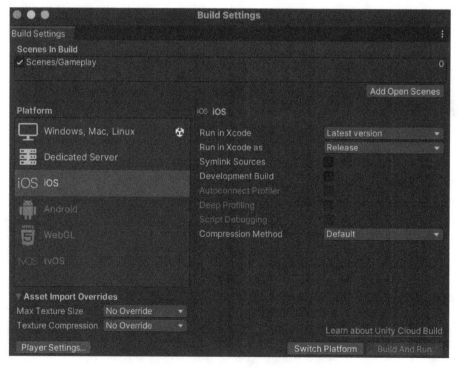

Figure 2.39 – Selecting the iOS option from the Platform list

Note that this will make Unity reimport all of the assets in our game, which may be time-consuming as you build larger and larger projects. This now also means that when we build our project, it will create an Xcode project instead of just an app, which we will need to open and work with once it's built.

3. If we didn't do so earlier when building for Android, we must modify the properties needed to modify the bundle identifier for our game. To modify this, we'll need to open up the **Player Settings** menu, which we can get to by clicking on the **Player Settings...** button in the **Build Settings** menu or by going to **Edit | Project Settings | Player**.

4. From the top of the menu, change the **Company Name** property to either your company name or some type of identifier; I used JohnPDoran. Then scroll down until you get to the **Other Settings** option, and from there, you'll see the **Package Name** property is using whatever we set for our **Company Name** and **Product Name** properties, but we can customize it if we'd like by checking the **Override Default Package** name property.

> **Note**
>
> If you have already changed this property when building for Android, it will already be done; there's no need to do this again.

5. Now, we can try to build the project by clicking on the **Build** button and saving it in the same Export folder we created earlier—in this case, I created a new folder inside of it and named it MobileDev_iOS:

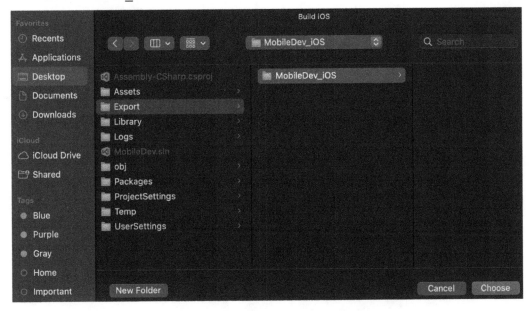

Figure 2.40 – Selecting a build location

> **Tip**
>
> You can press the down arrow button to search for folders in the Finder window that pops up.

6. Once the project has been built, we will be taken to a Finder window at the location where we created the project. From there, we can double-click on the `.xcodeproj` file to open the project inside Xcode:

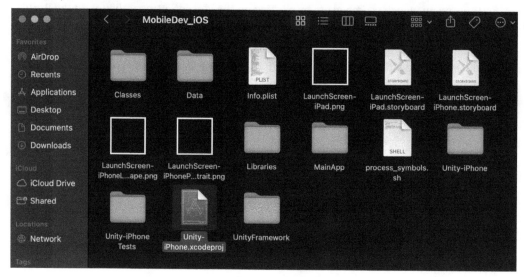

Figure 2.41 – Location of the build's Xcode project

7. In Xcode, after waiting for everything to load in, you'll notice a yellow triangle with a ! in the center of it in the top-center console. If you click on it, you'll see some information appear on the left-hand side.

8. Double-click on the **Update to recommended settings** option on the left-hand side of the screen and then click on the **Perform Changes** button in the window that pops up:

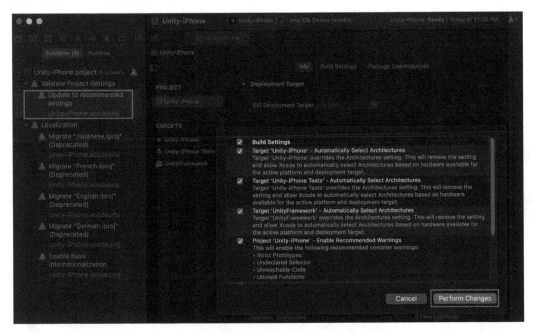

Figure 2.42 – Perform Changes

9.   Then, go to the middle of the window, and under **TARGETS**, select the **Unity-iPhone** option:

Figure 2.43 – Selecting the Unity-iPhone option

10.   Afterward, in the **Signing & Capabilities** section, check the **Automatically manage signing** option and click on **Enable Automatic** when the popup appears. Then, assign your team to your profile in the window that pops up.

11. Once all the preceding steps are done, plug in your phone via USB, and when you unlock it, it may ask if you wish to trust this device; hit the **Trust** button. After loading all of the symbols it needs (wait until the top-middle section says **Ready**), at the top right, instead of **Generic iOS Device**, change it to the device you've connected. You may need to unplug and replug your phone after installing the symbols to have it pick up the device.

12. When you click the **Play** button, a window will appear, noting the device it will be building to. Once you've confirmed all the details are correct, click the **Run** button:

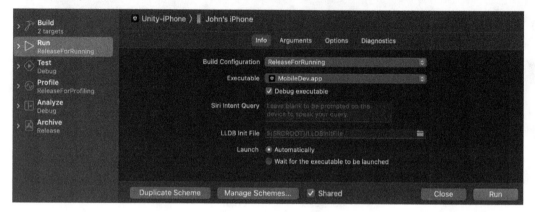

Figure 2.44 – The Play settings window

13. Your phone may be busy, so you may need to wait a bit before you can build to the device. You may get a window asking you to access the key access in your keychain. Go ahead and click **Allow**, entering your device password if required. You'll also need to unlock your phone at some point so it can make the installation.

If all goes well, you should see your app automatically start playing on your device:

Figure 2.45 – Playing our game on an iOS device

With that, we also have the game running on the iOS side.

14. If you go to your home screen, you should notice that the app will now be on your iOS device, as you can see in the following screenshot:

Figure 2.46 – The location of the iOS app

> **Note**
>
> When building in the following manner, apps will only work for a limited time, possibly up to a week without the paid license. If your game crashes immediately and it worked correctly beforehand, this is most likely the culprit. Redeploy the device again to check whether that is the issue before modifying your actual project.

Running the project via the iOS simulator

Much like how we were able to use an Android emulator on the PC to play a simulated version of our game project, it is also possible to do the same exact thing on iOS by using the iOS simulator:

1. Back in the Unity Editor, go to the **Player** settings. From there, go to the **Other Settings** section and change the **Target SDK** property from **Device SDK** to **Simulator SDK**:

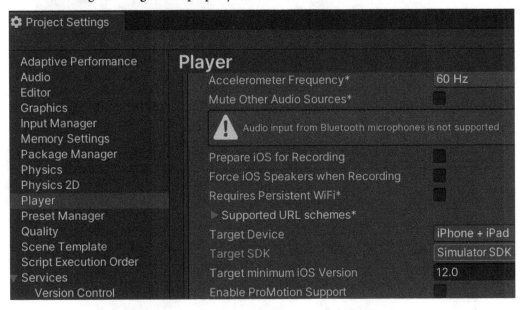

Figure 2.47 – Setting Target SDK to Simulator SDK

2. Rebuild the project. This time I created a new folder to specify that this build was meant for the iOS simulator:

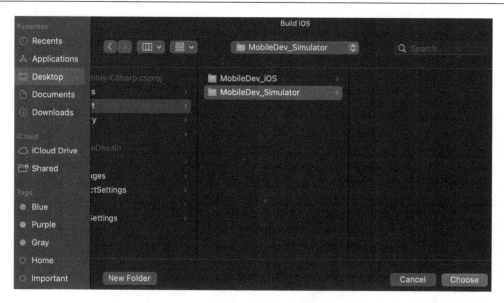

Figure 2.48 – Select a build folder

3. Open the new project, and from there, in the top section, you'll now see a simulator device selected instead of the **Any iOS device** option given in the previous build. You can also click on the option to open a drop-down list where you can select a particular device you'd like to build to:

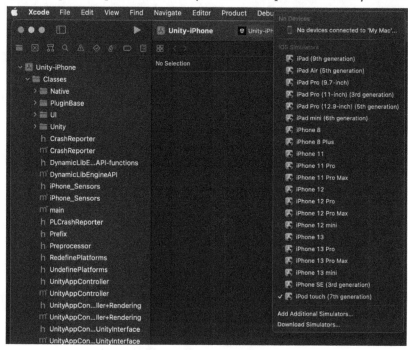

Figure 2.49 – Selecting a simulator device

4. Once you have your device selected, press the **Play** button and wait until it completes building the project. If all goes well, you should be able to see the simulator open up, and you can then play your game:

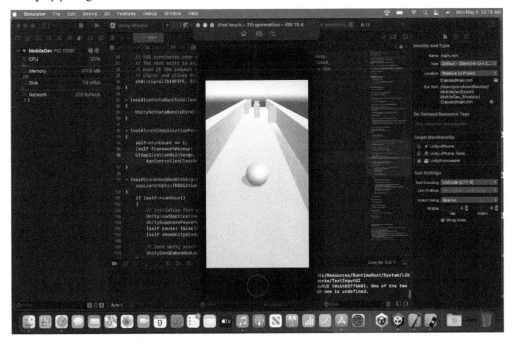

Figure 2.50 – Playing the game on the simulator

And with that, we've seen just how easy it is to build our project in a simulator if needed; just make sure to switch the **Target SDK** property back to **Device SDK** when making a build for actual devices.

Summary

We now have our game running on Android and iOS devices, and we have learned the steps we'll need to take each time we want to deploy our games on these devices.

While I will not be writing about exporting to both kinds of devices again until we get to *Chapter 13, Building a Release Copy of Our Game*, it's a good idea for you to see how the changes that we will make will work with both platforms and keep testing on each platform to make sure that your project works correctly and at a frame rate that you are okay with.

This is especially important to note, as running the project on your PC via the editor or an emulator will not always accurately represent how the game will run on a different device. As a result, you may find that certain aspects of your game that run fine on your mobile device will cause your computer to be choppy instead. The thing is, you won't know unless you are always checking the games on devices, so I highly advise that you do so.

Our game is working on mobile devices now, but it will not react to anything we do on the devices due to how we wrote our input code. In the next chapter, we will explore how we can add input to our project as well as the design considerations we need to make regarding how the different forms of input will change our game.

Part 2: Mobile-Specific Features

This part of the book will focus on developing mobile-specific features in your Unity project. By the end of this part, you will have all the knowledge necessary to create a feature-rich mobile game with a polished UI and integrated monetization and social media features.

This part has the following chapters:

- *Chapter 3, Mobile Input/Touch Controls*
- *Chapter 4, Resolution-Independent UI*
- *Chapter 5, Advanced Mobile UI*
- *Chapter 6, Implementing In-App Purchases*
- *Chapter 7, Advertising Using Unity Ads*
- *Chapter 8, Integrating Social Media into Our Project*

3
Mobile Input/Touch Controls

How players interact with your project is probably one of the most important things in it to get right. While player input is added for all projects, no matter what platform you are using, this is one area that can make or break your mobile game.

If the controls that are implemented don't fit the game that you're making, or if the controls feel clunky, players will not play your game for long stretches of time. While many people consider Rockstar's *Grand Theft Auto* series of games to work well on consoles and PC, playing the games on a mobile device provides a larger barrier of entry, due to all of the buttons on the screen and the replacement of joysticks with virtual versions that don't provide haptic feedback in the same manner as other platforms.

Mobile and tablet games that tend to do well typically have controls that are simple, finding as many ways to streamline the gameplay as possible. Many popular games require a single input, such as Dong Nguyen's *Flappy Bird* and Ketchapp's *Ballz*.

There are various ways for games to interact with a mobile device that are different when compared to traditional games such as gestures and pinches, and we will explore a number of those in this chapter.

In this chapter, we will cover the different ways that inputs will work on mobile devices. We will start with the input that is already built into our project, using the mouse, and then move on to touch events, gestures, the use of the accelerometer, and accessing information via the Touch class.

This chapter will be split into a number of topics. It will contain a simple, step-by-step process from beginning to end. Here is the outline of our tasks:

- Using mouse input
- Moving via touch
- Using Unity Remote
- Implementing a gesture
- Scaling a player using pinches

- Using an accelerometer

- Detecting touch on game objects

Technical requirements

This book utilizes *Unity 2022.1.0b16* and *Unity Hub 3.3.1*, but the steps should work with minimal changes in future versions of the editor. If you would like to download the exact version used in this book (and there is a new version out), you can visit Unity's download archive at `https://unity3d.com/get-unity/download/archive`.

You can also find the system requirements for Unity at `https://docs.unity3d.com/2022.1/Documentation/Manual/system-requirements.html` under the **Unity Editor system requirements** section.

You can find the code files present in this chapter on GitHub at `https://github.com/PacktPublishing/Unity-2022-Mobile-Game-Development-3rd-Edition/tree/main/Chapter03`.

Using mouse input

Before we dive into mobile-only solutions, I do want to point out that it is possible to write input that works on both mobile and PC by using mouse controls. Mobile devices support using mouse clicks as taps on the screen, with the position of the tap/click being the location where the finger has been pressed. This form of input provides just the position where the touch happened and indicates that a press has happened; it doesn't give you all of the features that the mobile-only options do. We will discuss all of the features you have using mobile-specific input later on in this chapter, but I think it's important to note how to have click events on the desktop as well. I personally use the desktop often for ease of testing on both a PC and my device, so I don't have to deploy to a mobile device to test every single change made in a project.

To use desktop-based mouse click events for the movement of a player, first, inside Unity, open up your `PlayerBehaviour` script and update the `FixedUpdate` function to the following:

```
/// <summary>
/// FixedUpdate is a prime place to put physics
/// calculations happening over a period of time.
/// </summary>

void FixedUpdate()
{
    // Check if we're moving to the side
    var horizontalSpeed = Input.GetAxis("Horizontal") *
        dodgeSpeed;
```

```
/* If the mouse is held down (or the screen is pressed
 * on Mobile) */
if (Input.GetMouseButton(0))
{
    /* Get a reference to the camera for converting
     * between spaces */
    var cam = Camera.main;

    /* Converts mouse position to a 0 to 1 range */
    var screenPos = Input.mousePosition;
    var viewPos = cam.ScreenToViewportPoint(screenPos);

    float xMove = 0;

    /* If we press the right side of the screen */
    if (viewPos.x < 0.5f)
    {
        xMove = -1;
    }
    else
    {
        /* Otherwise we're on the left */
        xMove = 1;
    }

    /* Replace horizontalSpeed with our own value */
    horizontalSpeed = xMove * dodgeSpeed;
}

rb.AddForce(horizontalSpeed, 0, rollSpeed);

}
```

We have added a number of things to the preceding script. First, we check whether the mouse button had been held down or not through the use of the Input.GetMouseButton function. The function will return true if the mouse is held down, and false if it is not. The function takes in a parameter, which is for what mouse button we'd like to check, providing 0 for the left button, 1 for the right, and 2 for the middle button. For mobile, however, only 0 will be picked up as a click.

> **Note**
>
> For more information on the Input.GetMouseButton function, check out https://docs.unity3d.com/ScriptReference/Input.GetMouseButton.html.

We can get the position that the mouse is at by using the `Input.mousePosition` property. However, this value is given to us in screen space. What is screen space? Well, let's first talk about how we traditionally deal with positions in Unity by making use of world space.

Screen space versus world space

When dealing with positions in Unity through the **Inspector** window, we have the **(0,0,0)** point in the middle of our game's world, which we call the origin, and then we refer to everything else based on an offset from there. We typically refer to this method of positioning as **world space**. Assuming that we have our camera pointing toward the origin, world space looks like this:

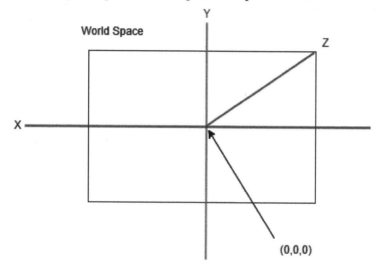

Figure 3.1 – An example of world space

The lines are the *x*, *y*, and *z* axes of our world. If I were to move an object to the right or left, it would move along the *x* axis positively or negatively respectively. When in school, you may have learned about using graphs and points, and world space works very much like that.

> **Note**
>
> Children of parented objects use a different system in the **Inspector** window, in that they are given positions relative to their parents instead. This system is called *local space*.

When using mouse input, Unity gives us this information in another space, **screen space**. In this space, the position is based on where the camera is and isn't involved with the actual game world. This space is also just in 2D, so there's only an *x* and *y* position, with *z* always being stuck at **0**:

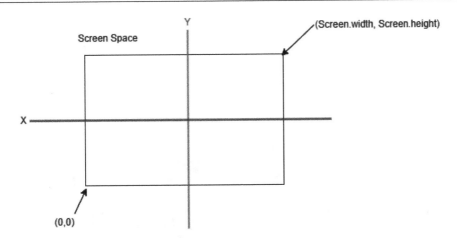

Figure 3.2 – An example of screen space

In the preceding case, the bottom left of the screen would be **(0,0)** and the top right would be **(Screen. width, Screen.height)**. *Screen.width* and *Screen.height* are values in Unity that will give us the screen size of the screen window in pixels.

We could use these values as provided and then compare what side of the screen the player pressed, but in our case, I think it'd be better to convert the position into an easier space to work with. One such space is the **viewport space**, which goes from **(0,0)** to **(1,1)**:

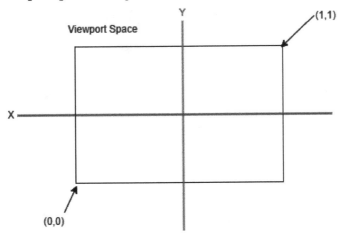

Figure 3.3 – An example of viewport space

Instead of searching whether our *x* position is less than half of the screen width, I can instead just check whether the value of viewPos.x is less than 0.5, which is what we are doing in the preceding code. If the value is less than 0.5, it's on the left side of the screen, so we return -1; otherwise, it's on the right side, so we give 1.

> **Note**
>
> Note that some of Unity's functions will use *Vector3* instead of *Vector2* in order to work with 3D spaces as well.

Once we know that, we can then set the horizontal speed variable to move to the left or right based on our movement.

Save the script and dive back into Unity, and you will see the following:

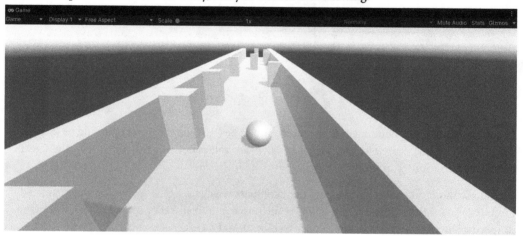

Figure 3.4 – The current status of the game

As you can see in the preceding screenshot, we can now use either the mouse (via the `Input. GetMouseButton` function and the `Input.mousePosition` variable) or our keyboard (via the `GetAxis` function), as described previously, to move our player.

This form of input works well enough for what we're doing right now, but I'm assuming that you'll want to know how to use the mobile device's own way of moving, so we will go ahead and learn how to replicate the same functionality using touch instead.

Moving using touch controls

Unity's Input engine has a property called `Input.touches`, which is an array of the `Touch` objects. The `Touch` struct contains information on the touch that occurred, with information such as the amount of pressure on the touch and how many times you tapped the screen. It also contains the position property, such as `Input.mousePosition`, that will tell you what position the tap occurred at, in pixels.

> **Note**
>
> For more information on the Touch struct, check out `https://docs.unity3d.com/ScriptReference/Touch.html`.

Let's look at the steps to use touch instead of mouse inputs:

1. Adjust our preceding code to look something like the following:

```csharp
/// <summary>
/// FixedUpdate is a prime place to put physics
/// calculations happening over a period of time.
/// </summary>

void FixedUpdate()
{
    // Check if we're moving to the side
    var horizontalSpeed = Input.GetAxis("Horizontal")
        * dodgeSpeed;

    /* Check if Input has registered more than 0
       touches */
    if (Input.touchCount > 0)
    {
        /* Get a reference to the camera for
           converting between spaces */
        var cam = Camera.main;

        /* Store the first touch detected */
        var firstTouch = Input.touches[0];

        /* Converts mouse position to a 0 to 1 range
        */
        var screenPos = firstTouch.position;
        var viewPos =
            cam.ScreenToViewportPoint(screenPos);

        float xMove = 0;

        /* If we press the right side of the screen */
        if (viewPos.x < 0.5f)
        {
            xMove = -1;
        }
```

```
    else
    {
        /* Otherwise we're on the left */
        xMove = 1;
    }

    /* Replace horizontalSpeed with our own value
    */
    horizontalSpeed = xMove * dodgeSpeed;
}


rb.AddForce(horizontalSpeed, 0, rollSpeed);

}
```

Now, note that this code looks very similar to what we've written in the preceding section. With that in mind, instead of copying and pasting the appropriate code twice and making changes, as a number of starting programmers would do, we can instead take the similarities and make a function. For the differences, we can use parameters to change the value instead.

2. Keeping that in mind, let's add the following function to the `PlayerBehaviour` class:

```
/// <summary>
/// Will figure out where to move the player
/// horizontally
/// </summary>
/// <param name="screenPos">The position the player
/// has touched/clicked on in screen space</param>
/// <returns>The direction to move in the x
    axis</returns>
private float CalculateMovement(Vector3 screenPos)
{
    /* Get a reference to the camera for converting
     * between spaces */
    var cam = Camera.main;

    /* Converts mouse position to a 0 to 1 range */
    var viewPos =
        cam.ScreenToViewportPoint(screenPos);

    float xMove = 0;

    /* If we press the right side of the screen */
    if (viewPos.x < 0.5f)
    {
```

```
        xMove = -1;
    }
    else
    {
        /* Otherwise we're on the left */
        xMove = 1;
    }

    /* Replace horizontalSpeed with our own value */
    return xMove * dodgeSpeed;
}
```

In the preceding code, instead of using `Input.mousePosition` or the touch position, we use a parameter for the function. Also, unlike previous functions we've written, this one will actually use a return value; in this case, it will give us a floating-point value. We will use this value in the `Update` function to set `horiztonalSpeed` to a new value when this function is called. Now that the function exists, we can call it when appropriate.

3. Now, update the `Update` function, as follows:

```
/// <summary>
/// FixedUpdate is a prime place to put physics
/// calculations happening over a period of time.
/// </summary>

void FixedUpdate()
{
    // Check if we're moving to the side
    var horizontalSpeed = Input.GetAxis("Horizontal")
        * dodgeSpeed;

    /* Check if we are running either in the Unity
        editor or in a * standalone build.*/
    #if UNITY_STANDALONE || UNITY_WEBPLAYER ||
        UNITY_EDITOR
        /* If the mouse is held down (or the screen is
            tapped * on Mobile */
        if (Input.GetMouseButton(0))
        {
            var screenPos = Input.mousePosition;
            horizontalSpeed =
                CalculateMovement(screenPos);
        }
    /* Check if we are running on a mobile device */
    #elif UNITY_IOS || UNITY_ANDROID
```

```
        // Check if Input has registered more than
        // zero touches
        if (Input.touchCount > 0)
        {
            /* Store the first touch detected */
            var firstTouch = Input.touches[0];
            var screenPos = firstTouch.position;
            horizontalSpeed =
                CalculateMovement(screenPos);
        }
    #endif

        rb.AddForce(horizontalSpeed, 0, rollSpeed);

}
```

In the preceding example, I am using a #if directive based on the platform selected. Unity will automatically create #define, depending on what has been selected as the platform we are deploying for. What this #if does, along with #elif and #endif, is allow us to include or exclude code from our project based on these directives.

In Visual Studio, note that if you're building for iOS or Android, the code within the UNITY_IOS || UNITY_ANDROID section is grayed out, meaning that it won't be called currently because we are running the game in the *Unity Editor*. However, when we export the code to our platform, the appropriate code will be used.

> **Note**
>
> To take a look at all of the other platform-dependent #define directives, check out https://docs.unity3d.com/Manual/PlatformDependentCompilation.html.

Making use of the aforementioned directives, we can specify the code for different versions of our project, which is vital when dealing with multi-platform development.

> **Note**
>
> In addition to Unity's built-in `#define` directives, you can create your own by going to **Edit | Project Settings | Player**, scrolling down to **Other Settings** in the **Inspector** window, and changing **Scripting Define Symbols**.
>
> This can be great for targeting specific devices or for showing certain pieces of debug information, in addition to a number of other things.

4.   Save the script and dive back into Unity.

Upon exporting our game to your Android device, note that the controls now work correctly using our newly created touch code. This allows us to have something that works on mobile as well as PC.

We already know that we can export our game to an Android device, but there is another way that we can test our game on a device without having to do a full export. This can be done by downloading a special app, which will allow us to stream our games from our computer to our mobile device and is what we will be discussing next.

Using Unity Remote

Another way to check how our game works using mobile devices is through an application that Unity has created called the **Unity Remote**. Created with Unity 5, it has been a while since the application has been updated, but it still works with the current version of Unity; however, it does require us to do some additional work and setup.

Android setup For Unity Remote

In order to set up a phone to use Unity Remote, we will need to download the app and learn how to enable debugging mode, so in this section, we're going to see just how to do that:

1.   To start, open up the *Google Play* app, and from there in the search bar, type in `unity remote`:

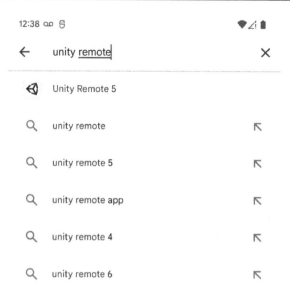

Figure 3.5 – Searching for the Unity Remote application

2. Select the **Unity Remote 5** app. Afterward, you'll be brought to the screen in order to install it, so click on the **Install** button and wait for it to finish downloading.

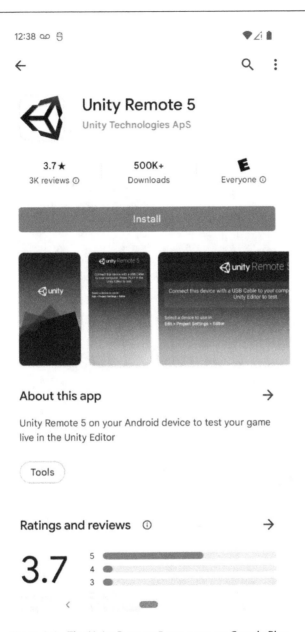

Figure 3.6 – The Unity Remote 5 app page on Google Play

3. Once it's completed, you should see it show up on your phone, ready to be opened.

Figure 3.7 – Application on your device

4.   Click on the application, and you'll be brought to a screen that asks you whether the application is allowed to take pictures and record video. This is due to the features that your games may use, so feel free to choose whether your game can use those features.

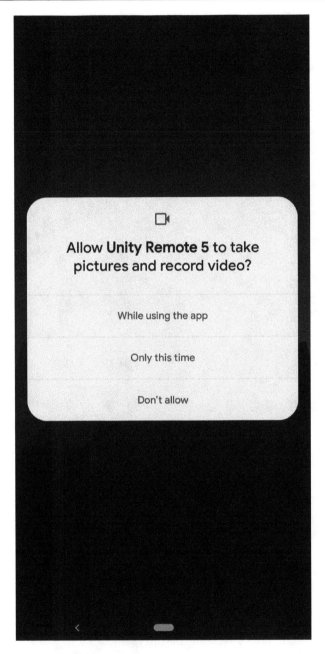

Figure 3.8 – The permissions screen

5.   Afterward, you should see a screen that looks like this:

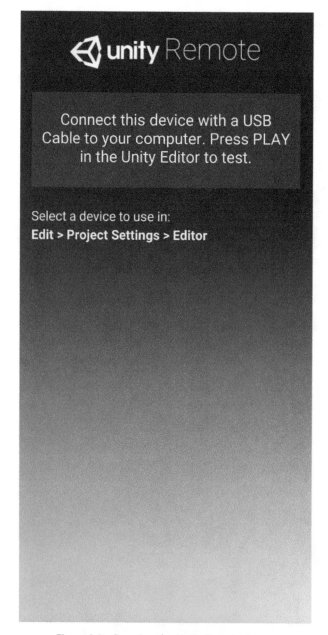

Figure 3.9 – Running the Unity Remote 5 app

This is the setup screen that you should see before playing your games, but if you try to play your project right now, nothing would happen; therefore, there's still a few things that we need to do in preparation.

Enabling developer mode and debugging

To start off with, we're going to need to change our phone to be in developer mode so that we can enable debugging:

1. First, in the Unity Editor, go to the **Project Settings** menu and open up the **Editor** section. From there, under the **Unity Remote** options, change **Device** from **None** to **Any Android Device**.

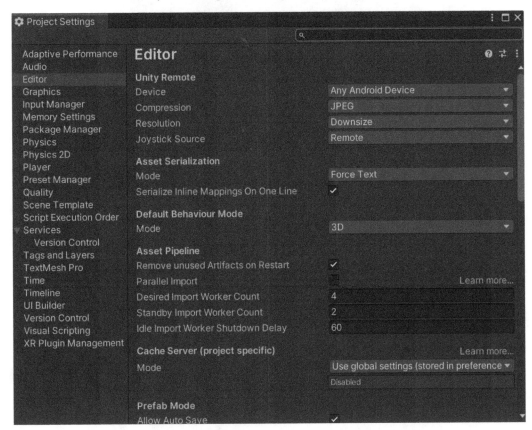

Figure 3.10 – Setting the Unity Remote device

2. If you have not done so already, connect your phone to your PC via USB. From the **Settings** menu, you'll want to select the **USB accessory connected** notification from your notifications.

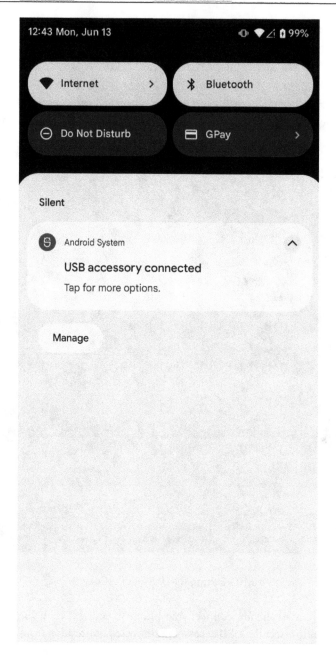

Figure 3.11 – The notifications window upon plugging in the phone to the computer

3.   From the menu that pops up, select the **USB tethering** option.

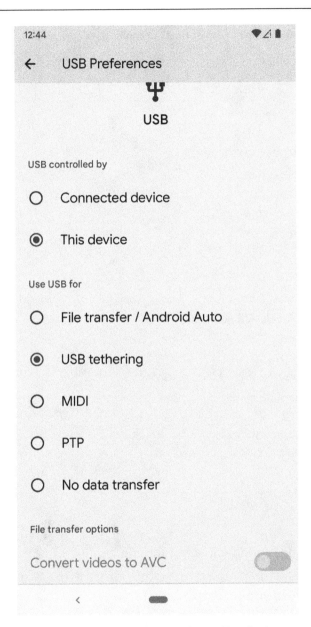

Figure 3.12 – Changing the mode to USB tethering

If you don't see this on your device, you may look for the **Mobile Hotspot and Tethering** section of your phone or using your internet search engine of choice to see how to enable USB tethering for your device.

4. Then, on the device, go to **Settings** | **About phone**.

5.   Tap the **Build number** property seven times to enable *developer mode*.

Figure 3.13 – The About phone menu on my phone

6. From there, go to the **Developer options** section. I used the **Settings** window's search function to find the exact location.

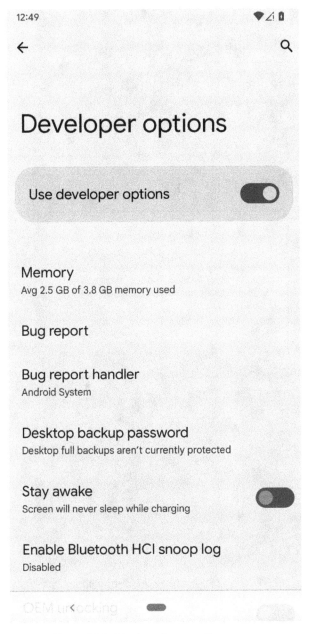

Figure 3.14 – The Developer options menu

7. From there, scroll down and select the **USB debugging** option. You may see a window explaining what USB debugging is for. Click on the **OK** button.

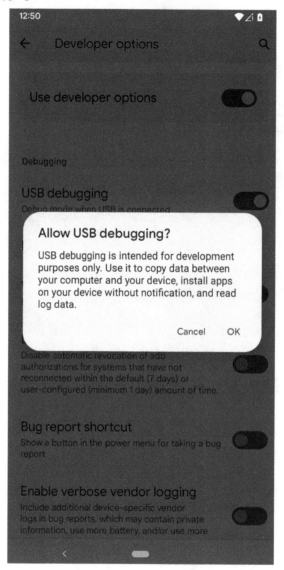

Figure 3.15 – Enabling USB debugging

8. Next, you'll have a window popup that says **Allow USB debugging?**. Click on the **Allow** button.

9. Now, you should be able to return to the *Unity Remote 5* application. Back on your PC, click on the **Play** button, and you may see the computer appear to freeze for a bit, but after a short period of time, you should see your phone change to reflect the gameplay on the PC:

Figure 3.16 – Unity Remote gameplay

You may see some blurriness or graphical issues when playing the game on your device using Unity Remote. This is because Unity is sending an image of what the game looks like to the device to interact with; the game is not actually on the device. The quality isn't anywhere near what the game on the actual device would be, but it does allow us to check the current state of our game on the actual device itself!

The enabling of developer mode and debugging also has the benefit of allowing us to deploy our game to our device straight through the build menu, without having to install it manually. To do so, go to the **Build Settings** menu, and under the **Run Device** option, select your phone.

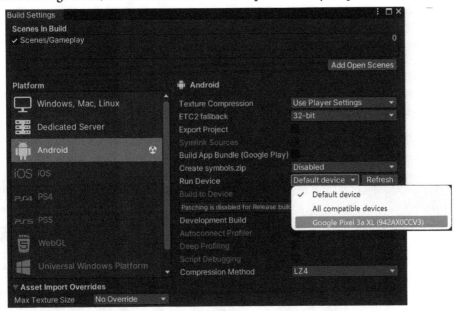

Figure 3.17 – Setting a run device

Now, if you select **Build and Run** when the game finishes, the build you should see is the game directly running upon opening your phone:

Figure 3.18 – The game installed directly on the device

Now that we've learned how to use Unity Remote on an Android device, we can now see how we can set up Unity Remote on an iOS device.

Unity Remote setup for iOS

Getting Unity Remote set up on iOS is possible on a Mac computer or a Windows computer that has *iTunes* installed. However, the steps will be similar to working with Android, aside from not needing to enable debugging. For the purpose of this section, I will be using a Mac:

1. First, in the Unity Editor, go to the **Project Settings** menu and open up the **Editor** section. From there, under the **Unity Remote** options, change **Device** from **None** to **Any iOS Device**.

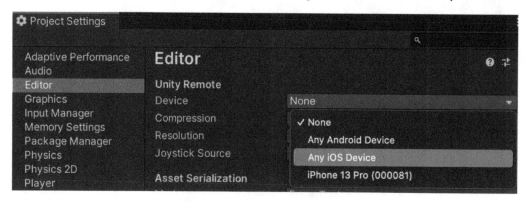

Figure 3.19 – Selecting the Any iOS Device option

2. Then, from your iOS device, open up the App Store and search for unity remote.

Figure 3.20 – Searching for the Unity Remote app

3. Select the Unity Remote 5 app and install it on your device. Once it has finished installing, it should be located on your phone:

Figure 3.21 – Unity Remote installed

4. Open up the app, and you should see something similar to the following, asking you whether you'd like to trust this computer. Go ahead and hit the **Trust** button:

Figure 3.22 – The Trust This Computer option

5. From your computer, go ahead and play the game. It may take a moment, but you should see the game streaming to your device, and you can play as usual:

Figure 3.23 – Footage of Unity Remote streaming our game

As noted when we built the Android version, you may see some blurriness or graphical issues when playing the game on your device using Unity Remote. This is because Unity is sending an image of what the game looks like to the device to interact with; the game is not actually on the device. The quality isn't anywhere near what the game on the actual device would be, but it does allow us to check the current state of our game on the actual device itself!

And with that, we can now play our games on our respective devices without having to do a build! This can be a great way to quickly check whether things are working correctly on your device without having to do a build every time. Now, let's take a look at some of the mobile-specific ways that we can interpret input.

Implementing a gesture

Another type of input that you'll find in mobile games is that of a swipe, such as in Kiloo's *Subway Surfers*. This allows us to use the general movement of the touch to dictate a direction for us to move in. This is usually used to have our players *jump* from one position to another or move quickly in a certain direction. So, we'll go ahead and implement that using the following steps, instead of our previous movement system:

1. In the PlayerBehaviour script, go ahead and add some new variables for us to work with:

    ```
    [Header("Swipe Properties")]
    [Tooltip("How far will the player move upon swiping")]
    public float swipeMove = 2f;

    [Tooltip("How far must the player swipe before we will
    ```

```
        execute the action (in inches)")]
public float minSwipeDistance = 0.25f;

/// <summary>
/// Used to hold the value that converts
/// minSwipeDistance to pixels
/// </summary>
private float minSwipeDistancePixels;

/// <summary>
/// Stores the starting position of mobile touch
/// events
/// </summary>
private Vector2 touchStart;
```

In order to determine whether we are swiping, we will need to first check the start and the end of our movement. We will store the starting position in the touchStart property. We will also have the swipeMove property to set how far we will *jump* when the swipe happens. Lastly, we have the minSwipeDistance variable, which will make sure that the player has moved on the *x* axis a little before actually making the jump – in this case, we want the user to move at least a quarter of an inch in order for the input to be counted as a swipe.

Also note that the Header attribute has been added to the top of the first variable. This will add a header to the **Inspector** tab, making it easier to break apart different sections of your script. If you were to save the script and dive into Unity, you should see that this new attribute has been added when you select the player:

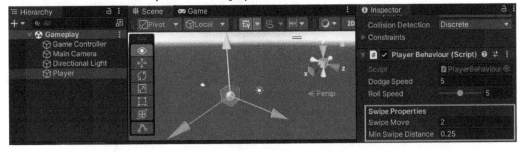

Figure 3.24 – The newly added mobile input/touch controls under Swipe Properties

Our next step is to convert the MinSwipeDistance value from inches into the pixel equivalent, which can be used to see how far the user's swiping motion moves the player's character.

2. Go back to the `PlayerBehaviour` script and update the `Start` function to add the following highlighted code:

```
// Start is called before the first frame update
public void Start()
{
    // Get access to our Rigidbody component
    rb = GetComponent<Rigidbody>();

    minSwipeDistancePixels = minSwipeDistance *
        Screen.dpi;

}
```

The `Screen.dpi` value stands for **dots per inch** and generally can be thought of as how many pixels are there per inch on the screen. By multiplying the value of `minSwipeDistance` by `Screen.dpi`, we know how long the movement in pixels needs to be for it to be counted as a swipe.

> **Note**
>
> For more information on the `Screen.dpi` variable, check out `https://docs.unity3d.com/ScriptReference/Screen-dpi.html`.

Now that we know the length of a swipe, we need to add the ability to trigger one. As we mentioned before, we have been using the `FixedUpdate` function for our player's movement. This is because Unity's physics engine is only updated once between each `FixedUpdate`, which is generally called less often than the `Update` function.

We use the `Input.GetAxis` and `Input.GetMouseButton` functions, which return `true` every single frame that the button is held down and will continue to respond during `FixedUpdate` loops as well. This works great for events that happen over time, but `FixedUpdate` can miss the start and ending frames where input events happen, which is required for swipe events and certain actions, such as jumping, in games. If you want something to happen the moment an input starts or finishes, you will likely want to utilize the `Update` function instead, and that is what we will be doing with our gesture.

3. Now, back in the `PlayerBehaviour` script, add the following function to the project:

```
/// <summary>
/// Update is called once per frame
/// </summary>
private void Update()
{
    /* Check if we are running on a mobile device */
```

```
#if UNITY_IOS || UNITY_ANDROID

    /* Check if Input has registered more than
       zero touches */
    if (Input.touchCount > 0)
    {
        /* Store the first touch detected */
        Touch touch = Input.touches[0];


        SwipeTeleport(touch);

    }


#endif
}
```

In the preceding code, we added a new behavior called `SwipeTeleport` that will only be called if the game is running on a mobile device. It hasn't been created yet, but this will take in the Touch event and use its properties to move the player if a swipe happens.

We will then create a function to handle this new swiping behavior, as follows:

```
/// <summary>
/// Will teleport the player if swiped to the left or
/// right
/// </summary>
/// <param name="touch">Current touch event</param>
private void SwipeTeleport(Touch touch)
{
    /* Check if the touch just started */
    if (touch.phase == TouchPhase.Began)
    {
        /* If so, set touchStart */
        touchStart = touch.position;
    }


    /* If the touch has ended */
    else if (touch.phase == TouchPhase.Ended)
    {
        /* Get the position the touch ended at */
        Vector2 touchEnd = touch.position;


        /* Calculate the difference between the
           beginning and end of the touch on the x
           axis. */
        float x = touchEnd.x - touchStart.x;
```

```
    /* If not moving far enough, don't do the
       teleport */
    if (Mathf.Abs(x) < minSwipeDistancePixels)
    {
        return;
    }

    Vector3 moveDirection;

    /* If moved negatively in the x axis, move
       left */
    if (x < 0)
    {
        moveDirection = Vector3.left;
    }
    else
    {
        /* Otherwise player is on the right */
        moveDirection = Vector3.right;
    }

    RaycastHit hit;

    /* Only move if player wouldn't hit something
    */
    if (!rb.SweepTest(moveDirection, out hit,
    swipeMove))
    {
        /* Move the player */
        var movement = moveDirection * swipeMove;
        var newPos = rb.position + movement;

        rb.MovePosition(newPos);
    }
  }
}
```

In this function, instead of just using the current touch position, we instead store the starting position when the touch begins. When the player lifts their finger, we get the position as well. We then get the direction of that movement and then apply it to the ball, checking whether we'll collide with something before actually causing the movement.

4. Save your script and dive back into Unity, exporting your project to your mobile device or an emulator.

Figure 3.25 – A visual of the game after performing a swipe

Now, whenever we swipe to the left or right, the player will move accordingly. Let's learn about another action that we can use while playing the game in the next section.

Scaling the player using pinches

The concept of using touch events to modify things in the game can also be applied to other methods of touch interaction, such as using finger pinches to zoom in and out. To see how to do this, let's adjust the PlayerBehaviour script so that we can change the player's scale, using two fingers to pinch or stretch out the view:

1. Open up the PlayerBehaviour script and add the following properties:

```
[Header("Scaling Properties")]

[Tooltip("The minimum size (in Unity units) that the
    player should be")]
public float minScale = 0.5f;

[Tooltip("The maximum size (in Unity units) that the
    player should be")]
```

```
public float maxScale = 3.0f;

/// <summary>
/// The current scale of the player
/// </summary>
private float currentScale = 1;
```

2. Next, add the following function:

```
/// <summary>
/// Will change the player's scale via pinching and
/// stretching two touch events
/// </summary>
private void ScalePlayer()
{
    /* We must have two touches to check if we are
     * scaling the object */
    if (Input.touchCount != 2)
    {
        return;
    }
    else
    {
        /* Store the touches detected. */
        Touch touch0 = Input.touches[0];
        Touch touch1 = Input.touches[1];

        Vector2 t0Pos = touch0.position;
        Vector2 t0Delta = touch0.deltaPosition;

        Vector2 t1Pos = touch1.position;
        Vector2 t1Delta = touch1.deltaPosition;

        /* Find the previous frame position of each
           touch. */
        Vector2 t0Prev = t0Pos - t0Delta;
        Vector2 t1Prev = t1Pos - t1Delta;

        /* Find the the distance (or magnitude)
           between the * touches in each frame. */
        float prevTDeltaMag =
            (t0Prev - t1Prev).magnitude;
```

```
float tDeltaMag = (t0Pos - t1Pos).magnitude;

/* Find the difference in the distances
 * between each frame. */
float deltaMagDiff =
    prevTDeltaMag - tDeltaMag;

/* Keep the change consistent no matter what
 * the framerate is */
float newScale = currentScale;
newScale -= (deltaMagDiff * Time.deltaTime);

// Ensure that the new value is valid
newScale = Mathf.Clamp(newScale, minScale,
    maxScale);

/* Update the player's scale */
transform.localScale = Vector3.one * newScale;

/* Set our current scale for the next frame */
currentScale = newScale;

    }
}
```

Instead of using a single touch event, in this example, we are using two. Using both touch events, we can see how the touches have changed over the course of the previous frame (the delta). We then use that difference to modify the scale of the player. To ensure the ball will always have a valid value, we use the `Mathf.Clamp` function to keep the values between what is set in `minScale` and `maxScale`.

3. Next, we need to call the function by updating the `Update` function:

```
/// <summary>
/// Update is called once per frame
/// </summary>
private void Update()
{
    /* Check if we are running on a mobile device */
    #if UNITY_IOS || UNITY_ANDROID

        /* Check if Input has registered more than
            zero touches */
        if (Input.touchCount > 0)
        {
```

```
                    /* Store the first touch detected */
                    Touch touch = Input.touches[0];

                    SwipeTeleport(touch);
                    ScalePlayer();
            }

        #endif
    }
```

4. Save your script and return to the Unity editor. Export your game, and you should be able to see the player scaling in action – by moving two fingers apart, you'll see the ball expand, and vice versa:

Figure 3.26 – The result of our pinch gesture in the current state of the game

> **Note**
>
> For those using LDPlayer, it is possible to replicate a pinch/zoom effect by pressing *Ctrl* and then scrolling the mouse wheel.

Hopefully, this demonstrates the power given by being able to use multi-touch and some of the advantages of utilizing touch events, instead of just a single mouse click. Next, we will explore another type of input method that PCs don't have.

Using the accelerometer

Another type of input that mobile has, but PC doesn't, is the accelerometer. This allows you to move in the game by tilting the physical position of the phone. The most popular example of this is likely the movement of the player in games such as Lima Sky's *Doodle Jump* and Gameloft's *Asphalt* series. To do something similar, we can retrieve the acceleration of our device with the `Input.acceleration` property and use it to move the player. Let's look at the steps to do just that:

1. We may want to allow our designers to set whether they want to use the `Accelerometer` mode or `ScreenTouch`, which we used previously. With that in mind, let's create a new enum with the possible values to place in the `PlayerBehaviour` script above the **Swipe Properties** header:

```
[Tooltip("How fast the ball moves forwards
    automatically")]
[Range(0, 10)]
public float rollSpeed = 5;


public enum MobileHorizMovement
{
    Accelerometer,
    ScreenTouch
}


[Tooltip("What horizontal movement type should be
    used")]
public MobileHorizMovement horizMovement =
    MobileHorizMovement.Accelerometer;



[Header("Swipe Properties")]
[Tooltip("How far will the player move upon swiping")]
public float swipeMove = 2f;
```

The preceding script utilizes enum to define a custom type called `MobileHorizMovement`, which can be one of two values, `Accelerometer` or `ScreenTouch`. We then create a variable of this new type called `horizMovement`.

Now, if you save the `PlayerBehaviour` script and dive back into the **Inspector** tab, you will see we can select one of these two options (**Accelerometer** or **Screen Touch**). By using this drop-down menu, the game designer of the project can easily select which of the two options we'd like to use, and then we can expand to even more if want to in the future (which we will in the next chapter):

Figure 3.27 – Adjusting the Horiz Movement property from the Inspector

2. Next, let's update the Update function to use the following highlighted code within the #elif UNITY_IOS || UNITY_ANDROID block of code:

```
/* Check if we are running on a mobile device */
#elif UNITY_IOS || UNITY_ANDROID

    switch (horizMovement)
    {
        case MobileHorizMovement.Accelerometer:
            /* Move player based on accelerometer
                direction */
            horizontalSpeed = Input.acceleration.x *
                dodgeSpeed;
            break;

        case MobileHorizMovement.ScreenTouch:
            /* Check if Input registered more than
                zero touches */
            if (Input.touchCount > 0)
            {
                /* Store the first touch detected */
                var firstTouch = Input.touches[0];
                var screenPos = firstTouch.position;
                horizontalSpeed =
                    CalculateMovement(screenPos);
            }
            break;
    }

#endif

// Check if we are running on a mobile device
```

```
#elif UNITY_IOS || UNITY_ANDROID

if(horizMovement == MobileHorizMovement.Accelerometer)
{
// Move player based on direction of the accelerometer
horizontalSpeed = Input.acceleration.x * dodgeSpeed;
}

//Check if Input has registered more than zero touches if
(Input.touchCount > 0)
{
    if (horizMovement ==
    MobileHorizMovement.ScreenTouch)
    {
        //Store the first touch detected.
        Touch touch = Input.touches[0];
        horizontalSpeed =
            CalculateMovement(touch.position);
    }
}
#endif
```

If the `horizMovement` variable is set to **Accelerometer**, this new snippet of code will use the acceleration of our device instead of touches detected on the screen.

3. Save your script and export the project.

Figure 3.28 – Moving the player via the accelerometer

With that, you'll note that we can now tilt our screen to the right or left, and the player will move in the appropriate direction.

In Unity, acceleration is measured in *g*-force values, with 1 being 1 g of force. If you hold the device upright (with the home button at the bottom) in front of you, the *x* axis is positive along the right, the *y* axis is positive upward, and the *z* axis is positive when pointing toward you.

> **Note**
>
> For more information on the accelerometer, check out `https://docs.unity3d.com/Manual/MobileInput.html`.

It's great to know that our regular input is working, but you may want to check whether a game object in our scene has been touched so that the game can react to it. Let's do that next.

Detecting touch on game objects

To add something else for our player to do, as well as to demonstrate some additional input functionality, we'll ensure that if the player taps an obstacle, it will be destroyed. We will use the following steps to modify our existing code to add this new functionality, utilizing the concept of **raycasts**:

1. In the `PlayerBehaviour` script, add the following new function:

    ```
    /// <summary>
    /// Will determine if we are touching a game object
    /// and if so call events for it
    /// </summary>
    /// <param name="screenPos">The position of the touch
    /// in screen space</param>
    private static void TouchObjects(Vector2 screenPos)
    {
        /* Convert the position into a ray */
        Ray touchRay =
            Camera.main.ScreenPointToRay(screenPos);
        RaycastHit hit;

        /* Create a LayerMask that will collide with all
         * possible channels */
        int layerMask = ~0;

        /* Are we touching an object with a collider? */
        if (Physics.Raycast(touchRay, out hit,
        Mathf.Infinity, layerMask,
        QueryTriggerInteraction.Ignore))
        {
            /* Call the PlayerTouch function if it exists
             * on a component attached to this object */
    ```

```
            hit.transform.SendMessage("PlayerTouch",
            SendMessageOptions.DontRequireReceiver);
    }
}
/// <summary>
/// Will determine if we are touching a game object
/// and if so call events for it
/// </summary>
/// <param name="touch">Our touch event</param> private static
void TouchObjects(Touch touch)
{
// Convert the position into a ray
Ray touchRay =
    Camera.main.ScreenPointToRay(touch.position);
RaycastHit hit;
// Create a LayerMask that will collide with all
// possible channels
int layerMask = ~0;

// Are we touching an object with a collider?
if (Physics.Raycast(touchRay, out hit, Mathf.Infinity,
layerMask, QueryTriggerInteraction.Ignore))
{
    // Call the PlayerTouch function if it exists on a
    // component attached to this object
    hit.transform.SendMessage("PlayerTouch",
        SendMessageOptions.DontRequireReceiver);
}
}
```

Here, we use a different version to determine collisions – a raycast. This is basically an invisible vector leading in a given direction, and we will use it to check whether it collides with any object inside of our scenes. This is often used in games, such as first-person shooters, to determine whether a player has hit an enemy or not without spawning a projectile and moving it there.

The version of Physics.Raycast that we use here takes in five parameters:

- The first specifies what ray to use.

- The second is hit, which holds information about the collision if it occurred.

- The third parameter specifies how far to check for a collision.

- The fourth is a layer mask, which dictates with which objects you can collide. In our case, we want to collide with all colliders, so we use the bit-wise complement operator (~) to change 0 into the number possible by flipping all the bits used to create the number.

- Lastly, we have an enumeration called `QueryTriggerInteraction`, which we set to `Ignore`. This means that the `Tile End` objects with the triggers that we created in *Chapter 1, Building Your Game*, will not block our touch events, which would happen by default even if we couldn't see them.

> **Note**
>
> For more information on the bitwise complement operator (~), check out `https://docs.microsoft.com/en-us/dotnet/csharp/language-reference/operators/bitwise-and-shift-operators#bitwise-complement-operator-`.
>
> For more information on *raycasting*, check out `https://docs.unity3d.com/ScriptReference/Physics.Raycast.html`.

If we do hit something, we call a function named `SendMessage` on the object that we collided with. This function will attempt to call a function with the same name as the first parameter if it exists on any component of the game object. The second parameter lets us know whether we should display an error if it doesn't exist.

> **Note**
>
> For more info on the `SendMessage` function, check out `https://docs.unity3d.com/ScriptReference/GameObject.SendMessage.html`.

2. Now, in the `Update` function, let's actually call the aforementioned `TouchObjects` function and adjust the code so that we can test the functionality within the Unity Editor as well:

```
/// <summary>
/// Update is called once per frame
/// </summary>
private void Update()
{
    /* Check if we are running either in the Unity
       editor or in a
     * standalone build.*/
    #if UNITY_STANDALONE || UNITY_WEBPLAYER ||
        UNITY_EDITOR

    /* If the mouse is tapped */
    if (Input.GetMouseButtonDown(0))
    {
```

```
            Vector2 screenPos = new Vector2(
                Input.mousePosition.x,
                    Input.mousePosition.y);
            TouchObjects(screenPos);
        }


        /* Check if we are running on a mobile device */
        #elif UNITY_IOS || UNITY_ANDROID

            /* Check if Input has registered more than
               zero touches */
            if (Input.touchCount > 0)
            {
                /* Store the first touch detected */
                Touch touch = Input.touches[0];

                TouchObjects(touch.position);
                SwipeTeleport(touch);
                ScalePlayer();
            }

        #endif
}
```

3. Save the `PlayerBehaviour` script at this point.

4. Finally, we call a `PlayerTouch` function if it exists. So, let's open up the `ObstacleBehaviour` script and add the following code:

```
[Tooltip("Explosion effect to play when tapped")]
public GameObject explosion;

/// <summary>
/// If the object is tapped, we spawn an explosion and
/// destroy this object
/// </summary>
private void PlayerTouch()
{
    if (explosion != null)
    {
        var particles = Instantiate(explosion,
            transform.position,
                Quaternion.identity);
        Destroy(particles, 1.0f);
    }
```

```
        Destroy(this.gameObject);
    }


    public GameObject explosion;

    /// <summary>
    /// If the object is tapped, we spawn an explosion and
    /// destroy this object
    /// </summary>
    private void PlayerTouch()
    {
        if (explosion != null)
        {
            var particles = Instantiate(explosion,
                transform.position, Quaternion.identity);
            Destroy(particles, 1.0f);
        }

        Destroy(this.gameObject);
    }
```

This function will basically destroy the game object it is attached to, and create an explosion that will also destroy itself after 1 second.

Note

It is possible to get similar results to what we are writing by making use of Unity's OnMouseDown function. As we have already discussed, it is possible to use mouse events when developing for mobile. Keep in mind, though, that the use of that function is computationally more expensive than the method I'm suggesting here.

This is because when you tap the screen, every object that has an OnMouseDown method will do a **raycast** to check whether it was touched. When you have many objects on the screen, you'll note massive performance differences between 1 raycast and 100, and it's important to keep performance in mind when dealing with mobile development. For more information on this, check out http://answers.unity3d.com/questions/1064394/onmousedown-and-mobile.html.

---

5. Save the scripts and return to Unity.

We haven't created an explosion particle effect yet. To create this effect, we will make use of a *particle system*. We'll be diving into particle systems at a much deeper level in *Chapter 12, Improving Game Feel*, but, for now, we can consider a particle system as a game object that is made as simple as possible so that we can spawn many of them on the screen at once, without causing the game to slow down too much. This is mostly used for things such as smoke or fire, but, in this case, we will have our obstacle explode.

Use the following steps to create an explosion particle effect:

1. Create a particle system by going to **GameObject | Effects | Particle System**. While selected, give the object the name of `Explosion` and hit the *Enter* key.

2. Select the game object in the **Hierarchy** window and then open the **Particle System** component in the **Inspector** tab. In there, click on the **Renderer** section to expand it, and change **RenderMode** to **Mesh** and **Material** to **Default-Material** by clicking on the circle next to the name and selecting **Default-Material** from the menu that pops up:

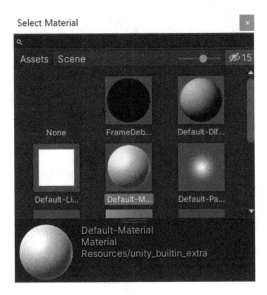

Figure 3.29 – Selecting the Default-Material material

This will make the particles look like the obstacles that we've already created, as a box with the default material.

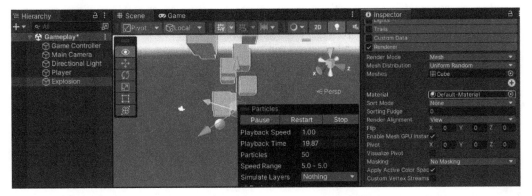

Figure 3.30 – The visual of the boxes

3. Next, under the top **Particle System** section, change the **Gravity Modifier** property to **1**. This ensures that objects will fall gradually, much like normal objects with rigid bodies do, but with less computation.

4. Then, under **Start Speed**, move to the right side and click on the downward-facing arrow, and from that menu, select **Random Between Two Constants**:

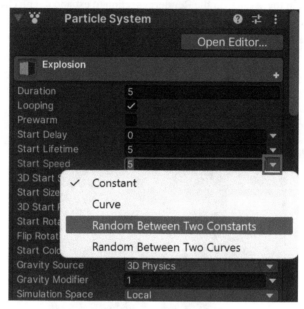

Figure 3.31 – Using a random value between two constants

5. This will change the single window to two, signifying the minimum and maximum values that can be used for this property. From there, set the two values to 0 and 8. This makes the objects spawned start at speeds between *0* and *8*.

6. Then, change **Start Size** to something between **0** and **0.25**. This will ensure that we are creating a bunch of cubes that are smaller than the one we are planning to replace.

7. Change **Duration** to 1 and uncheck the **Looping** option. This ensures that the particle system will last only for *1* second, and unchecking looping means that the particle system will activate only once by default.

> **Note**
>
> You can still see the effect of each of the changes made, by clicking on the **Play** button on the bottom-right menu of the **Scene** window with the **Particle System** object selected.

8. Finally, change the **Start Lifetime** property to **1** to ensure that all of the particles will be dead before the game object is destroyed.

9.   Under the **Emission** section, change **Rate over Time** to **0**. Then, under **Bursts**, click on the + button and then set **Count** to **50**:

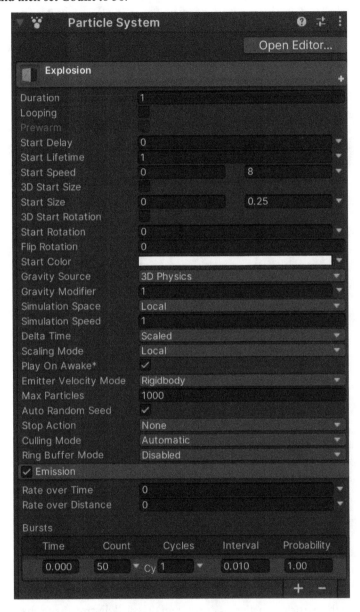

Figure 3.32 – Creating a single burst upon creation

This means that 50 particles will be spawned right at the beginning of the particle system being created, much like an explosion.

10. Then, check **Size over Lifetime** and click on the text next to the checkmark to show more details. From there, change the **Size** property by selecting a curve that decreases gradually so that at the end, they'll all be **0.0**. This can be done by first selecting the curve itself and then going to the **Particle System Curves** section at the bottom of the **Inspector** window. If you do not see the contents shown in the following screenshot, you can click and drag the name upward to make it pop out. From there, you can click on the option that has the downward-facing curve:

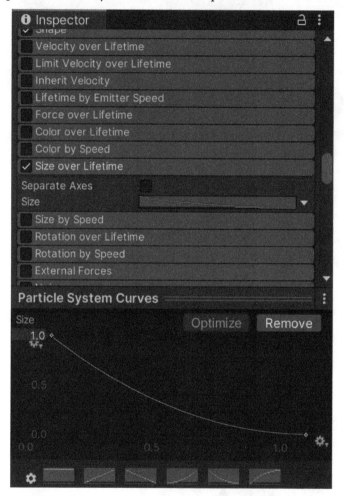

Figure 3.33 – Setting the Size over Lifetime curve

This will make the particles smaller gradually, and they will destroy themselves only after they become invisible (a scale of **0.0**).

11. Finally, check the **Collision** property and open it, setting the **Type** property to **World**. This will cause the particles to hit the ground.

12. Then, make your object a prefab by dragging and dropping it from the **Hierarchy** tab into the **Project** tab in the **Assets | Prefabs** folder. Once the prefab is created (you should see the text on the object in the Hierarchy turn blue), remove the original from the scene by selecting it and pressing the *Delete* key.

13. Next, assign the **Explosion** property of **Obstacle Behaviour (Script)** in the **Obstacle** prefab:

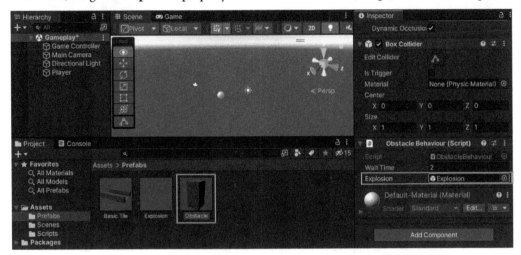

Figure 3.34 – Assigning the Explosion property in the Obstacle prefab

14. Save your project and run the game:

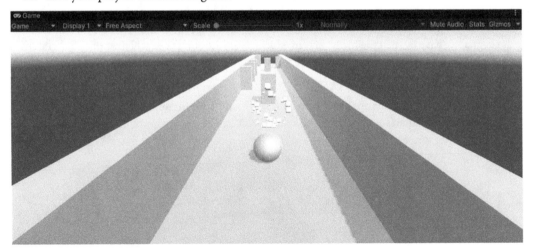

Figure 3.35 – Exploding obstacles on touch

Now, when we tap on one of the obstacles, we can see the object gets destroyed and an explosion effect is played!

If you export the game to your mobile device, you should see the same functionality as well:

Figure 3.36 – The current state of the game

From now on, whenever we tap on the obstacles on our mobile device, they will be destroyed.

Summary

In this chapter, we have learned the main ways in which games are controlled when working on mobile devices. We also learned how we can use mouse inputs, touch events, gestures, and the accelerometer to allow players to interact with our game.

In the next chapter, we will explore the other main way that players interact with a game by diving into the world of user interfaces and creating menus that can be enjoyed, no matter what device a user is playing the game on.

4
Resolution-Independent UI

When working on mobile devices, one of the things that you'll need to spend a fair bit of time on is the **user interface** (**UI**). Unlike when developing projects for a PC, where you only need to care about a single resolution or aspect ratio, there are many different devices out there with different resolutions and aspect ratios when building for mobile. For instance, we have phones that can fit in one of our pockets, and also tablets, which are huge. Not only that but mobile games can also be played horizontally or vertically. Some new phones even allow you to fold them to either increase or decrease the screen size dynamically.

A **graphical user interface** (**GUI**) is the way that players interact with games. You've actually used a GUI in all of the previous chapters (the Unity Editor) and also when interacting with your operating system. Without a GUI of some sort, the only way you'd be able to interact with a computer is with a **command-line interface** (**CLI**) – that is, Command Prompt in Windows and Terminal for Linux and macOS.

When working on GUIs, we want them to contain only information that is important to the player at any given time while also being simple and intuitive. There are people whose main job is programming and/or designing UIs, and there are college degrees in the subject as well. So, while we won't talk about everything to do with using GUIs, I do want to touch on the aspects that should be quite helpful when working on your own projects in the future.

When building for mobile, it's very important that you design your UI to be resolution-independent – that is, to ensure that the UI will scale and adjust itself to fit any screen size that is given to it. As a game developer, you will be able to target a large number of devices if your game is resolution-independent or responsive.

This chapter will be split into a number of topics. The chapter is a simple step-by-step process from beginning to end. The following is the outline of our tasks:

- Creating a title screen
- Adding UI elements to the screen
- Adding on-screen controls

- Implementing a pause menu

- Pausing the game

Technical requirements

This book utilizes Unity 2022.1.0b16 and Unity Hub 3.3.1, but the steps should work with minimal changes in future versions of the editor. If you would like to download the exact version used in this book, and there is a new version out, you can visit Unity's download archive at https://unity3d.com/get-unity/download/archive. You can also find the system requirements for Unity at https://docs.unity3d.com/2022.1/Documentation/Manual/system-requirements.html in the **Unity Editor system requirements** section.

You can find the code files present in this chapter on GitHub at https://github.com/PacktPublishing/Unity-2022-Mobile-Game-Development-3rd-Edition/tree/main/Chapter04.

Creating a title screen

Now, before we start adding UI elements to our game, let's first set up some groundwork and foundational knowledge by creating something that we will need anyway – a title screen:

1. To start, we'll go ahead and create a new scene for us to work with by going to **File | New Scene**. There will be a window that pops up asking which template should be used. In this case, we will select **Basic (Built-in)** and then click on the **Create** button.

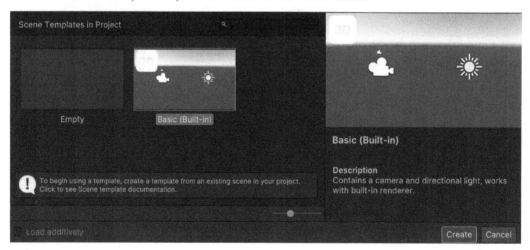

Figure 4.1 – Creating a Basic scene

When dealing with a UI, we will often want to see a visual representation of what will be drawn on the screen, so we will want to make use of 2D mode to have a better representation of what our UI will look like in the final version of the game.

2. To do that, go to the **Scene** view tab – you'll see the control bar menu with a **2D** button on it underneath that. Click on it, and you should see the camera automatically move into something that looks similar to the following screenshot:

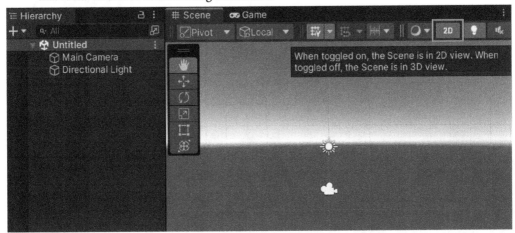

Figure 4.2 – Selecting 2D mode

The **2D** button switches the camera between 2D and 3D views. In 2D mode, you'll note that the Scene Gizmos are gone due to the fact that the only option is to look perpendicularly at the *XY* plane (the *x* axis pointing to the right and the *y* axis pointing upward) and that our camera has changed to an orthographic view.

3. We have to create a **Text** object with the name of our game. Go to the menu and select **GameObject | UI | Text – Text Mesh Pro**.

4. If this is your first time using **TextMeshPro**, there may be a **TMP Importer** window that pops up. If so, click on the **Import TMP Essentials** button.

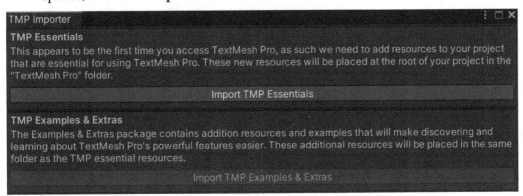

Figure 4.3 – TMP Importer window

> **Tip**
>
> Note that while this book uses **TextMesh Pro** for drawing text, the following steps from the scripting portion also work with the legacy Unity UI system and **Text** objects, and all the concepts in this chapter work the same with both systems.

5.   You will see three new objects, in the **Hierarchy** view, **Canvas**, **Text (TMP)**, and **EventSystem**:

   -   **Canvas**: This is the area where all of the UI elements will reside, and if you try to create a UI element without one already existing, Unity will create one for you like it just did here. From the **Scene** view tab, it will draw a white rectangle around itself to show you how large it is and will resize itself depending on how large the **Game** view is:

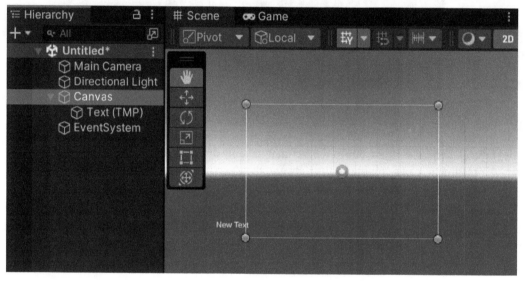

Figure 4.4 – Zooming out to display the Canvas

> **Note**
>
> If you double-click on an object in the **Hierarchy** window, the camera will automatically move and zoom so you can see the object within the **Scene** window. The GameObject contains a **Canvas** component, which allows you to dictate how the image will be rendered (and a **Canvas Scaler** component to make your art scale, depending on the resolution of the device the game is running on and the **Graphic Raycaster** component, which determines whether any objects on the **Canvas** have been hit. We will dive into the **Canvas Scaler** component later on in this section.

> **Important note**
>
> For more information on the **Canvas** object, check out `http://docs.unity3d.com/Manual/UICanvas.html`. In particular, the discussion on the render modes is quite useful in understanding the ways that UI elements can be rendered onto the screen.

- **Text (TMP)**: This object is our actual text object, which has all of the properties that allow us to position the object anywhere on the **Canvas** object and change the text, color, size, and so on that will be displayed.

> **Note**
>
> For more info on TextMesh Pro, check out `https://docs.unity3d.com/Packages/com.unity.textmeshpro@3.0/manual/index.html`.

- **EventSystem**: This object allows users to send events to objects in our game based on various input types, whether keyboard presses, touch events, or gamepads. There are properties in this object that allow you to specify how you'd like your users to interact with your UI, and if you try to create a UI element without one existing, Unity will create one for you as it did here. If you want to have any kind of interactive material in your level using Unity's UI system, such as buttons, sliders, and so on, you must have an object with the **EventSystem** component attached within the level or the events will not trigger.

> **Note**
>
> For more information on the **EventSystem** object, check out `http://docs.unity3d.com/Manual/EventSystem.html`.

6. By default, you may or may not see where our textbox was created. If you aren't able to see it, you can go to the **Hierarchy** window and then double-click on the **Text (TMP)** object. If all went well, we should have something like this:

Figure 4.5 – Zooming in to the Text (TMP) object

7. The next thing we will do is make it easier to tell what this object is. So, with that in mind, scroll all the way up on the **Inspector** tab with the **Text** object selected and change its name to Title Text. To make it a bit easier to see, with the object selected, go to the **Inspector** tab and scroll down to the **TextMeshPro – Text (UI)** component, and then change the **Vertex Color** property to **black**.

We can tell whether the object is going to be visible in the game by seeing whether it is within the white box created for **Canvas**. One thing to note is that instead of the default **Transform** component that all of the game objects we've seen so far used, our **Text** object has a **Rect Transform** component in the same place.

The Rect Transform component

The **Rect Transform** component is probably the most different thing about working in the UI system, so it's a good idea to learn as much as we can about it. Rect Transform is different from the regular Transform in that while the Transform component represents a single point or the center of an object, Rect Transform represents a rectangle, in which the UI element will reside. If an object with a Rect Transform has a parent, which also has a Rect Transform, then the child will specify how the object should be positioned relative to its parent.

> **Note**
>
> For more information on positioning objects and information on **Rect Transform**, check out http://docs.unity3d.com/Manual/UIBasicLayout.html.

To get a better idea of what the properties of the **Rect Transform** component mean, change the **Pos X** and **Pos Y** values to 0, which will center our object around the object's anchors; you can then double-click on the object in the **Hierarchy** tab to center the camera at its new position and can zoom in/out using the mouse wheel:

Figure 4.6 – Title Text centered on the Canvas

Our object's anchors are visible from the **Scene** tab via four small rectangles, creating an X shape in the center of our **Scene** tab, if you have the **Title Text** object selected (double-click on it to center the object on the screen).

> **Important note**
>
> As I mentioned previously, note that the white box that is displayed here for the **Canvas** may look different on your screen based on the aspect ratio you've set from the **Game** tab view (mine is set to **Free Aspect**, so it scales based on that to fill the space). If you go to the **Game** tab, you can select them from the drop-down menu on the left-hand side.

Next, we'll take a look at the two main elements present that work differently in the **Rect Transform** component: anchors and pivots.

Anchors

Found inside the **Rect Transform** component, anchors give you the ability to *hold on* to a corner or part of the Canvas so that if the Canvas were to move and/or change, the pieces of the UI would stay in the appropriate place. These specify the edges of your element using a percentage of the parent's size. For example, if we opened the **Anchors** property from the **Rect Transform** component and set the **Min X** property to 0, the UI element would stick to the left edge of its parent.

The properties above the anchors are your position relative to the anchor that has been set. This can be quite useful when it comes to things such as supporting multiple resolutions without scaling the art assets created. In our case, we will want to have our title position itself relative to the top of the camera. Let's look at the steps to take when working with anchors:

1. Click on the **Anchor Presets** menu in the upper-left corner of the **Rect Transform** component (the box to the left of the **Pos X** and **Width** values). From there, it shows some of the most common anchor positions used in games for easy selection. In our case, we will want to pick the top-center option:

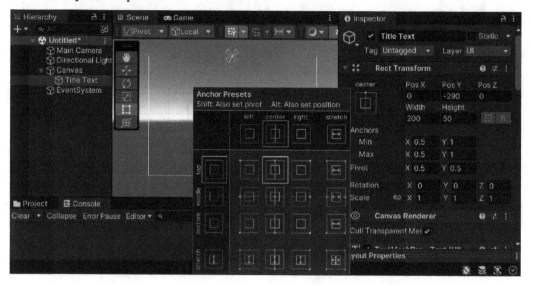

Figure 4.7 – Selecting the top-center option on the Anchor Presets menu

2. Note that after selecting it, the **Pos Y** value changes to another number (in my case, -290). This is saying that our object is positioned **290** units below the anchor's *y* position (in screen space, 1 unit is 1 pixel). If we changed the **Pos Y** value to 0, the object would be centered along the *y* **axis**'s anchor, which would place the object with half of it off the screen, which is not good, as you can see in the following example:

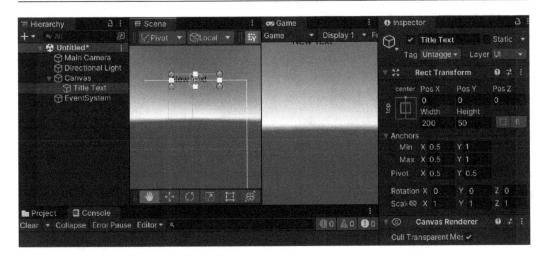

Figure 4.8 – Changing Pos Y to 0

I placed the **Game** tab next to the **Scene** tab to make it easier to see the issue; you can do this by dragging and dropping the **Game** tab to the edge of the screen.

> **Tip**
> To reset any layout changes, you may go to the **Layout** menu in the top-right part of the screen and select **Default**.

If we changed our **Title Text** object's **Pos Y** value to -25 (subtracting half its **Height** value), it would be positioned correctly. However, hardcoding this value will be an issue if we decide we want to change the **Height** value later on, as we will have to remember to adjust this again. It would be a lot nicer if we had something to make **Pos Y** at 0 the edge of the map relative to our height, and, thankfully, we have the **Pivot** property to fix that.

3. Next, change the **Pivot Y** value to 1 and then change **Pos Y** to 0 if you changed it previously and it doesn't change automatically:

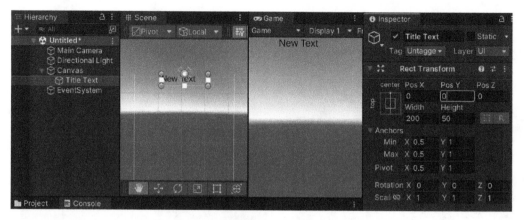

Figure 4.9 – Adjusting Pivot and Pos Y values

As you can see, the text is now hugging the top due to the pivot setting being changed.

Pivots

Pivots are markers that note where we want things to be in relation to our object. This means that objects will be moved, rotated, and/or scaled via this position. To see how this changes the way things react, try changing the **Rotation Z** property with **Pivot Y** values of 0, 0.5, and 1, and note the differences in how things are rotated.

> **Important note**
>
> Note that it is possible to set the **Pivot**, **Position**, and **Anchors settings** of an object via the **Anchors Preset** menu I mentioned previously if you hold down the *Alt* + *Shift* keys while clicking on the object. This way, all of the steps we discussed will happen all at once, but it's a good idea to get a foundation of what everything means before jumping straight into using shortcuts.

Now that we have a basic understanding of how to work within the m space, let's start finalizing our **Title Text** object.

Adjusting and resizing the title text

Now that we have our object positioned correctly, let's give some visual flair to our title text using the following steps:

1. Select the **Title Text** object from the **Hierarchy** tab, and then move over to the **Inspector** tab and scroll down to the **TextMeshPro -Text (UI)** component. From there, change the text in the **Text** property to Endless Roller and set the **Alignment** property of the object to be centered vertically and horizontally. Afterward, change **Font Size** to 40. Note that now the text shows up in two lines and is not within the confines of the size that we defined in the **Rect Transform** component.

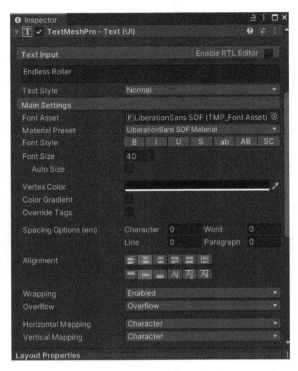

Figure 4.10 – Settings used for the TextMeshPro - Text (UI) component

2. With that in mind, scroll up to **Rect Transform** and change the **Width** value to 300 and keep **Height** at 50. We will also want it to be offset from the top of the world, so let's change **Pos Y** to -30 to give it a little offset:

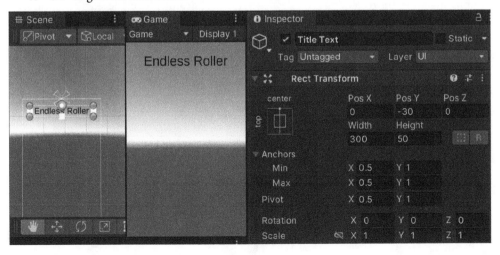

Figure 4.11 – Offsetting the title text

Now, this looks great for this resolution; however, if we were to play the game at a larger resolution, it may look like this:

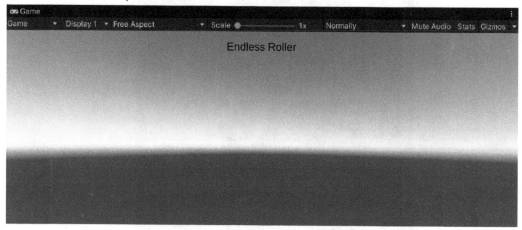

Figure 4.12 – Current state of the title screen

Having a UI that doesn't scale can be good if you're trying to have a **Heads-Up Display** (HUD) in your game, but for the title screen, it's usually a good idea to have the title of the screen be larger; so with that in mind, we will use the **Canvas Scaler** component to adjust how the screen will change based on the resolution we give it.

3. Select the **Canvas** object from the **Hierarchy** component, and then from the **Inspector** window, go to the **Canvas Scaler** component. From there, change **UI Scale Mode** to **Scale with Screen Size**.

The key property here is **Reference Resolution**. This is the resolution that we want to base our menu on—if the resolution is made bigger, it will scale up; if it's made smaller, it will scale down. You will likely have a resolution in mind based on your mockups or an image file you've made; however, for reference, the following are some of the most common screen resolutions at the time of writing this book.

Here are some sample Apple device resolutions:

Device Name	Resolution
iPhone 12 Pro Max/13 Pro Max	2778 x 1284
iPhone 12/12 Pro/13 Pro	2532 x 1170
iPhone 12/13	2532 x 1170
iPhone 12 mini/13 mini	2340 x 1080
iPhone 11 Pro Max	2688 x 1242
iPhone 11 Pro	2436 x 1125
iPhone 11	1792 x 828
iPhone 14 Pro Max	2796 x 1290

iPhone 14 Pro	2556 x 1179
iPhone 14	2532 x 1170 (Same as 12/13)
iPhone 14 Plus	2778 x 1284 (Same as Phone 12 Pro Max/13 Pro Max)
iPhone SE (2020)	1334 x 750
iPhone XS Max	1242 x 2688
iPhone XS	1125 x 2436
iPhone XR	828 x 1792
iPhone X	2436 x 1125
iPhone 7 Plus/8 Plus	1080 x 1920
iPhone 7/8	750 x 1334
iPhone 6S Plus	1080 x 1920
iPhone 6S	750 x 1334
iPad Pro (1st-5th gen 12.9")	2048 x 2732
iPad 9th gen	2160 x 1620
iPad Air 4th gen	2388 x 1668
iPad Mini (6th gen)	2266 x 1488

Here are some sample Android device resolutions:

Device Name	Resolution
Samsung Galaxy S22 Ultra	3080 x 1440
Samsung Galaxy S22	2340 x 1080
Samsung Galaxy Z Fold3	2208 x 1768
Samsung Galaxy S20 Ultra/S21 Ultra	3200 x 1440
Samsung Galaxy S20/S21	2400 x 1080
Samsung Note 10+	2280 x1080
Google Pixel 5 XL	2960 x 1440
Google Pixel 5	2340 x 1080
Google Pixel 4 XL	1440 x 2960
Google Pixel 4	2280 x 1080
Samsung Galaxy S10/S10+	3040 x 1440
Google Pixel 3 XL	2960 x 1440
Google Pixel 3/3a XL	2160 x 1080
Google Pixel 3a	2220 x 1080
Samsung Galaxy S8/S8+	2960 x 1440
Google Pixel 2 XL	2560 x 1312

Nexus 6P	1440 x 2560
Nexus 5X	1080 x 1920
Google Pixel/Pixel 2	1080 x 1920
Google Pixel XL/Pixel 2 XL	1440 x 2560
Samsung Galaxy Note 5	1440 x 2560
LG G5	1440 x 2560
One Plus 3	1080 x 1920
Samsung Galaxy S7	1440 x 2560
Samsung Galaxy S7 Edge	1440 x 2560
Nexus 7 (2013)	1200 x 1920
Nexus 9	1536 x 2048
Samsung Galaxy Tab 10	800 x 1280
Chromebook Pixel	2560 x 1700

> **Note**
>
> To see a list of popular cell phone screen resolutions, check out `http://screensiz.es/phone` or `https://www.ios-resolution.com/`.

I am using a Google Pixel 3a XL, which has a resolution of 2160 x 1080, and an iPhone 13 Pro Max, which has a 2778 x 1284 resolution, so I think that would be a good place to start. However, if you are creating art assets, it's a good idea to create the UI at the largest resolution you plan on supporting and then build for other resolutions from there.

Unity has some of the most common resolutions built in, which can be seen/changed from the dropdown in the **Game** window view mentioned previously.

4. In the **Inspector** view, go to the **Canvas Scaler** component and change the **Reference Resolution** value to `1920 x 1080` if it isn't there already.

5. Next, under **Match**, move it all the way over to **Height**. This will ensure that when the height of our screen changes, that's when we will modify the scale of our UI.

6. Next, let's make the text a bit larger. Select the **Title Text** object and from **Rect Transform**, change the **Width** value to `1000` and **Height** to `200`, and then change the **Text** component's **Font Size** value to `130`:

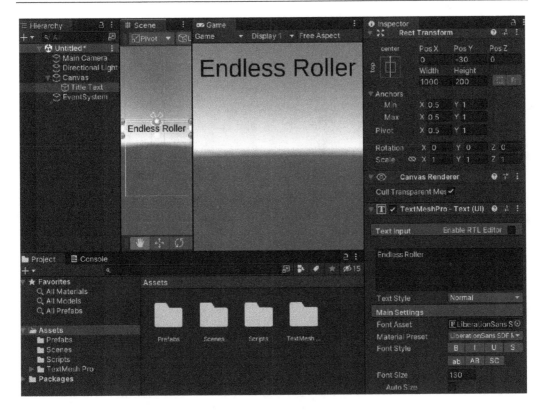

Figure 4.13 – Adjusting the title text to be large

7.   Now, if we play the game with a higher resolution, it will display our title nicely, scaling up to fit the larger size that we have:

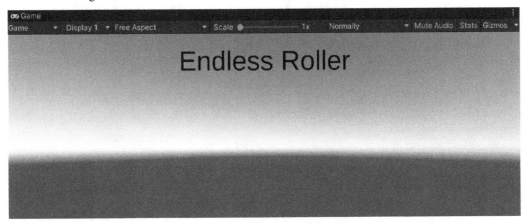

Figure 4.14 – Scaling the title screen

8. Go to the **Game** view control bar and pick a smaller resolution, such as **800x480 Landscape (800x480)**, and you'll note that the text will scale down to fit nicely as well:

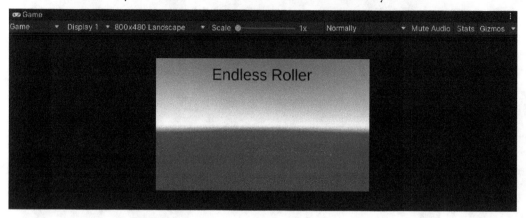

Figure 4.15 – Title screen at a smaller resolution

As you can see, the **Canvas Scaler** component will adjust the size of the text depending on the resolution of the device. Next, we will see how we can quickly test different resolutions as well.

> **Note**
>
> For more information on the **Canvas Scaler** component, check out `https://docs.unity3d.com/Manual/script-CanvasScaler.html`.

Selecting different aspect ratios

As I mentioned previously, in the **Game** view, if we go to the control bar and select the first option, there is a drop-down menu where we can pick different resolutions to test our game, so we can find potential issues before exporting it to our devices:

Figure 4.16 – Different resolution options

There are a number of resolutions built in for us by default, but we can also make our own using the + button at the bottom. I suggest that you make two new selections for your phone for landscape mode and for portrait mode at the resolutions you are trying to reach if they're not included by default (in my case, 1920 x 1080, 1080 x 1920, 2778 x 1284, and 1284 x 2778):

So, at this point, we can see that in a landscape ratio, it works fairly well, but let's try a portrait one:

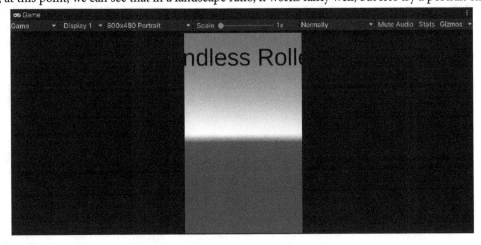

Figure 4.17 – Current Portrait view

Oops! Currently, the text is overflowing past the bounds of the screen. Looks like will have to fix that:

1. Select the **Title Text** object and check the **Auto Size** property in the **Inspector** tab under the **TextMeshPro – Text (UI)** component. This automatically scales the text to fit the space we have if the width and height were to change, which they currently don't, but we will change that next. From the **Auto Size options**, change the **Max** value to a larger value such as 200.

2. Now, go to the **Rect Transform** component, and under **Anchors**, change the **Min X** value to 0.25 and **Max X** to 0.75:

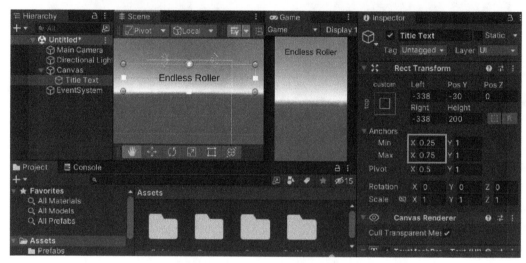

Figure 4.18 – Setting the Anchors values

Note that the **Pos X** and **Width** values. They have now been replaced with the **Left** and **Right** properties, which are currently set to -338 and -338. This means that the area being taken up by this is -338 units away from our anchor at 25%, and -338 units away from our max anchor at 75%. We want the screen to resize to be at those anchors, so we will change both the **Left** and **Right** values to 0.

3. Save our Scene as a new file inside the Scenes folder called MainMenu, and then play the game:

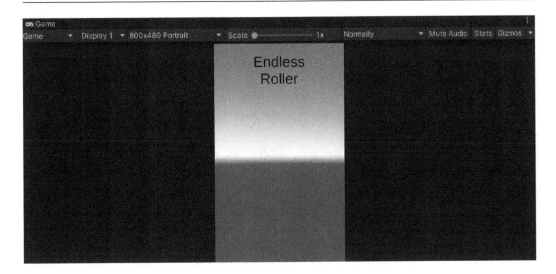

Figure 4.19 – The title text automatically adjusts to fit the screen

As you can see in the preceding screenshot, the text now fits a lot nicer. You'll also note that no matter what resolution we are using, this text takes up an amount of room that's fitting for the game's title. Now that we have the text displaying correctly, let's add the ability to move from the main menu into the game properly.

Working with buttons

Unlike our title, for things that we want our players to touch, it's a good idea to make the buttons the same size in each device, as our fingers are the same size, no matter what device we are using. To show a possible solution for this, we will create a new Canvas using a different scaling technique:

1. Stop the game if it is currently running. We will first rename our current **Canvas** object Canvas - Scale w/Screen. This way, we can easily tell whether we are using the correct Canvas for this or not.

2. Now that we have that one ready, we can create our new one. Go to the top menu bar and then select **GameObject | UI | Canvas**. Rename this new Canvas Canvas - Scale Physical. Then, under the **Canvas Scaler** component, change **UI Scale Mode** to **Constant Physical Size**:

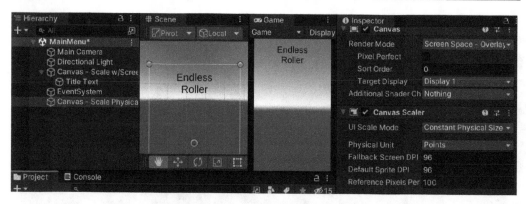

Figure 4.20 – Creating a Physical Canvas

Using this method, Unity will attempt to scale the size of this Canvas so that each element has the same physical size, regardless of the resolution. Since we're going for buttons that we intend to press with our fingers, this makes a lot of sense.

3.   Now, with this Canvas (**Canvas - Scale Physical**) selected in the **Hierarchy** view, go to the menu and select **GameObject | UI | Button - TextMeshPro** to create a new button inside this Canvas.

Note

You can also do this by right-clicking on the `Canvas - Scale Physical` object from the **Hierarchy** window and selecting **UI | Button - TextMeshPro**.

At this point, you will see a new child object to **Canvas** called **Button**, and if you were to extend that object, you'd see that it has a **Text (TMP)** child also:

Figure 4.21 – Showing off the Text (TMP) object

The next question is, what size should our buttons be? Google suggests in their Material guidelines for Android that at least 48 x 48 **density-independent pixels** should be used (**dp** for short), whereas, at their **Worldwide Developers Conference** (**WWDC**), Apple recommended at least 44 x 44 dp. Either way, that comes somewhere around 8mm x 8mm, or 0.3 inches x 0.3 inches.

> **Note**
>
> To read the material guidelines, check out `https://material.io/design/layout/spacing-methods.html#touch-click-targets`. Or for Material 3's guidelines, check out `https://m3.material.io/components/buttons/specs#85e63496-f905-4978-ae35-69ab83b70536`

If you were to look at the game right now and check out some of the different resolution options, you may be a bit scared due to the size of the button, depending on the resolution:

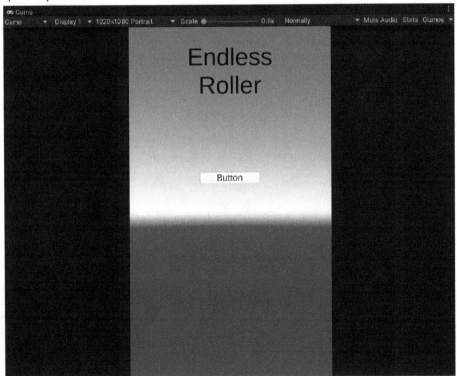

Figure 4.22 – Small button

That's because our button size is assuming that the **dots per Inch** (**DPI**) value is 96, when on devices such as the Google Pixel 3a XL and the iPhone 6/7/8 Plus, it is around 400. For now, I'll change the **Aspect Ratio** value to **16:9 Landscape** to see something closer to what we'll use on our device when we play there:

Figure 4.23 – Game at a 16:9 aspect ratio

4. Stop the game if it is currently running. Afterward, from the **Hierarchy** window, expand the **Button** object, and from there, select the **Text (TMP)** child object. From there, go to the **Inspector** window and change the **TextMeshPro - Text (UI)** component's text value to `Play`.

> **Note**
>
> If you're interested in finding out what the DPI for your device is, check out `http://dpi.lv/`.

5. Next, let's make some adjustments to the **Button** object itself.

    From the **Hierarchy** window, select the **Button** object. Rename it `Play Button` at the top of the **Inspector** window to make it clear what the object is.

6. Next, go to the **Rect Transform** component and change the **Pos X** and **Pos Y** values to `0` to center the button in the middle of the screen. Afterward, the size of the button is quite large, so let's change the **Width** property to `75` and the **Height** property to `35`:

Figure 4.24 – Adjusting the button's size

We now have a button, but it doesn't actually do anything yet. Let's fix that now.

7. Let's create a script to contain the functionality that we want. From the **Project** view, open the `Scripts` folder, and let's create a new C# script called `MainMenuBehaviour`.

8. Once your IDE has opened, use the following code:

```
using UnityEngine;
using UnityEngine.SceneManagement; // LoadScene

public class MainMenuBehaviour : MonoBehaviour
{
    /// <summary>
    /// Will load a new scene upon being called
    /// </summary>
    /// <param name="levelName">The name of the level
    /// we want to go to</param>
    public void LoadLevel(string levelName)
    {
        SceneManager.LoadScene(levelName);
    }
}
```

The `LoadLevel` function will load a level based on the name that we provide to it making use of Unity's Scene Manager, which we added using a statement at the top of our code so that we would have access to that namespace.

9. Save the script and go back to the Unity editor. To call Unity's UI events from the editor, we will need to have a game object with the `MainMenuBehaviour` component attached to it to call this function. We could use one of the currently existing objects, but we'll just create a new object, making it easier to be found in the future.

10. With that in mind, create an empty game object (**Game Object | Create Empty...**) in your scene called `Main Menu` and then add the `MainMenuBehaviour` script to it. Then, drag and drop it to the top of the **Hierarchy** tab to make it easier to access in the future and reset its position for the sake of neatness:

Figure 4.25 – Creating the Main Menu object

11. Select your **Play Button** object from **Hierarchy**, go to the **Inspector** tab, and scroll down to the **Button** component from there. Then, in the **On Click ()** section, click on the + icon to add something for our button to do.

12. Then, drag and drop the **Main Menu** object from the **Hierarchy** tab into the area that currently says **None (Object)**, which is added to the list.

13. Click on the dropdown that currently says **No Function** and then select **MainMenuBehaviour. LoadLevel**. Then, in the textbox that appears below that, type in the name of our game's level, Gameplay:

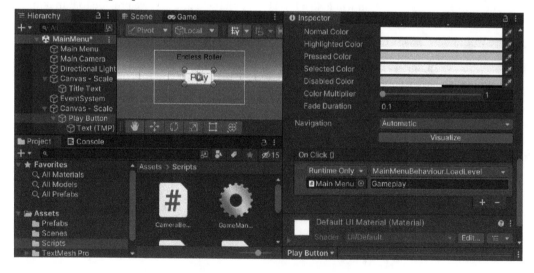

Figure 4.26 – Adding functionality to the button

14. Save your scene by going to **File | Save**. Lastly, open **Build Settings** as we did before by going to **File | Build Settings** and add our **MainMenu scene** to the list at index **0** by selecting **Add Open Scenes** and then dragging the **MainMenu** level to the top, so that the main menu level will be the scene that starts off when we start the game:

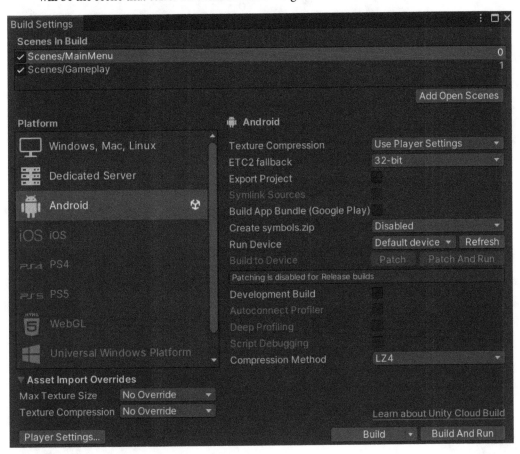

Figure 4.27 – Starting the game with the main menu

15. Save your project and Scene, then click on the **Play** button:

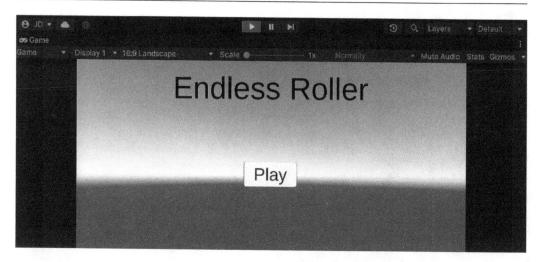

Figure 4.28 – Current state of the main menu

At this point, our main menu is working well, and we can get into the game without any issues by clicking on the **Play** button:

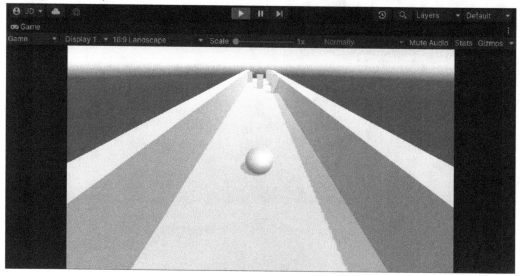

Figure 4.29 – Current state of the gameplay scene

Now that we have a foundational knowledge of the UI system and we have our title screen, we will move on to building something else that most games will need: a pause menu.

Adding a pause menu

When playing games, especially mobile games, there may come a time when you need to stop playing them at any moment. Having a pause menu will allow our players the convenience of deciding when they want to stop the game in its current state and resume it at a time that is convenient for them. This will also allow us to dive into some additional concepts in using Unity's UI system, so with that in mind, let's start building one:

1. Open up the **Gameplay** scene by going to the **Project** window, opening the Assets/Scenes folder, and double-clicking on **Gameplay**, saving the **MainMenu** level if you didn't do so already:

Figure 4.30 – Opening the Gameplay scene

Before we worry about how we are going to open our pause menu, let's go ahead and create the pause menu that we'll be opening first.

2. The first thing we'll do is dim our screen when we enter the pause menu. An easy way to do that is to have an image scale to cover our entire screen, which is what the **Panel** object does by default. We can create it by selecting **Game Object | UI | Panel**. Note that this creates a **Canvas** object and an **EventSystem** object in addition to the **Panel** object, as one doesn't exist in this scene already.

3. Rename the **Panel** object Pause Menu. Then, with the object selected from the **Inspector** window, go to the **Image** component and we will then change the **Color** property to black with higher transparency by increasing the alpha channel (**A**) to 178:

Figure 4.31 – Setting the Panel's color

The **Image** component works in a similar manner to **Sprite Renderer** for 2D games, with information on an image to draw and the color to use for it.

4.   Switch to the **Game** window to get a better look at what the **Panel** object is doing to the screen. The current image has a thin border, which I'm not a fan of, in this case. You may keep it if you'd like, but I'm going to remove it and change the **Source Image** value to **None (Sprite)** by selecting the current one and pressing the *Delete* key:

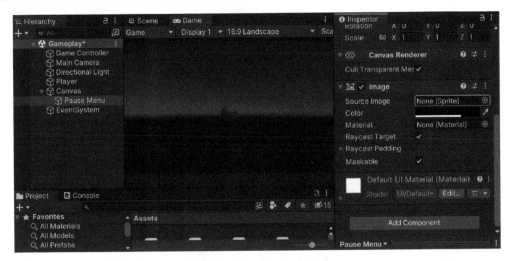

Figure 4.32 – Creating the backdrop

Now that we have this, we will need to populate the menu with content. In this case, we will have a **Text - TextMeshPro** object saying that the game is paused, and some buttons allowing the player to resume, restart, or return to the main menu.

5.   Let's create another panel to hold our pause menu contents. We want this panel to be a child of our **Pause Menu** object, so we can do this easily by going to the **Hierarchy** window, right-clicking on **Pause Menu**, and selecting **UI | Panel**:

Figure 4.33 – Creating a child via the Hierarchy window

Now, for this panel, I don't want it to take up the entire screen, so I will use another component to modify its size based on the resolution we receive. In this case, I will use an **Aspect Ratio Fitter** component.

6. In the **Inspector** window, scroll all the way down and then select **Add Component** and start typing in Aspect. From there, select **Aspect Ratio Fitter** and then press the *Enter* key.

7. Afterward, go to our newly added component and change the **Aspect Mode** value to Fit In Parent to ensure that the panel will always fit within our screen and set **Aspect Ratio** to 0.5. This means that the panel will be twice as high as it is wide (width over height, which means ½ or 0.5).

If you go to the **Game** window and switch aspect ratios, you'll note that the menu will stay in a similar shape.

> **Note**
>
> For more information on the **Aspect Ratio Fitter** component, check out https://docs.unity3d.com/Manual/script-AspectRatioFitter.html.

8. This is good, but I don't want to have the panel stuck directly to the edge of our screen, so we will make this object invisible by clicking on the checkmark by the **Image** component. This will disable the component and stop the component's functionality.

9. Then, right-click on the **Panel** object and create another panel by going to **UI | Panel**. Rename this new object Pause Menu Contents and then change the **Rect Transform** component's left, right, top, and bottom values to 10 to give us a border around the screen.

10. We will use physical buttons like last time, so let's move to the **Canvas** object, and under the **Canvas Scaler** component, change **UI Scale Mode** to **Constant Physical Size**:

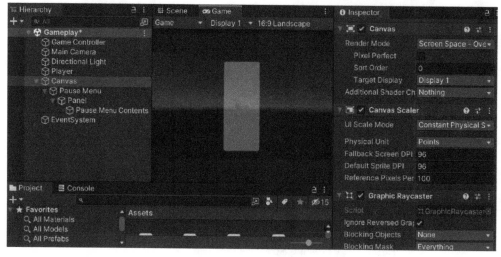

Figure 4.34 – Pause Menu Contents setup

We could place everything manually as we did previously, but in this case, we may want to use another feature that Unity's UI system has: layout groups.

Layout groups will resize the children of an object so that a component will automatically fit the area of the parent. There are several different layout groups, including grid-based, horizontal, and vertical layout groups. In our case, the menu will probably be vertical.

> **Important note**
>
> For more information on Unity's way of automatically creating layouts, check out `https://docs.unity3d.com/Manual/UIAutoLayout.html`.

11. Select the **Pause Menu Contents** object in the **Hierarchy** window and then switch to the **Inspector** window. From there, scroll all the way down to the **Add Component** option and select it. Type in `Vertical Layout Group` and select **Vertical Layout Group** by pressing the *Enter* key.

12. Let's create some children to fit into our menu. From the **Hierarchy** window, right-click on the **Pause Menu Contents** object and select **UI | Button - TextMeshPro**.

13. This creates a button, but you'll note that it looks pretty much like a normal button. Let's open up its child **Text** object and change the text to `Resume`. Then, we'll check the **Auto Size** property and change the **Min** value to 0. To keep all of the button text on one line, we can also change the **Wrapping** property to **Disabled**. We don't want the text to hug the button, so scroll up on the **Inspector** window, and under the **Rect Transform** component, change the **Left, Top, Right**, and **Bottom** values to 5.

14. Afterward, select the **Pause Menu Contents** object, and under the **Inspector** window, go to the **Vertical Layout Group (Script)** component and change the **Child Alignment** value to **Middle Center**. Then, change the **Child Control Size** value to have **Width** toggled.

15. Then, in the **Vertical Layout Group** component, click on the arrow to the left of the **Padding** property to open it up and then set all of the sides to 5:

This will add five pixels of padding in each direction within all of the children of the layout group.

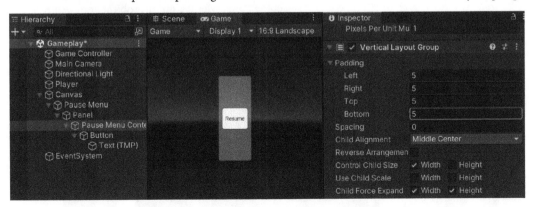

Figure 4.35 – Adding padding

16. Now, duplicate this button twice and change the text to Restart and Main Menu. Then, to make it easy to tell the difference between them, let's change the objects' names to Resume Button, Restart Button, and Main Menu Button.

17. Next, right-click on the **Pause Menu Contents** object and select **UI | Text - TextMeshPro**. Change the object's text to Paused and change its alignment to be centered, and just like the buttons, we will check the **Auto Size** value, set the **Min** value to 0, and set **Wrapping** to **Disabled**. I also went to the **Rect Transform** component and set **Height** to 30. Note how the order in which the children are placed in the hierarchy changes the order in which they are displayed. With that in mind, drag the **Text** object to the top:

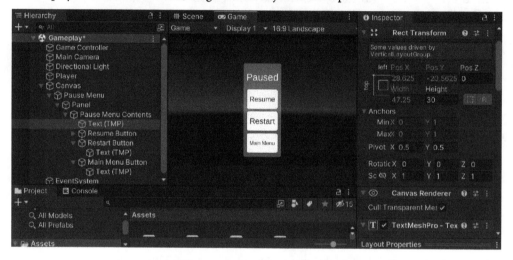

Figure 4.36 – Pause Menu setup

This looks nice, but there's also a lot of spacing here. So, if we'd like, we can instead condense the contents of our menu to just fit what we have there.

18. To do this, we can go to **Hierarchy** and select the **Pause Menu Contents** object and then add a **Content Size Fitter** component. Once it is added, we will change **Vertical Fit** to **Preferred Size**.

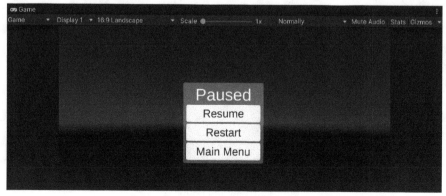

Figure 4.37 – Effect of the preferred size option

19. This will scrunch all the buttons together, so we can change the **Spacing** property of **Vertical Layout Group** to 5 and add some space between the buttons:

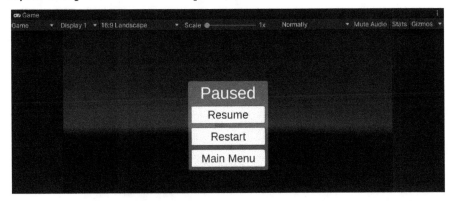

Figure 4.38 – Current view of the pause menu

20. Now that we have the buttons themselves, let's actually make them do something. In the **Project** window, open up the `Scripts` folder and create a new C# script called `PauseScreenBehaviour`, and double-click on it to open up the IDE of your choice.

21. Once it's opened, use the following code:

```
using UnityEngine;
using UnityEngine.SceneManagement; // SceneManager

public class PauseScreenBehaviour : MainMenuBehaviour
{
    /// <summary>
    /// If our game is currently paused
    /// </summary>
    public static bool paused;

    [Tooltip("Reference to the pause menu object to
        turn on/off")]
    public GameObject pauseMenu;

    /// <summary>
    /// Reloads our current level, effectively
    /// "restarting" the game
    /// </summary>
    public void Restart()
    {
        SceneManager.LoadScene(SceneManager
            .GetActiveScene().name);
```

```
    }

    /// <summary>
    /// Will turn our pause menu on or off
    /// </summary>
    /// <param name="isPaused"></param>
    public void SetPauseMenu(bool isPaused)
    {
        paused = isPaused;

        /* If the game is paused, timeScale is 0,
            otherwise 1 */
        Time.timeScale = (paused) ? 0 : 1;

        pauseMenu.SetActive(paused);
    }

    void Start()
    {
        /* Must be reset in Start or else game will be
            paused upon restart */
        paused = false;
    }
}
```

In this script, we will first use a `static` variable, which is called `paused`. When we declare a `static` variable, we ensure that there will only ever be one of those variables inside this class, which all instances will share. One of the advantages of this is that we can access the property in other scripts using the class name followed by a period and then the attribute's name (in this case, `PauseScreenBehaviour.paused`). We will use this concept later on when we want to open the menu through code.

We then have two public functions, which we will call via the UI elements. First, we have a `Restart` function, which will use Unity's Scene Manager to return us to the currently loaded level, effectively restarting the game. It is important to note that `static` variables do not reset when restarting in Unity, so that's why I set `paused` to `false` in the `Start` function to ensure that when we come to the level, it is unpaused.

Finally, we have a `SetPauseMenu` function, which will turn the pause menu on or off based on the value of `isPaused`. It also sets the `Time.timeScale` property, where `0` means that nothing will happen and `1` means normal time. This property will modify the `Time.deltaTime` variable, effectively canceling out movement that we have as long as we use it.

22. Save your script and dive back into Unity.

23. Then, we'll create a new empty game object by going to **GameObject | Create Empty**. We'll name it `Pause Screen Handler` and then attach the **Pause Screen Behaviour (Script)** component to it.

24. Next, assign the **Pause Menu** variable to the **Pause Menu** game object in the **Hierarchy** tab:

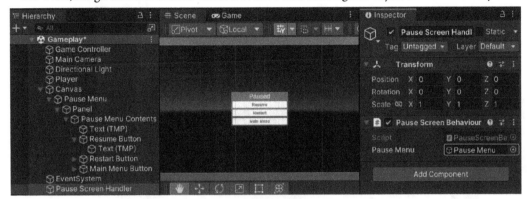

Figure 4.39 – Assigning the Pause Menu property

25. Now that we have the script, we can now change the buttons to actually do something. Go to the **Inspector** window with the **Resume Button** object selected, go to the **Button** component's **On Click ()** section, and click on the + button to add an action to occur.

26. Drag and drop the **Pause Menu Handler** object from the **Hierarchy** window into the box on the bottom-left side of the **On Click ()** action in the **Inspector** window. Next, go to the dropdown and select **Pause Screen Behaviour | SetPauseMenu**. By default, it's on `false` due to not being checked, so this should work for us:

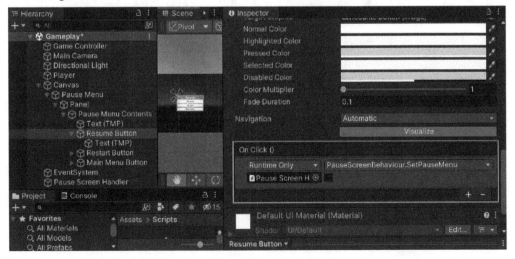

Figure 4.40 – Calling the SetPauseMenu function from the Resume button

27. Likewise, do the same for the **Restart** button object – this time, calling the Restart function.

28. Next, do the same for the **Main Menu Button** object, except call LoadLevel and put the name of our main menu level in the string place (MainMenu, in my case).

> **Note**
>
> The PauseScreenHandler script already contains LoadLevel due to the fact that we are inheriting from the MainMenuBehaviour class.

29. Save our game and go ahead and run it:

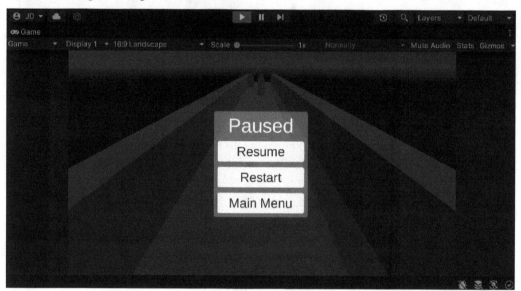

Figure 4.41 – The current state of the game

As you can see in the preceding screenshot, if we start the game, the menu appears correctly—we can click the **Main Menu** button to get to the main menu, and **Resume** continues the game.

At this point, we have some issues: once the menu is gone, there is no way to get it back; the game should start unpaused, and the game should actually pause. Let's tackle these issues next.

Pausing the game

To get the game to pause correctly, we will tweak some scripts we've written previously using the following steps:

1. Open the PlayerBehaviour script and add the code highlighted in bold to the FixedUpdate function:

```
/// <summary>
/// FixedUpdate is a prime place to put physics
/// calculations happening over a period of time.
/// </summary>

void FixedUpdate()
{
    /* If the game is paused, don't do anything */
    if (PauseScreenBehaviour.paused)
    {
        return;
    }

    // Check if we're moving to the side
    var horizontalSpeed = Input.GetAxis("Horizontal")
        * dodgeSpeed;

    // Rest of the FixedUpdate function...
```

The added code makes it so that if the game is paused, we will not do anything within the function.

2. We then also need to add the same script to the top of the Update function as well:

```
/// <summary>
/// Update is called once per frame
/// </summary>
private void Update()
{
    /* Using Keyboard/Controller to toggle pause menu
    */
    if (Input.GetButtonDown("Cancel"))
    {
        // Get the pause menu
        var pauseBehaviour =
            GameObject.FindObjectOfType
                <PauseScreenBehaviour>();
```

```
        // Toggle the value
        pauseBehaviour.SetPauseMenu
            (!PauseScreenBehaviour.paused);
    }

    /* If the game is paused, don't do anything */
    if (PauseScreenBehaviour.paused)
    {
        return;
    }

    /* Check if we are running either in the Unity
        editor or in a standalone build.*/
    #if UNITY_STANDALONE || UNITY_WEBPLAYER ||
        UNITY_EDITOR

    // Rest of the Update function…
```

3. Save your script and return to the Unity editor. Now, the game, by default, should be unpaused, so let's go ahead and select the **Pause Menu** object in the **Hierarchy** view and then click on the active button in the **Inspector** view to disable it:

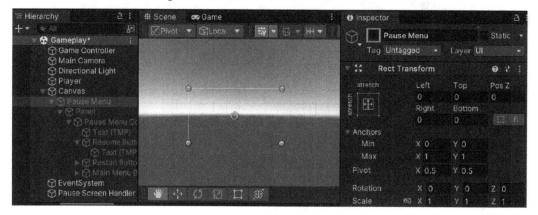

Figure 4.42 – Disabling the pause menu

4. Save your scene and then go ahead and play the game. While playing, hit the *Esc* key and you should see the pause menu appear and the game is paused! We can also use **Resume** or hit *Esc* again to resume the game.

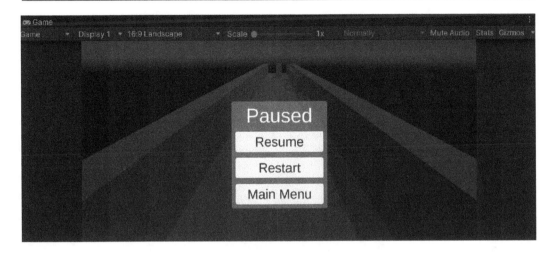

Figure 4.43 – The current state of the game

This is great, but it will only work if our player has a keyboard or controller attached to it. In the next chapter, we will see how we can have a button that players can click to turn on the menu. In addition, we may want to be able to move the player using some visual on-screen UI menu. That's what we will tackle next.

Summary

With that, we've got a good foundation to build on when creating UI elements for a mobile game. We first covered how to create a title screen, making use of buttons and **Text** objects. We then covered how to use panels, buttons, text, and layout groups to make your menus adapt to the size of your elements. We also touched on how layout groups can arrange our objects to fit in a pleasing manner.

In the next chapter, we will continue our exploration of UIs for games by seeing how we can add a pause screen button and an on-screen joystick, and adapting our GUIs for notch devices.

5

Advanced Mobile UI

In the last chapter, we were introduced to the Unity UI system and how to build resolution-independent UI elements, which are useful for all game projects that utilize different aspect ratios and resolutions. In this chapter, we will be exploring some mobile-specific aspects of working on a UI, such as requiring on-screen controls and adapting our UI to fit devices with notches.

This chapter will be split into a number of topics. The chapter is a simple step-by-step process from beginning to end. The following is the outline of our tasks:

- Adding a pause screen button
- Implementing an on-screen joystick
- Adapting GUIs for notch devices

Over the course of this chapter, we will take the pause screen that we implemented in the previous chapter and adapt it to work on a mobile device. We will then implement an on-screen joystick as an additional movement option, and lastly, have our UI automatically adapt to fit mobile devices that have notches.

Technical requirements

This book utilizes Unity 2022.1.0b16 and Unity Hub 3.3.1, but the steps should work with minimal changes in future versions of the editor. If you would like to download the exact version used in this book, and there is a new version out, you can visit Unity's download archive at https://unity3d.com/get-unity/download/archive. You can also find the system requirements for Unity at https://docs.unity3d.com/2022.1/Documentation/Manual/system-requirements.html in the **Unity Editor system requirements** section.

You can find the code files present in this chapter on GitHub at https://github.com/PacktPublishing/Unity-2022-Mobile-Game-Development-3rd-Edition/tree/main/Chapter05.

Adding a pause screen button

While many mobile games do support controllers through Bluetooth, most, if not all, of them allow the users to control the game via just the device. Increasingly, many mobile games will include on-screen buttons or analog sticks that players can use to control their avatars. In this section, we will see just how we can implement that if we wish.

To start off, let's build a pause menu button:

1. Since we are going to be creating multiple types of on-screen controls, let's create a panel to hold them all. From the **Hierarchy** view, right-click on the **Canvas** object and select **UI | Panel.** Rename the object to On Screen Controls. From the **Inspector** view, remove or disable the **Image** component, as we don't need to see the image.

   For this version of our controls, we will be using some 2D sprites to make it easier to tell what the various UI elements are. The sprites are included in the example code for this book if you'd like to use the exact ones I'm using.

2. From the **Project** window, create a new folder called Sprites and drag and drop the image files into the newly added folder. Since our project is a 3D one, Unity assumes we want them to be textures, but we want to use them with Unity's UI system. With that in mind, select all three sprites. From the **Inspector**, change **Texture Type** to **Sprite (2D and UI)**, then scroll all the way down, and then hit the **Apply** button.

> **Note**
>
> The sprites used here are from *Kenney's Onscreen Controls* pack. There are seven other possible styles that you could use, which are available from https://kenney.nl/assets/onscreen-controls.

3. Now that we have the sprites, let's build our first UI element, a pause button. From the **Hierarchy** view, right-click on the **On Screen Controls** object and select **UI | Button - TextMeshPro**.

4. Rename the new object Show Pause Button and use the **Anchor Presets** menu to place the object at the bottom right of the screen (use *Alt + Shift* to set **Pivot** and **Position** as well).

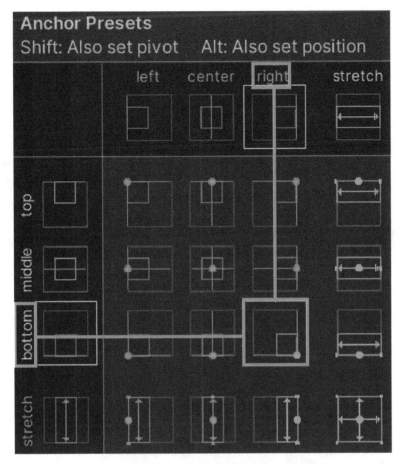

Figure 5.1 – Bottom-right option

5. Then, from the **Image** component, drag and drop our **pauseButton** sprite into the **Source Image** property. You'll notice it's stretched out, so click on the **Set Native Size** button to have the sprite automatically resize itself for us.

6. We don't actually need the text object included, so select the **Text (TMP)** object and hit the *Delete* key.

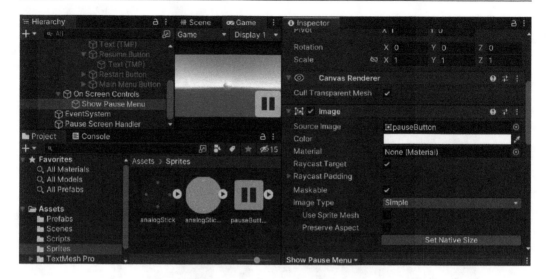

Figure 5.2 – Creating the pause button

7. Go back and select the **Show Pause Button** object and create an **On Click ()** event using the **SetPauseMenu** function on the **Pause Screen Behaviour** component on the **Pause Screen Handler** object. Then, click on the checkbox to set it to pause.

8. Go back to **Resume Button** and add another event to its button to turn the **Show Pause Menu** button back on when we leave.

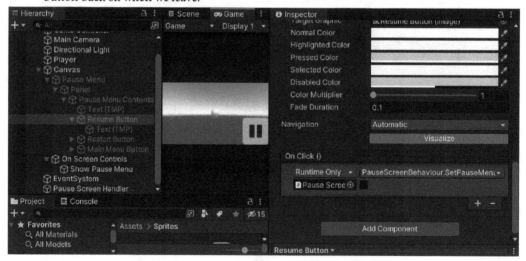

Figure 5.3 – Creating the Resume Button click action

Now, we want to remove our on-screen controls whenever we pause the game. This can be done through **Inspector**, but we can also do this through code.

9. Open the `PauseScreenBehaviour` script and add the following property to the script:

```
[Tooltip("Reference to the on screen controls menu")]
public GameObject onScreenControls;
```

10. Afterward, update the **SetPauseMenu** function to have the following new line:

```
/// <summary>
/// Will turn our pause menu on or off
/// </summary>
/// <param name="isPaused">is the game currently
    paused</param>
public void SetPauseMenu(bool isPaused)
{
    paused = isPaused;

    /* If the game is paused, timeScale is 0,
       otherwise 1 */
    Time.timeScale = (paused) ? 0 : 1;

    pauseMenu.SetActive(paused);
    onScreenControls.SetActive(!paused);
}
```

Note that we are using `!paused` and not `paused` like in the previous line. The `!` operator will take something that is `true` and make it `false`, and vice versa. This will cause the `onScreenControls` window to turn on when the game is not paused and off when it is.

Since we are already in the code editor, we can also use this time to fix something that will come up later: as mentioned previously, one problem that won't be apparent now unless you restart the level is the fact that `static` variables will keep their values each time we reload the game. In our case, we set `paused`, which turns `Time.timeScale` to 0. Thankfully, we can fix this fairly easily.

11. Open the `PauseScreenBehaviour` script and update the `Start` function to have the following, replacing the original line:

```
void Start()
{
    /* Must be reset in Start or else game will be
       paused upon
     * restart */
    SetPauseMenu(false);
}
```

12. Return to Unity and go to the **Pause Screen Handler** object. From the **Pause Screen Behaviour** script, set the **On Screen Controls** property to our **On Screen Controls** object.

Figure 5.4 – Updating Pause Screen Behaviour

13. Save your script and the scene, and then play the game:

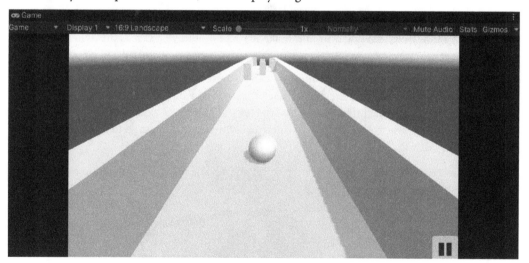

Figure 5.5 – The current state of the game

The pause menu now works correctly. This is a simple way to add on-screen controls to the screen. A more advanced version would be an analog stick that we can use to control the player's movement. Let's tackle that next.

Implementing an on-screen joystick

To implement this on-screen joystick, we will utilize two images: a background image and then a joystick image placed on top of it. We will then write code to allow the player to simulate that they are physically moving the joystick. Later, we learn how we can have the simulated joystick actually affect the game properly:

1. Right-click on the **On-Screen Controls** object and create an image by selecting **UI | Image**. We will then rename the object to `Joystick Background`.

2. From the **Image** component, set **Source Image** to the `analogStickBackground` sprite and click on the **Set Native Size** button.

3. From the **Rect Transform** component, hold down *Alt + Shift* and use the **Anchor Presets** menu to move **Joystick Background** to the bottom-left option.

4. Next, right-click on the **Joystick Background** object and create another image by selecting **UI | Image**. We will then rename the object to `Joystick`.

5. From the **Image** component, set **Source Image** to the `analogStick` sprite and click on the **Set Native Size** button.

Figure 5.6 – Creating the Joystick UI

6. We want this joystick to move, so to do that, we will create a new script. From the **Project** window, go to the `Scripts` folder and create a new C# script called `MobileJoystick`. Then, attach the `MobileJoystick` script to the `Joystick` object.

7. Open your code editor to the `MobileJoystick` script and add the following properties and initialization of those properties in the `Start` function:

```
/// <summary>
/// A reference to this object's RectTransform
/// component
/// </summary>
RectTransform rt;
/// <summary>
/// The original position of the stick used to
/// calculate the offset of movement
/// </summary>
Vector2 originalAnchored;
// Start is called before the first frame update
void Start()
{
    rt = GetComponent<RectTransform>();
    originalAnchored = rt.anchoredPosition;
}
```

8. To have the joystick do something when we are dragging it, we can add an interface to our script for when we are dragging and when we stop. To do so, we need to add the following `using` statement to the top of our script:

```
using UnityEngine.EventSystems; /* IDragHandler, IEndDragHandler
*/
```

9. After that, we add the following bold code to the class definition:

```
public class MobileJoystick : MonoBehaviour, IDragHandler,
IEndDragHandler
```

10. Now, we will get some errors because we haven't actually defined the functions given in the interfaces, let's do that now:

```
/// <summary>
/// Will allow the user to move the joystick
/// </summary>
/// <param name="eventData">Information about the
/// movement, we are only
/// using the position</param>
public void OnDrag(PointerEventData eventData)
{
    /* We use our parent's info since the joystick
       moves */
    var parent =
```

```
            rt.parent.GetComponent<RectTransform>();
    var parentSize = parent.rect.size;
    var parentPoint =
        eventData.position - parentSize;

    /* Calculate the point relative to the
       parent's local space */
    Vector2 localPoint =
        parent.InverseTransformPoint(parentPoint);

    /* Calculates what the new anchor point should
       be */
    Vector2 newAnchorPos =
        localPoint - originalAnchored;

    /* Prevent the analog stick from moving too
       far */
    newAnchorPos = Vector2.ClampMagnitude(
        newAnchorPos, parentSize.x/2);

    rt.anchoredPosition = newAnchorPos;

}


/// <summary>
/// Will be called when the player lets go of the
/// stick
/// </summary>
/// <param name="eventData">Information about the
/// movement, unused</param>
public void OnEndDrag(PointerEventData eventData)
{
    /* Reset the stick to it's original position
    */
    rt.anchoredPosition = Vector3.zero;
}
```

11. Save your script and return to the Unity editor. Play the game and try to click and drag the analog sticks:

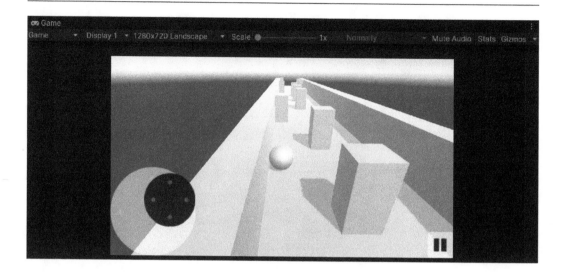

Figure 5.7 – Joysticks can now be moved

12. Now that they functionally work, let's have them actually affect the game. We need to have some way to communicate the information that MobileJoystick has. To do this, let's add a new property:

```
/// <summary>
/// Gets the value of the joystick in a -1 to 1
/// manner in the same way that Input.GetAxis does
/// </summary>
public Vector2 axisValue;
```

13. Next, add the following line to the OnDrag function:

```
// Update the axis value to the new position
axisValue = newAnchorPos / (parentSize.x / 2);
```

14. Then, add the following line to the OnEndDrag function:

```
axisValue = Vector2.zero;
```

15. Now we need to go to the PlayerBehaviour script. From there, we will add a new variable to tell us whether we have a MobileJoystick or not:

```
private MobileJoystick joystick;

// Start is called before the first frame update
public void Start()
{
    // Get access to our Rigidbody component
```

```
    rb = GetComponent<Rigidbody>();

    minSwipeDistancePixels = minSwipeDistance *
        Screen.dpi;

    joystick = GameObject.FindObjectOfType
        <MobileJoystick>();

}
```

16. This way, if the player has turned off `MobileJoystick`, we still want the game to work.

17. Next, we will need to update the `FixedUpdate` function to have the following changes:

```
/// <summary>
/// FixedUpdate is a prime place to put physics
/// calculations
/// happening over a period of time.
/// </summary>

void FixedUpdate()
{
    /* If the game is paused, don't do anything */
    if (PauseScreenBehaviour.paused)
    {
        return;
    }

    // Check if we're moving to the side
    var horizontalSpeed = Input.GetAxis("Horizontal")
        * dodgeSpeed;

    /* If the joystick is active and the player is
       moving the joystick, override the value */
    if (joystick && joystick.axisValue.x != 0)
    {
        horizontalSpeed = joystick.axisValue.x *
            dodgeSpeed;
    }

    /* Check if we are running either in the Unity
       editor or in a standalone build.*/
    #if UNITY_STANDALONE || UNITY_WEBPLAYER ||
        UNITY_EDITOR
        /* If the mouse is held down (or the screen is
```

```
                    tapped on Mobile */
        if (Input.GetMouseButton(0))
        {
            if(!joystick)
            {
                var screenPos = Input.mousePosition;
                horizontalSpeed =
                    CalculateMovement(screenPos);
            }
        }
/* Check if we are running on a mobile device */
#elif UNITY_IOS || UNITY_ANDROID

        switch (horizMovement)
        {
            case MobileHorizMovement.Accelerometer:
                /* Move player based on accelerometer
                    direction */
                horizontalSpeed = Input.acceleration.x
                    * dodgeSpeed;
                break;

            case MobileHorizMovement.ScreenTouch:
                /* Check if Input registered more than
                    zero touches */
                if (!joystick && Input.touchCount > 0)
                {
                    /* Store the first touch detected
                    */
                    var firstTouch = Input.touches[0];
                    var screenPos =
                        firstTouch.position;
                    horizontalSpeed =
                        CalculateMovement(screenPos);
                }
                break;
        }

#endif

rb.AddForce(horizontalSpeed, 0, rollSpeed);
```

```
    }
```

18. Save your scripts and return to the Unity editor. Save your scene and then play the game:

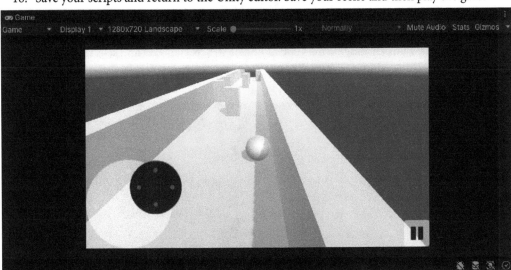

Figure 5.8 – Joystick moving the player

In this way, if we have the joystick enabled when the game starts, the game will use it to move the player. Alternatively, you can disable the joystick and your game will work in the same way as before.

At this point, our UI should work for the vast majority of cell phones. However, there are certain phones that contain "notches." We will see how to adjust our UI for that in the next section.

Adapting GUIs for notch devices

Since the first edition of this book, there have been many phones that have come out with sensor housings, more commonly known as "notches." Made popular with the iPhone X, this has grown to be a part of many phones that are out right now. While some people online state that entire-screen displays are the future, iOS devices, Android devices running 9.0 and above, and Unity have added support for notches built into devices, and we can use the Screen.safeArea property in Unity to ensure that all of our content is visible.

To get started, we will first go to the main menu to tweak the menu text:

1. Go to the **Project** view and open up the MainMenu Scene in the Scenes folder. In the *Adding a pause menu* section, we saw how we can use the **Panel** object in order to hold the contents we want to display. We will use this concept to account for the safe area.

2. With the level opened, go to the **Hierarchy** view and create a child panel for our title screen to be inside by right-clicking on the **Canvas - Scale w/Screen** object and selecting **UI | Panel**.

3. Afterward, make **Title Text** a child of the newly created panel by dragging and dropping the object on top of the newly created **Panel** object:

Figure 5.9 – SafeArea setup

4. From the **Project** view, go to the Scripts folder and create a new C# script called UISafeAreaHandler. Double-click on it to open your code editor and use the following code:

```csharp
using UnityEngine;

public class UISafeAreaHandler : MonoBehaviour
{
    RectTransform panel;

    // Start is called before the first frame update
    void Start()
    {
        panel = GetComponent<RectTransform>();
```

```
    }

    // Update is called once per frame
    void Update()
    {
        Rect area = Screen.safeArea;

        /* Pixel size in screen space of the whole
            screen */
        Vector2 screenSize = new Vector2(Screen.width,
            Screen.height);

        /* Set anchors to percentages of the screen
            used. */
        panel.anchorMin = area.position / screenSize;
        panel.anchorMax = (area.position + area.size)
            / screenSize;

    }
}
```

The `Screen.safeArea` property returns a variable of the `Rect` type, which contains an X and Y position and a width and height, just like the **Rect Transform** component we worked with previously in this chapter. This **Rect Transform** component gives a box containing the safe area that doesn't have notches inside it. Note that this property is in screen space and so will be given in pixels. For those Android phones running 8.1 or lower, `Screen.safeArea` will just return `Rect(0, 0, Screen.width, Screen.height)`, which will work due to the lack of a notch.

`Screen.safeArea` will change depending on the orientation that the device is currently in. Since we want to support all orientations (landscape and portrait mode), we'll have to check for the safe area changing at runtime, which is why we use the `Update` function to do modifications.

We previously saw that anchors can be used to specify the size of a panel. Anchors work in viewport space, which is to say that the values go from `(0, 0)` to `(1, 1)`. Since the `Rect` value given by `Screen.safeArea` is in screen (pixel) space, we divide by the screen size in pixels to convert to the points to viewport space.

Save the script and return to the Unity Editor. Then, attach the **UI Safe Area Handler** component to the **Panel** object that we just created.

5. Return to the Unity editor and transition to the **Game** window. At the top left, you'll see a dropdown that currently says **Game**; select it and change the value to **Simulator**. From there, you'll see a list of sample devices that you can select from a dropdown. Or click on the **Install Additional Devices** option to download a list of all of the possible options they have available. Due to us using the Screen.safeArea property, you should notice the panel tweak its size appropriately to fit everything within our screen:

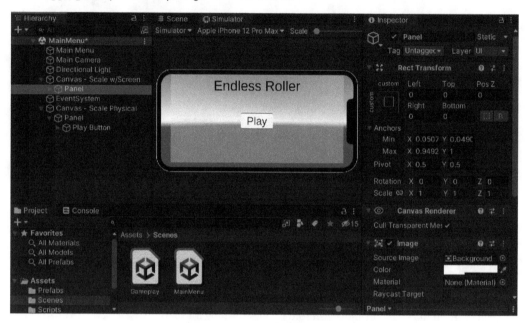

Figure 5.10 – Adjusting the notch value

The **Device Simulator** is a tool that aims to allow developers to see what their game will look like on many devices. For more information on it, check out https://docs.unity3d.com/Manual/device-simulator-view.html.

In portrait mode, the top portion of the screen is cut off for the notch and the bottom is cut off for the home button. We can also click on the buttons next to the **Rotate** text to see how our game will look on the device facing the other direction:

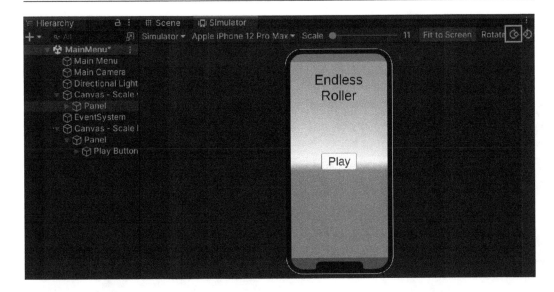

Figure 5.11 – Landscape mode

Switching to landscape mode, we lose the left/right side for the notch, and on iOS, it cuts off the other side as well. Just as in portrait mode, the top is cut off for the home button.

With this, we see that the menu adjusts itself correctly! However, there is a chance that the **Play** button no longer works. This is because both of our **Canvas** objects are drawn in the same sorting order, which means either can be on top of the other, similar to the concept of Z-fighting that you may know of if you've worked on 2D games in the past. Thankfully, we can fix that pretty easily.

6. Select the **Canvas - Scale w/Screen** object. From the **Inspector** window, go to the **Canvas** component and set **Sort Order** to -1. The button with a **Sort Order** value of 0 will always be on top of the contents of this Canvas.

    While the semi-transparent white panel is useful in illustrating the concept, we don't actually want our users to see it when the game is being played. With that in mind, let's turn off the image.

7. Select the **Panel** object. From the **Image** component, uncheck the checkbox to the left of the component's name to disable it.

Tip
If you wanted to still have the image visible and have the button still work, you can instead uncheck the **Raycast Target** property.

Now that the first Canvas is completed, we can now do the same actions for the other one:

1. Go to the **Canvas - Scale Physical** component and create another **Panel** object with the **UI Safe Area Handler** component attached to it, making sure to disable the **Image** component. Next, make the **Play** button a child of it:

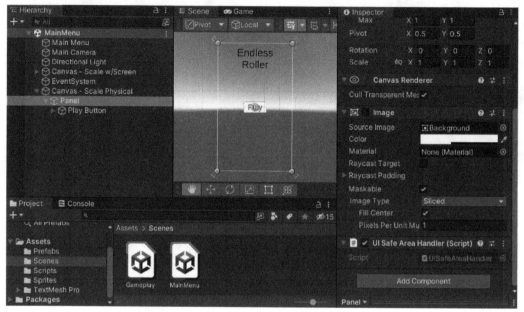

Figure 5.12 – Adjusting the Safe Area Handler

2. Save your Scene. Now that we have the main menu completed, we can tweak the Gameplay Scene as well.

3. Open the Gameplay Scene, select the **On Screen Controls** object, and then just add the **UI Safe Area Handler** component to it:

Figure 5.13 – Making the On Screen Controls use the UI Safe Area

4. To adjust the **Pause Menu**, we don't want to change the **Pause Menu** object as we want the black screen even in the notch areas. We have previously created a panel to hold the contents of the pause menu, but that object is using the **Aspect Ratio Fitter**, which will overwrite any anchor changes we would make in the code. To keep this functionality as well as **Content Size Fitters** in the child objects, we can just create a parent panel to act as a holder.

5. Make the **Pause Menu** object active again by selecting it in the **Hierarchy** window and then clicking on the checkbox by its name in the **Inspector** window. Right-click on the **Panel** object and create a **Panel** object by right-clicking and selecting **UI | Panel**. In the new panel, add the **UI Safe Area Handler** component and disable the **Image** component:

Figure 5.14 – Adjusting the Pause Menu to work with notches

6. Finally, since we are not working with the **Pause Menu** object anymore, select the **Pause Menu** object from the **Hierarchy** window, and in the **Inspector** window, uncheck the checkbox by the name to disable the object.

7. Save your Scene and play the game:

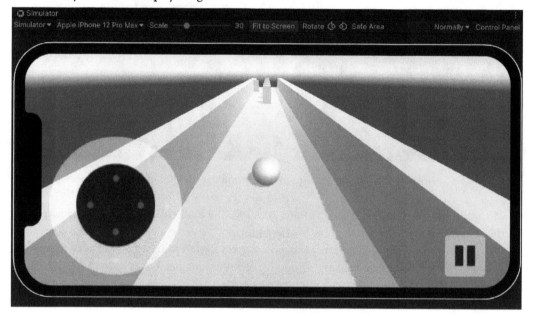

Figure 5.15 – UI now responds correctly to notches

As you can see, if we hold down the spacebar, we can see both menus working correctly!

Summary

In this chapter, we integrated the pause menu into our game itself and made it work with everything in our project. We then saw how we could create on-screen controls to give players another way to interact with the game using mobile devices. Finally, we saw how to have our game automatically adapt to fit within the allotted safe areas to handle the notches on phones. We will be exploring the previous concepts more deeply in later chapters, so keep these explanations in mind.

In the next chapter, we will dive into monetization and take a look at just how we can add Unity ads to our project.

6

Implementing In-App Purchases

As mentioned in *Chapter 7, Advertising Using Unity Ads*, there are many options out there when it comes to selling your game on a mobile platform. If you decide to go free-to-play, in addition to showing ads, there is also the ability to sell people additional content and/or advantages through the use of **In-App Purchases (IAPs)**. This can be a way to engage users of your game and convert them from free players into paying customers.

Typically, these can be options such as removing ads or offering themes to players, but you can also do things such as unlock new levels and add additional content so that people addicted to your game will be clamoring to give you more of their time. Alternatively, you can also think of your IAPs as items that players will want to buy in order to enhance their gameplay experiences, such as power-ups and upgrades.

In this chapter, we will integrate Unity's IAP system into our project and take a look at how to create an IAP that is for consumable content as well as permanently unlocking features. By the end of the chapter, we will see how to set up Unity's IAP system and create our first possible purchasable item, and then we will see how to restore purchases on certain devices before seeing additional resources for the various app stores that exist.

This chapter is split into a number of topics. It contains a simple step-by-step process from beginning to end. The following is the outline of our tasks:

- Setting up Unity IAP
- Creating our first purchase
- Adding a button to restore purchases
- Configuring purchases for the stores of your choice

Technical requirements

This book utilizes Unity 2022.1.0b16 and Unity Hub 3.3.1, but the steps should work with minimal changes in future versions of the editor. If you would like to download the exact version used in this book, and there is a new version out, you can visit Unity's download archive at `https://unity3d.com/get-unity/download/archive`. You can also find the system requirements for Unity at `https://docs.unity3d.com/2022.1/Documentation/Manual/system-requirements.html` in the *Unity Editor system requirements* section.

You can find the code files for this chapter on GitHub at `https://github.com/PacktPublishing/Unity-2022-Mobile-Game-Development-3rd-Edition/tree/main/Chapter06%20and%2007`.

Setting up Unity IAP

Unity IAP is a service that allows us to sell a variety of different items to players within our game projects and is currently supported by the iOS App Store, Mac App Store, Google Play, Windows Store, Amazon Appstore, and more, by default. So, using this, we can easily sell our items in many different places. We have already set up Unity Services in *Chapter 7, Advertising Using Unity Ads*, so this will be a lot easier to get going. Perform the following steps to add Unity IAP:

1. Open the **Services** window by going to **Window | Package Manager**, and then click on the **Services** button on the top toolbar.

2. From there, scroll down to the **In App Purchasing** item and then click on the **Install** button.

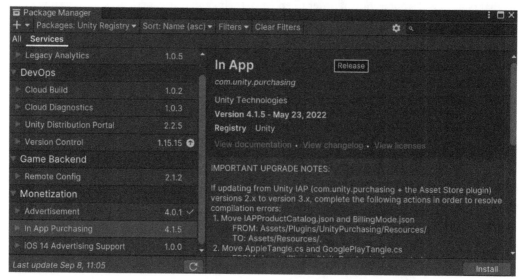

Figure 6.1: The In App Purchasing option from Package Manager

3. A window will pop up asking for you to confirm that you would like to activate the **Purchasing** service package. Click on the **Ok** button.

Figure 6.2: Activating the Purchasing service

4. Once completed, you can close out of **Package Manager** and then go into the **Project Settings** menu by going to **Edit | Project Settings** and then going to the **Services** section. If all went well, you should see an **In-App Purchases** menu section. Select it and you should notice that it has been toggled on.

> **Important note**
>
> The IAP package is created externally from the main engine itself because the code is meant to be extremely flexible and can be updated to fit any policies that are needed. We can then just update the package instead of having to update it to the latest version of Unity, which can be very important when working on a large project.

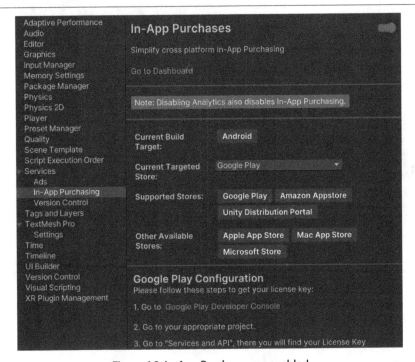

Figure 6.3: In-App Purchases are enabled

Now that we have the IAP system brought into our project, we can now utilize it to create our first purchasable object for our players.

Creating our first purchase

To make our first in-app purchase, we will make use of a feature of Unity that was just added to our project, Codeless IAP. It is called Codeless IAP because you do not need to write any code for the actual IAP transaction, just the script that defines what users get if they make a purchase. It's by far the easiest way to integrate IAPs into Unity games and a great way to start trying out IAPs in our project.

One of the most common IAPs is the ability to disable advertisements in mobile games. Using the following steps, let's add that functionality by creating a button that, when clicked, will disable advertisements:

1. Open up our Main Menu level by going to the **Project** window, opening the Assets/Scenes folder, and then double-clicking on the MainMenu file.

2. From there, return to the **Scene** window if not there already, and then click on the **2D** button to go into 2D mode since we'll be working with the UI.

3. We will first need to have something to sell and to do that, we will use the IAP Catalog, which we can access by going to **Services | In-App Purchasing | IAP Catalog…**:

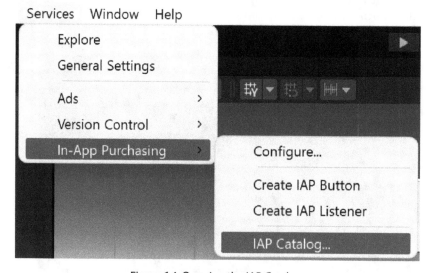

Figure 6.4: Opening the IAP Catalog

Once we get to the menu, it should look something like this:

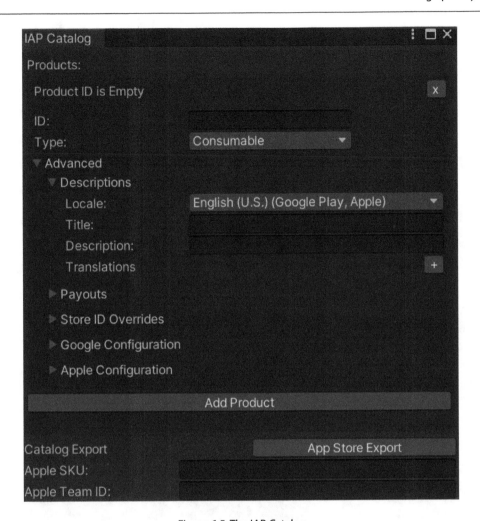

Figure 6.5: The IAP Catalog

Now, the first thing we'll need to do is create an ID for our product, which is how we will identify our product in different app stores. In our case, let's go with removeAds. Then, under **Type**, change it to **Non Consumable**:

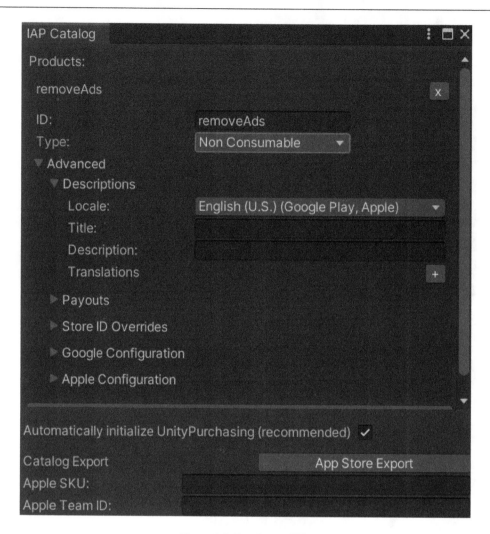

Figure 6.6: Creating an IAP

By non-consumable, we mean that the players only need to buy this once, and the game will keep that in mind for later. The others are consumable, meaning that they are used for things that can be bought over and over again, such as special power-ups and subscriptions. These give access to some kind of content for a period of time, possibly recurring until a user cancels them.

4. Next, we can close out of **IAP Catalog** by clicking on **X** in the top-right corner of the window.

5. Select the **Canvas - Scale Physical** object in the **Hierarchy** window. From there, select **Services |**
    In-App Purchasing | Create IAP Button, and we should see a new button created in our scene:

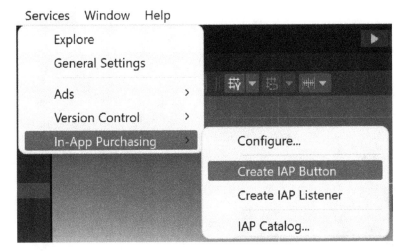

Figure 6.7: Creating an IAP button

This button will be used to perform an IAP to remove the ads in the game. The button currently uses Unity's legacy text system, but it can easily be adjusted to use `TextMeshPro` if you'd like.

To ensure that both the **Start** and **Remove Ads** buttons show up correctly on the screen, we will create a menu that can hold both of them. This means creating another panel as a child of our Safe Area panel.

From the **Hierarchy** window, select our **Panel** object and, in the **Inspector** window, rename it `SafeAreaHolder`.

6. Afterward, create a child **Panel** object of `SafeAreaHolder` and have it fill the entire screen as done before. Add a **Vertical Layout Group** component to it. From there, change **Child Alignment** to **Middle Center** and set all **Padding** and **Spacing** to `10`.

7. Then, add a **Content Size Fitter** component and set the **Vertical Fit** and **Horizontal Fit** fields to **Preferred Size**.

8. Rename the newly added button `Remove Ads Button` and then add a **Horizontal Layout Group** component to it with all **Padding** options set to `10` and at the **Child Controls Size** property check both the **Width** and **Height** options. Also, add a **Content Size Fitter** component to it with both **Fit** options set to **Preferred Size**. Then, in the child **Text (Legacy)** object's **Text** component, change the **Text** property to show `Remove Ads` instead.

Tip

For a reminder on what these instructions mean and what each step does, check out *Chapter 4, Resolution-Independent UI*.

---

1. Finally, drag and drop the two buttons onto the **Panel** object, with the **Play** button in the top half and the **Remove Ads** button below it, as follows:

Figure 6.8: The Remove Ads button added to the scene

2. Next, with the **Remove Ads** object selected, move to the **Inspector** tab, and scroll down to the **IAP Button** component. Under **Product ID:**, click the dropdown, and select **removeAds**. You'll note that the IAP Button class has an **On Purchase Complete (Product)** function, which works similarly to **On Click** as we've used with **Button** components in the past. With that in mind, we will need to create a function that we would like to call when the player presses the button.

In *Chapter 7, Advertising Using Unity Ads*, we created a static variable inside the UnityAdController class called showAds. We will use this variable to check whether we should show ads.

We will need to open up the MainMenuBehaviour script and add the following functions to the class:

```
public void DisableAds()
{
    UnityAdController.showAds = false;

    /* Used to store that we shouldn't show ads */
    PlayerPrefs.SetInt("Show Ads", 0);
}


protected virtual void Start()
```

```
{
    /* Initialize the showAds variable */
    bool showAds = (PlayerPrefs.GetInt("Show Ads", 1)
        == 1);
    UnityAdController.showAds = showAds;
}
```

Here, we are using Unity's `PlayerPrefs` system in order to save whether a player should be shown ads or not. `PlayerPrefs` is cool because it saves information between playthroughs of the game and is used often for things such as high scores and player preferences (hence the name). To reset the properties for testing, you can go to **Edit** | **Clear All PlayerPrefs**. `PlayerPrefs` may be removed if the app is uninstalled or if the app's data is cleared, so we will later add a **Restore Purchases** button that will allow the players to restore their purchases on platforms that allow it. For platforms that don't, you'll want to make an API call to the server to check whether the current user has already purchased the non-consumable IAP item. More details on this will be covered in the *Adding a button to restore purchases* section of this chapter.

> **Note**
>
> For more information on PlayerPrefs, check out `https://docs.unity3d.com/ScriptReference/PlayerPrefs.html`.

Note that I made the `Start` function `virtual`, which means that inherited classes can also use this as a foundation for their own scripts. We also marked the function as `protected`, which works the same as a `private` function but it also is accessible in child classes.

3. With that in mind, we will also need to update the `Start` function of `PauseScreenBehaviour` to the following:

```
protected override void Start()
{
    /* Initialize Ads if needed */
    base.Start();

    if (!UnityAdController.showAds)
    {
        /* If not showing ads, just start the game */
        SetPauseMenu(false);
    }

}
```

The `override` keyword will replace the default behavior of `Start`. However, when we call `base.Start()`, we are ensuring that the preceding content from `MainMenuBehaviour` will be called—in this case, we ensure that `UnityAdController` has the correct value set.

4. Finally, we will need to adjust the `ObstacleBehaviour` script to handle not playing ads as well. Update the `ShowContinue` function to use the following:

```
// Other code above...

/* Come back after 1 second and check again */
yield return new WaitForSeconds(1f);
}
else if (!UnityAdController.showAds)
{
    /* It's valid to click the button now */
    contButton.interactable = true;

    /* If player clicks on button we want to just
       continue */
    contButton.onClick.AddListener(Continue);

    UnityAdController.obstacle = this;

    /* Change text to allow continue */
    btnText.text = "Free Continue";

    /* We can now leave the coroutine */
    break;
}

else
{
    /* It's valid to click the button now */
    contButton.interactable = true;

    // More code below...
```

5. We will also need to make a slight adjustment to the `ResetGame` method by removing or commenting out the following lines:

```
/*If we find the button, we can use it */
if (continueButton)
{
    //if (UnityAdController.showAds)
    //{
        // If a player clicks on a button, we want to
           play an ad
        // and then continue
```

```
            StartCoroutine(ShowContinue(continueButton));
    //}
    //else
    //{
        /* If we can't play an ad, no need for the
           continue button */
    //    continueButton.gameObject.SetActive(false);
    //}


    }
```

6. Save your script and dive into Unity.

7. From the **Hierarchy** window, select the **Remove Ads** button. Go into the **Inspector** tab and then scroll down to the **IAP Button** component. Go ahead and click on the plus button underneath the **On Purchase Complete (Product)** option, and then add the Main Menu object to the little box below the **Runtime Only** dropdown. Then, select **Main Menu Behaviour | DisableAds** from the dropdown to the right:

Figure 6.9: Adding the DisableAds function call to Purchase

8. Now, save our scene and start the game:

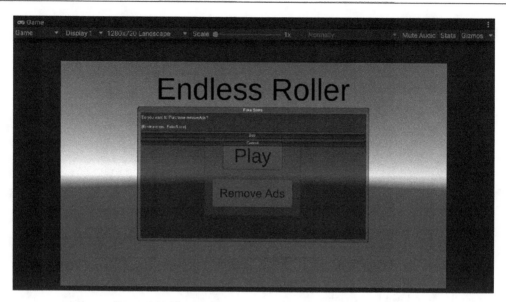

Figure 6.10: The purchase menu appears to work correctly

Now, if we click on the **Remove Ads** button, it will ask whether we want to make the purchase. If we do, it will then make it so that when we go into the game, there are no ads. Likewise, now when we die, it will display a **Free Continue** button:

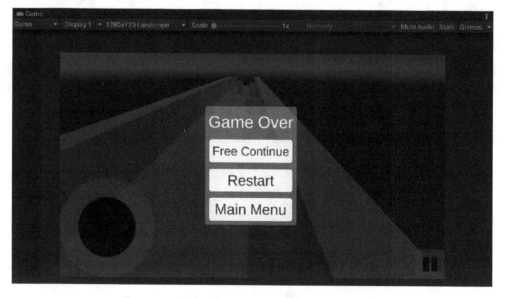

Figure 6.11: Making sure the purchase works correctly

With that, we now have created a simple purchase in Unity.

> **Note**
>
> If you're interested in learning more about Codeless IAP, checkout `https://docs.unity3d.com/Manual/UnityIAPCodelessIAP.html`.

With this, you can now build as many products as you'd like to have in your game. However, certain platforms also have requirements with regard to the functionality to restore previous purchases. In the next section, we will see how to do that.

Adding a button to restore purchases

On platforms that support it (Google Play and Universal Windows Applications, most notably), if you purchase something, uninstall, and then reinstall a game using Unity IAP, it automatically restores any products the user owned during the first initialization following reinstallation.

For those on iOS, users must have the ability to restore their purchases via a button due to Apple requiring them to reauthenticate their password beforehand. Not doing so will prevent our game from being accepted on the iOS App Store, so it's a good idea to include this functionality if we wish to deploy it there. Let's look at the steps to do just that:

1. Go to the **Hierarchy** window and select the **Remove Ads Button** object. Once selected, duplicate it by pressing *Ctrl + D*.

2. Change the duplicate's name by selecting it and changing its name to `Restore Button` in the **Inspector** window.

3. From the **Hierarchy** window, open up the **Text** object and change the text to `Restore Purchases` as well.

4. Now, select the **Restore** object, and then, in the **IAP Button** component, go to **Button Type** and select **Restore**:

Figure 6.12: Adding the Restore button

You should note that the properties of the **IAP Button** component have changed and now only allow you to set **Button Type**, as there is nothing left to customize.

5. Save your scene and jump into Unity.

6. When you start the game and try to click on **Restore**, you'll get a warning in the **Console** window stating that this isn't a supported platform:

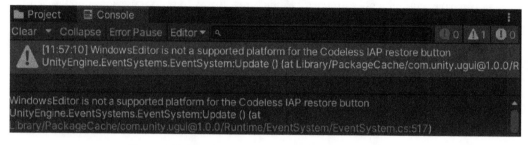

Figure 6.13: Warning upon trying to restore on Windows

So, with that in mind, we can adjust our game so that the button will only show up if we are currently running on a supported platform.

7. Go to the `Scripts` folder and create a C# script called `RestoreAdsChecker`. Once it opens, use the following script for it:

```csharp
using UnityEngine;

/// <summary>
/// Will show or remove a button depending on whether
/// we can restore ads or not
/// </summary>
public class RestoreAdsChecker : MonoBehaviour
{

    // Use this for initialization
    void Start()
    {
        bool canRestore = false;

        switch (Application.platform)
        {
            // Windows Store
            case RuntimePlatform.WSAPlayerX86:
            case RuntimePlatform.WSAPlayerX64:
            case RuntimePlatform.WSAPlayerARM:

            // iOS, OSX, tvOS
```

```
case RuntimePlatform.IPhonePlayer:
case RuntimePlatform.OSXPlayer:
case RuntimePlatform.tvOS:
    canRestore = true;
    break;
    }

    gameObject.SetActive(canRestore);
    }

}
```

This script goes through all of the stores listed in Unity's IAPButton class, and if they are something that can be restored, we set canRestore to true; otherwise, it will stay false. Finally, we will remove the object if we cannot restore it, without having to create specific things for different builds.

8. Save the script and dive back into Unity.

9. Attach our newly created RestoreAdsChecker component to our **Restore Button** object:

Figure 6.14: Adding the Restore Ads Checker component

10. Save your project and start up the game:

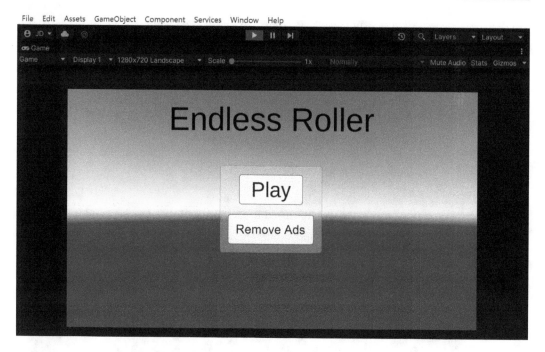

Figure 6.15: The result of the RestoreAdsChecker component

Now, due to the **RestoreAdsChecker** component that we added on our PC build of the game, the **Restore** button doesn't show up, but if we export for iOS, it will show up on our device!

> **Note**
>
> For more information on restoring transactions and how this functionally works, check out `https://docs.unity3d.com/Manual/UnityIAPRestoringTransactions.html`.

This ensures that our game has this particular feature on each of the different platforms that support it. With that in mind, we will next look at some of the specific stores and places you may wish to add support for IAPs in your game.

Configuring purchases for the stores of your choice

Unfortunately, we do not have enough room in the book to go step by step through the process for every store, but I do have pages that you can reference to go through the entire process for the following stores:

- The Apple App Store and Mac App Store: `https://docs.unity3d.com/Manual/UnityIAPAppleConfiguration.html`

- Google Play Store: `https://docs.unity3d.com/Manual/UnityIAPGoogleConfiguration.html`

- The Windows Store: `https://docs.unity3d.com/Manual/UnityIAPWindowsConfiguration.html`

- Amazon Appstore: `https://docs.unity3d.com/Manual/UnityIAPAmazonConfiguration.html`

There are some potential issues when trying to publish to multiple Android IAP stores (such as Samsung and Google) with the same build. You can find information on resolving those issues at `https://docs.unity3d.com/Manual/UnityIAPCrossStoreInstallationIssues.html`.

Summary

In this chapter, we covered how to create IAPs by making use of Unity in your project. We first covered how to set up Unity's IAP system and then dived into using Codeless IAP to easily add a purchasable item to your game. We then created the functionality to restore our purchase if we uninstall and reinstall our game and went over where we can go to set up our purchases depending on the store we want to target. These new skills give you the ability to make additional revenue from your game while also allowing you to target multiple stores and platforms, making it possible for even more people to see it.

Now, of course, having all these ways to make money isn't going to help us if no one plays our game. In the next chapter, we will get social, learning how we can make use of social media to share our score and get other players interested in our title.

Further reading

For more tips and tricks on improving your freemium strategy, I suggest that you check out the following article by Pepe Agell at `https://www.chartboost.com/blog/inapp-purchases-for-indie-mobile-games-freemium-strategy`.

7

Advertising Using Unity Ads

When working on mobile titles, you need to think about how you are going to sell your game. Deciding on how to best sell a game can be difficult. Of course, you can sell your game for a price, and there is a possibility that it will be successful, but you'll be limiting your audience numbers to a much lower amount. This could work well for a niche game, but if you're trying to make a game with a broad appeal where you want to get as many players as possible to play your title, you may have some issues.

Having a price on the game can be a major hurdle in getting initial customers who will share the game via word of mouth and contribute to having more people play your game. To solve this potential issue, you do have the option of making your game free.

Afterward, you can give players the opportunity to purchase things or show advertisements when playing the game.

That's not to say that having a bunch of advertisements in a free game is the best option either. Having too many ads, or even the wrong kind of ads, can drive users away, which can be even worse. Many developers have their own opinions on whether it's a good idea to use ads or not, but that's not the purpose of this chapter. In this chapter, we will look into the different options available to us in terms of advertising over the course of our game and show how to implement them, should you choose to add this content to your game.

This chapter is split into a number of topics. It contains a simple step-by-step process, from beginning to end. The following is the outline of our tasks:

- Setting up Unity Ads
- Creating a simple ad
- Adding in-ad callback methods
- Opt-in advertisements with rewards
- Integrating a cooldown timer

In this chapter, we will integrate the Unity Ads framework into our project and learn how to create both simple and complex versions of advertisements. This is done by first setting up Unity's Ads system, then creating a simple ad before adding additional callback options. We will then see how we can give additional incentives to view ads by utilizing opt-in rewards and adding a cooldown timer to prevent players from watching too many ads.

Technical requirements

This book utilizes Unity 2022.1.0b16 and Unity Hub 3.3.1, but the steps should work with minimal changes in future versions of the editor. If you would like to download the exact version used in this book, and there is a new version out, you can visit Unity's download archive at `https://unity3d.com/get-unity/download/archive`. You can also find the system requirements for Unity at `https://docs.unity3d.com/2022.1/Documentation/Manual/system-requirements.html` in the **Unity Editor system requirements** section.

You can find the code files present in this chapter on GitHub at `https://github.com/PacktPublishing/Unity-2022-Mobile-Game-Development-3rd-Edition/tree/main/Chapter06%20and%2007`.

Setting up Unity Ads

Unity Ads is a video ad network for iOS and Android that can monetize your existing player base by showing ads. Unity Ads offers video ads that can be shown as either rewarded or non-rewarded placements. As the name suggests, rewarded ads will give the users a reward or incentive that will help them while playing the game. Before we can enable Unity Ads, we must first enable Unity's Services suite. To activate Unity Services, you have to link your project to a Unity Services Project ID, which is how Unity can tell the difference between the different projects you are creating. So let's see how to do that:

1. Open the **Services** window by going to **Window | General | Services** or by pressing *Ctrl + 0*. This will open up the Unity Package Manager and will automatically select the **Advertisement** option:

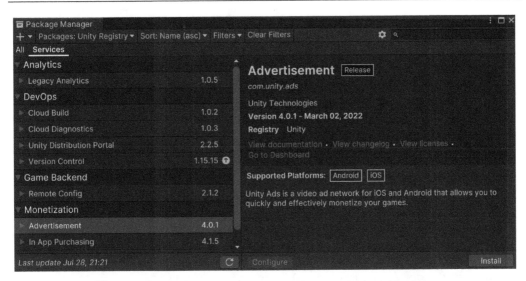

Figure 7.1 – The Advertisement option in the Unity Package Manager

2. Click on the **Install** button and wait for it to finish installing. Upon finishing the installation, you should see a window that looks like the following:

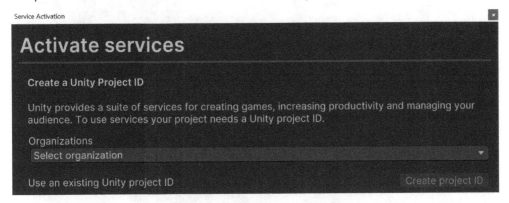

Figure 7.2 – Service Activation window

You can also access this menu by going to **Services | Ads | Configure** after the package has been installed.

Assuming that you haven't worked with Unity Services before, you will need to create **Organization** and **Project Name details**.

3. Click on the dropdown and select your username and then click on the **Create project ID** button. The project name is automatically created according to the name of your project when you first created it, but you can change this in the **Settings** section of the **Services** window.

> **Important note**
>
> Unity automatically creates an organization using your account username; however, if you need to create another one, you can do so at `https://id.unity.com/organizations`.

4. You'll then be asked questions about your game. If your game is not directed toward children, go ahead and select **No** from the drop-down menu and then click on the **Save** button. Otherwise, select **Yes** and then click on **Save**.

> **Important note**
>
> When you indicate that your game is designed for children under the age of 13 years, ads will not be behaviorally targeted to users in your game. Behavioral targeting can yield a higher **effective cost per thousand impressions (eCPM)** by showing ads that are more relevant to your users, but its use is prohibited with users under the age of 13 due to **Children's Online Privacy Protection Rule Act (COPPA)** regulations. For more info on this, check out `https://forum.unity.com/threads/age-designation.326930/`.

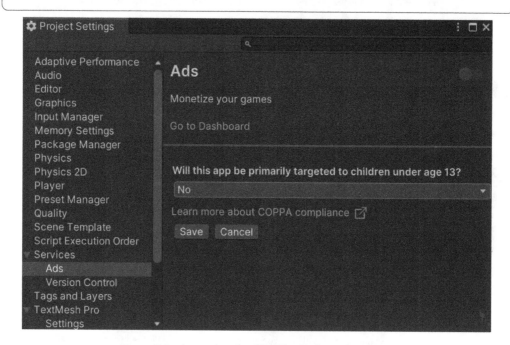

Figure 7.3 – Answering the COPPA compliance question

5. Then, when brought to the **Ads** menu, click on the toggle at the top right to turn it on. Ads should be toggled on at this point.

6. If you scroll down, you'll see a property called **Game Id**; note down those values as we will need them in order to initialize Unity Ads at the start of the game.

7. To get started, it would be a good idea for us to have all of the ad-related behavior to share a script, so we will create a new class called `UnityAd Controller` by going to the **Project** window, opening the `Assets/Scripts` folder, and selecting **Create | C# Script**.

8. Open up the file in the IDE of your choice, and use the following code:

```csharp
using UnityEngine;
using UnityEngine.Advertisements; /* Advertisement class */
public class UnityAdController : MonoBehaviour
{
    /// <summary>
    /// If we should show ads or not
    /// </summary>
    public static bool showAds = true;

    /// <summary>
    /// Replace with your actual gameId
    /// </summary>
    private string gameId = "1234567";

    /// <summary>
    /// If the game is in test mode or not
    /// </summary>
    private bool testMode = true;

    /// <summary>
    /// Unity Ads must be initialized or else ads will
    /// not work properly
    /// </summary>
    private void Start()
    {
        /* No need to initialize if it already is done
        */
        if (!Advertisement.isInitialized)
        {
            Advertisement.Initialize(gameId,
                testMode);
        }
    }

}
```

The preceding code does a number of things. We first state that we are using the `UnityEngine.Advertisments` namespace to get access to the `Advertisement` class. If you only intend to implement video, interstitial, and banner ads for your monetization strategy, this is the API that Unity suggests to use. In addition to this, in order to use Unity Ads, you must call the `Advertisement.Initialize` function, which I do inside of the `Start` function of this object.

9. From the **Project** window, open up the **MainMenu** scene and, once inside, create an empty GameObject (**GameObject | Create Empty**) and name it `Unity Ad Controller`. Once created, attach the **Unity Ad Controller** script to it:

Figure 7.4 – Creating the Unity Ad Controller object

10. Because this object is spawned at the **MainMenu** level, it is loaded at the beginning of the game, which is perfect for what we will use it for.

At this point, we have finished the setup process required to utilize Unity Ads by enabling Unity Analytics and then turning the **Ads** menu on. With the setup process complete, we can now proceed to actually adding a simple ad to our project.

Displaying a simple ad

Advertisements are a possible way to generate revenue from players playing your game. As mentioned previously, Unity Ads has two different types of ads that we can display: simple and rewarded. Simple ads are easy to use, hence the name, and allow users to have simple full-screen interstitial ads. This can be really useful when moving between levels or perhaps when the player wants to restart the game. Let's see how we can implement that feature now. Implement the following steps:

1. To get started, we will need to add a new function to the `UnityAdController` class:

```
/// <summary>
/// Will get the appropriate Ad ID for the platform we
/// are on
```

```
/// </summary>
/// <returns>A usable Ad ID</returns>
private static string GetAdID()
{
    string adID = "Interstitial_";

    if (Application.platform ==
        RuntimePlatform.IPhonePlayer)
    {
        adID += "iOS";
    }
    else
    {
        adID += "Android";
    }

    return adID;
}


/// <summary>
/// Will load and display an ad on the screen
/// </summary>
public static void ShowAd()
{
    // Load an Ad to play
    Advertisement.Load(GetAdID());

    // Display it after it is loaded
    Advertisement.Show(GetAdID());
}
```

Here, we created a static method called ShowAd. We made this static so that we can access the function without actually having to create an instance of this class in order to call it. The function will load an advertisement into memory and then, when it is ready, we will call the Show() function to display it on the screen. We also created a helper function called GetAdID in order to give us the correct ad type to use depending on the platform we are deploying to.

2. Save your script and then open up the MainMenuBehaviour file and add the following highlighted code:

```
/// <summary>
/// Will load a new scene upon being called
/// </summary>
/// <param name="levelName">The name of the level we
/// want to go to</param>
```

```
public void LoadLevel(string levelName)
{
    if (UnityAdController.showAds)
    {
        /* Show an ad */
        UnityAdController.ShowAd();
    }


    SceneManager.LoadScene(levelName);
}
```

This will have an advertisement play each time we call the `LoadLevel` function if it is supported. We also added a new parameter with a default value. The nice thing about this is that we can optionally decide when we want to show an ad.

For instance, we may want to make it so that when we restart the game, we don't play an ad.

3. Now let's see this in action. Play the game and then click on the **Play** button:

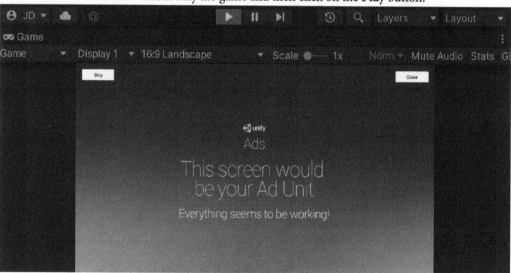

Figure 7.5 – An example ad being shown

As you can see in the preceding screenshot, the ad works correctly. This screen is what is shown when playing the game in the editor. It has buttons to allow us to test whether a player skips or watches a video in full. When we disable test mode, we will then see live video ads.

You'll also see this happen if, once in the game, you open the pause menu and click on the **Main Menu** button.

> **Important note**
>
> If this does not work and/or show up, check the **Player Settings** menu you learned about previously and ensure that your current platform is set to Android or iOS.

This provides us with the easiest way of getting an ad to show up in our game, but there are still a number of things we need to do to ensure our ads work properly, which we will look at next.

> **Important note**
>
> Another type of ad that can be used is banner ads. These work similarly to default ads but you'd use `Banner` instead of `Interstitial` when calling `GetAdID`.
>
> For more information on this, check out `https://docs.unity.com/monetization-dashboard/AdUnits.html`.

Utilizing ad callback methods

The code we wrote for the `LoadLevel` function works perfectly fine when we go to the main menu of the game; however, if we dive into the game itself from the main menu, the game will still be going on in the background with the ad blocking the player from playing the game.

When running your app on an actual mobile device, the Unity project will pause while Unity Ads are shown. However, if you are testing in the Unity Editor, the game is not paused while the placeholder ads are shown. However, we can simulate that behavior ourselves using the `Advertisement.ShowOptions` class.

We will pause the game when an ad is shown and then resume the game once the ad is finished. To do so, perform the following steps:

1. Let's first open up the `UnityAdController` class and add the following variable and update the `Start` function to the following:

```
/// <summary>
/// A static reference to this object
/// </summary>
public static UnityAdController instance;

/// <summary>
/// Unity Ads must be initialized or else ads will not
/// work properly
/// </summary>
private void Start()
{
    /* No need to initialize if it already is done */
```

```
    if (!Advertisement.isInitialized)
    {
        instance = this;
        // Use the functions provided by this to allow
        // custom
        Advertisement.Initialize(gameId, testMode);
    }
}
```

The `instance` variable is going to be used to give the `Advertisement.Show` function a second parameter to reference the object to run code on.

2. Update the `ShowAd` function to have the second parameter added to our function:

```
/// <summary>
/// Will load and display an ad on the screen
/// </summary>
public static void ShowAd()
{
    // Load an Ad to play
    Advertisement.Load(GetAdID());

    // Display it after it is loaded
    Advertisement.Show(GetAdID(), instance);
}
```

For the second parameter, the `Advertisement.Show` function takes in an `IUnityAdsShowListener` object. I at the start of the name here indicates that this type is an interface. This is a keyword in C#, designating something like a contract, promising that whatever you provide to this function contains the functionalities required by the interface.

3. Now update the class definition to the following:

```
public class UnityAdController : MonoBehaviour,
IUnityAdsShowListener
```

By adding the comma and then `IUnityAdsShowListener`, we are stating that we will implement the methods provided by the `IUnityAdsShowListener` interface.

In C#, whenever we add an interface to our class definition, we are making a promise that we will include an implementation for all of the methods that were declared inside of that interface, and if we don't, our code won't compile. This is needed because later on we are going to pass in an object of type `IUnityAdsShowListener` to Unity's code and it will use those methods at the appropriate times.

To see what those methods are, from your IDE, you may be able to right-click on the IUnityAdsShowListener option and select **Go to Definition**. From there, you may see something like the following:

```
namespace UnityEngine.Advertisements
{
    public interface IUnityAdsShowListener
    {
        void OnUnityAdsShowClick(string placementId);
        void OnUnityAdsShowComplete(
            string placementId,
                UnityAdsShowCompletionState
                    showCompletionState);
        void OnUnityAdsShowFailure(string placementId,
            UnityAdsShowError error, string message);
        void OnUnityAdsShowStart(string placementId);
    }
}
```

We will need to create four methods inside our own class with the exact same names, parameters, and return types.

> **Important note**
>
> For more information on interfaces and how they work in C#, check out https://www.tutorialsteacher.com/csharp/csharp-interface.

4. After doing this, we need to implement the functions used by the interface:

```
#region IUnityAdsShowListener Methods
/// <summary>
/// This callback method handles logic for the ad
/// starting to play.
/// </summary>
/// <param name="placementId">The identifier for the
    Ad Unit showing the content.</param>
public void OnUnityAdsShowStart(string placementId)
{
    /* Pause game while ad is shown */
    PauseScreenBehaviour.paused = true;
    Time.timeScale = 0f;
}

/// <summary>
```

```
/// This callback method handles logic for the ad
/// finishing.
/// </summary>
/// <param name="placementId">The identifier for the
/// Ad Unit showing the content</param>
/// <param name="showCompletionState">Indicates the
/// final state of the ad (whether the ad was skipped
/// or completed).</param>
public void OnUnityAdsShowComplete(string placementId,
UnityAdsShowCompletionState showCompletionState)
{
    /* Unpause game when ad is over */
    PauseScreenBehaviour.paused = false;
    Time.timeScale = 1f;
}


/* This callback method handles logic for the user clicking on
the ad. */
public void OnUnityAdsShowClick(string placementId) { }


/* This callback method handles logic for the Ad Unit failing to
show. */
public void OnUnityAdsShowFailure(string placementId,
UnityAdsShowError error, string message) { }
#endregion
```

Each of these four functions does something when we are creating ads. Of note is the `OnUnityAdsShowStart` method, where we pause the game, and then the `OnUnityAdsShowComplete` method where we unpause. We utilize a region here in order to make it easier to compartmentalize our code.

> **Important note**
>
> For more information on the #region block, check out https://docs.microsoft.com/en-us/dotnet/csharp/language-reference/preprocessor-directives/preprocessor-region.

5. Next, we will make it so that `PauseScreenBehaviour` doesn't override this new change. So, we will replace the `Start()` function with the following:

```
void Start()
{
    if (!UnityAdController.showAds)
    {
        /* If not showing ads, just start the game */
```

```
        SetPauseMenu(false);
    }

}
```

The preceding snippet is important because otherwise the game will immediately be turned off when the level loads in the `Start` function, after we tell the game to pause, which is called after the level loads. This is needed for the PC version of the game, as there is nothing else to unpause the static value.

6.   Save our scripts and start the game up again:

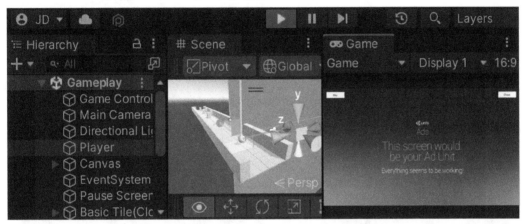

Figure 7.6 – The game is paused until the player ends the ad

With that, when we transition from the main menu to the game, we will pause the game until we are ready to jump in. Now that we can see how to work with basic advertisements that aren't optional, let's give players the opportunity to see an ad for some kind of benefit.

Opt-in advertisements with rewards

According to AdColony, the most recommended form of mobile game ad according to 58% of mobile developers is the rewarded video ad. By that, we're referring to making ads an opt-in experience where players choose to see an ad and receive some kind of bonus in return. That way, users feel it's a choice for them whether or not to watch the ad, and they feel more compelled to watch it because they will get something out of it.

Rewarded ad placements typically yield higher **effective Cost Per 1000 Impressions (eCPMs)** since they offer more engagement from users by allowing them to opt in before watching an ad in exchange for some in-game reward.

> **Note**
>
> If you're interested in learning more about why reward ads are recommended, check out `https://www-staging.adcolony.com/blog/2016/04/26/the-top-ads-recommended-by-mobile-game-developers/`.

In our game, we could add the choice of restarting the game or seeing an ad to continue the game. This means that we will need to create some kind of menu in order for the player to select whether or not to see the ad, so let's add that next:

1. Stop the game if you haven't done so already, and then open up the **Gameplay**

2. scene. Afterward, let's create a **Game Over** menu by first going to the **Hierarchy** window and expanding the **Canvas** game object if you have not done so already. Then, select the **Pause Menu** object and duplicate it by pressing *Ctrl + D*. Rename this new object `Game Over` and then turn off the **Pause Menu** so that we can see the **Game Over** object clearly. To make it easier to see, feel free to toggle to the 2D mode we used previously when creating the UI elements of our game.

3. Next, expand the **Game Over** object and both of the **Panel** children, then change the **Pause Menu Contents** object's name to `Game Over Contents` and change the child **Text (TMP)** object's **TextMeshPro - Text** component to say `Game Over` instead.

4. Now, change the **Resume** button to say `Continue (Play Ad)` and change the button object's name to `Continue Button`:

Figure 7.7 – Game Over menu setup

5. We'll first need to update the `ObstacleBehaviour` script to handle it; add the following highlighted code:

```
using UnityEngine;
using UnityEngine.UI; // Button

public class ObstacleBehaviour : MonoBehaviour
{

[Tooltip("How long to wait before restarting the game")]
public float waitTime = 2.0f;

public GameObject explosion;

private GameObject player;

private void OnCollisionEnter(Collision collision)
{
    // First check if we collided with the player
    if (collision.gameObject.GetComponent
        <PlayerBehaviour>())
    {
        // Destroy (Hide) the player
        collision.gameObject.SetActive(false);
        player = collision.gameObject;

        // Call the function ResetGame after waitTime
        // has passed
        Invoke("ResetGame", waitTime);
    }
}

/// <summary>
/// Will restart the currently loaded level
/// </summary>
private void ResetGame()
{
    //Bring up restart menu
    var go = GetGameOverMenu();
    go.SetActive(true);

    // Get our continue button
    var buttons =
    go.transform.GetComponentsInChildren<Button> ();
```

```csharp
            Button continueButton = null;

            foreach (var button in buttons)
            {
                if (button.gameObject.name == "Continue
                    Button")
                {
                    continueButton = button;
                    break;
                }
            }

            // If we found the button we can use it
            if (continueButton)
            {
                if (UnityAdController.showAds)
                {
                    // If player clicks on button we want to
                    // play ad and then continue
                    continueButton.onClick.AddListener
                    (UnityAdController.ShowAd);
                    UnityAdController.obstacle = this;
                }
                else
                {
                    // If can't play an ad, no need for
                    // continue button
                    continueButton.gameObject.SetActive(false);
                }

            }
        }

        /// <summary>
        /// If the object is tapped, we spawn an explosion and
        /// destroy this object
        /// </summary>
        private void PlayerTouch()
        {
            if (explosion != null)
            {
                var particles = Instantiate(explosion,
                    transform.position, Quaternion.identity);
```

```
            Destroy(particles, 1.0f);
        }

        Destroy(this.gameObject);
    }

    /// <summary>
    /// Retrieves the Game Over menu game object
    /// </summary>
    /// <returns>The Game Over menu object</returns>
    GameObject GetGameOverMenu()
    {
        var canvas = GameObject.Find("Canvas").transform;
        return canvas.Find("Game Over").gameObject;
    }

    /// <summary>
    /// Handles resetting the game if needed
    /// </summary>
    public void Continue()
    {
        var go = GetGameOverMenu();
        go.SetActive(false);
        player.SetActive(true);

        // Explode this as well (So if we respawn player
        // can continue)
        PlayerTouch();
    }

}
```

6. First, add the following variable and update the `OnCollisionEnter` function to the following:

```
        /// <summary>
        /// A reference to the player object
        /// </summary>
        private GameObject player;

        private void OnCollisionEnter(Collision collision)
        {
            // First check if we collided with the player
            if (collision.gameObject.GetComponent
                <PlayerBehaviour>())
```

```
    {
        // Destroy the player
        //Destroy(collision.gameObject);

        // Destroy (Hide) the player
        player = collision.gameObject;
        player.SetActive(false);

        // Call the function ResetGame after
        // waitTime has passed
        Invoke("ResetGame", waitTime);
    }
}
```

In this instance, we remove the code that was destroying the `player` object and hide it instead. The reason we do this is so that, if the player decides to play the ad, we can then unhide it and resume the game as normal.

7. We will use the `Button` class next, so we want to add the following to the top of the `ObstacleBehaviour` script:

```
using UnityEngine.UI;
```

8. With that done, we will then update the `ResetGame` function to the following:

```
/// <summary>
/// Will restart the currently loaded level
/// </summary>
private void ResetGame()
{
    //Bring up restart menu
    var go = GetGameOverMenu();
    go.SetActive(true);

    // Get our continue button
    var buttons =
        go.transform.GetComponentsInChildren<Button>();
    Button continueButton = null;

    foreach (var button in buttons)
    {
        if (button.gameObject.name == "Continue
            Button")
        {
            continueButton = button;
```

```
            break;
        }
    }

    /*If we found the button we can use it */
    if (continueButton)
    {
        if (UnityAdController.showAds)
        {
            // If player clicks on button we want to
            // play ad and then continue
            continueButton.onClick.AddListener(
                UnityAdController.ShowAd);
            UnityAdController.obstacle = this;
        }
        else
        {
            /* If can't play an ad, no need for
                continue button */
            continueButton.gameObject.SetActive(false);
        }

    }
}
```

We also destroy what the player hit. So, if we do restart the game, then the player will be able to start from right where they initially began.

9. Next, add the following two helper functions:

```
/// <summary>
/// Retrieves the Game Over menu game object
/// </summary>
/// <returns>The Game Over menu object</returns>
GameObject GetGameOverMenu()
{
    var canvas = GameObject.Find("Canvas").transform;
    return canvas.Find("Game Over").gameObject;
}

/// <summary>
/// Handles resetting the game if needed
/// </summary>
public void Continue()
{
```

```
            var go = GetGameOverMenu();
            go.SetActive(false);
            player.SetActive(true);

            /* Explode this as well (So if we respawn player
               can continue) */
            PlayerTouch();
    }
```

With that in mind, we also created a `Continue` function, which will set up the game to be continued if we need to do so.

10. Open up the `UnityAdController` script and add the following variable declaration at the top of the file:

```
    /// <summary>
    /// For holding the obstacle for continuing the game
    /// </summary>
    public static ObstacleBehaviour obstacle;
```

11. Afterward, staying in the `UnityAdController` script, update the `OnUnityAdsShow-Complete` function to the following:

```
    /// <summary>
    /// This callback method handles logic for the ad
    /// finishing.
    /// </summary>
    /// <param name="placementId">The identifier for the Ad Unit
    showing the content</param>
    /// <param name="showCompletionState">Indicates the final state
    of the ad (whether the ad was skipped or completed).</param>
    public void OnUnityAdsShowComplete(string placementId,
    UnityAdsShowCompletionState showCompletionState)
    {
        /* If there is an obstacle, we can remove it to
           continue the game */
        if (obstacle != null && showCompletionState ==
           UnityAdsShowCompletionState.COMPLETED)
        {
            obstacle.Continue();
        }

        /* Unpause game when ad is over */
        PauseScreenBehaviour.paused = false;
        Time.timeScale = 1f;
    }
```

Our additions first check whether there is an obstacle that our player has hit. If there is, we then check the value of the `showCompletionState` variable that is provided by the function. We utilize the `UnityAdsShowCompletionState` enum to verify that the player actually completed the ad and did not click on the **Skip** button.

12. We want to make sure that Unity's Advertisement system works in both scenes, so we can copy-paste the **Unity Ad Controller** object from the **Main Menu** and we can also add it through code. To do so, open up the `GameManager` script and add the following highlighted code to the `Start` function:

```
/// <summary>
/// Start is called before the first frame update
/// </summary>
private void Start()
{
    /* If there is no UnityAdController, we can add it
       through code */
    if (!GameObject.FindObjectOfType
      <UnityAdController>())
    {
        var adController = new GameObject("Unity Ad
            Controller");
        adController.AddComponent<UnityAdController>();
    }

    // Set our starting point
    nextTileLocation = startPoint;
    nextTileRotation = Quaternion.identity;

    for (int i = 0; i < initSpawnNum; ++i)
    {
        SpawnNextTile(i >= initNoObstacles);
    }
}
```

13. Save your scripts and return to the Unity Editor.

14. Click on the **Game Over** object and disable it, save our scene, and then open the **Main Menu** scene and dive into the game.

Tip

If you do not see the ads there, it may be due to the fact that Unity Ads was not initialized. This is done in the **Main Menu** scene, so you'll need to go there first before you see the ads.

At this point, when we die in the game, we'll be shown a **Game Over** screen:

Figure 7.8 – Game Over screen

If we click on **Continue (Play Ad)**, we will have an ad play. If the player skips it, nothing will happen, but if they watch all the way through, it should take them back into the game as if nothing happened:

Figure 7.9 – Continuing the game

With that, our ad system is working correctly. We have now seen how we can integrate the use of ads into our gameplay and provide a reason for players to actually want to see this content.

Adding in a cooldown timer

Ads are great for developers; however, according to Unity's Monetization FAQs, each user is only able to view 25 ads per day. With that in mind, we will likely want to make it so that players can only trigger ads every once in a while. This also has the benefit of making players want to come back to our game after a period of time.

> **Important note**
>
> For more information on Unity's Monetization FAQs, check out `https://docs.unity.com/ads/FAQ.html`.

We will now implement a feature where our **Continue** option will only work once in a while with a short delay that we can easily customize if we like:

1. To get started, go back to the `UnityAdController` script and add the following new variable to it, shown in the highlighted code:

```csharp
using System; // DateTime
using UnityEngine;
using UnityEngine.Advertisements; /* Advertisement class */

public class UnityAdController : MonoBehaviour,
IUnityAdsShowListener
{
    /// <summary>
    /// A static reference to this object
    /// </summary>
    public static UnityAdController instance;

    /// <summary>
    /// If we should show ads or not
    /// </summary>
    public static bool showAds = true;

    // Nullable type
    public static DateTime? nextRewardTime = null;


    /// <summary>
    /// For holding the obstacle for continuing the
    /// game
    /// </summary>
```

```
      public static ObstacleBehaviour obstacle;
  // Rest of UnityAdController...
```

The `nextRewardTime` variable is of the `DateTime` type, which we haven't talked about previously. Basically, it's a structure that represents a point in time that we can compare to other points in time and is built into .NET Framework. We'll use this to store the time that needs to pass before the player is able to play another ad if needed. Note that `DateTime` is part of the `System` namespace. That is why we added the `using System;` line in the preceding code as well.

> **Important note**
>
> For more information on the `DateTime` class, check out `https://msdn.microsoft.com/en-us/library/system.datetime(v=vs.110).aspx`.

You may notice the ? symbol next to the type of this variable. When we do this, we create what's called a nullable type. The advantage of using them is that they can be `null` in addition to having normal values. We do this so that we don't have to fill in a default value just for the sake of having one.

> **Important note**
>
> For more information on nullable types, check out `https://www.tutorialspoint.com/csharp/csharp_nullables.htm`.

2. To add a time delay between ads showing, we will create a new function for this purpose:

```
public static void ShowRewardAd()
{
    nextRewardTime = DateTime.Now.AddSeconds(15);

    ShowAd();
}
```

Now when we show a reward ad, we set `nextRewardTime` to 15 seconds from when the function is called. Of course, we can just as easily set this to minutes or hours using the `AddMinutes` and `AddHours` function.

3. Save your script and then open up the `ObstacleBehaviour` script. At the top of the script, add the following new `using` statements:

```
using System; // DateTime
using System.Collections; // IEnumerator
```

4. Afterward, we will need to modify the bottom part of the ResetGame() function to have the following code:

```
// Rest of ResetGame above...

        /*If we found the button we can use it */
        if (continueButton)
        {
            if (UnityAdController.showAds)
            {
                // If player clicks on button we want
                // to play ad and then continue
                StartCoroutine(ShowContinue(
                    continueButton));
            }
            else
            {
                /* If can't play an ad, no need for
                    continue button */
                continueButton.gameObject.SetActive(
                    false);
            }

        }
    }
```

Now, instead of just adding a listener to this button, we have replaced it with a call to the StartCoroutine function, which takes in a function that we haven't written yet. I think it's probably a good idea to talk a little bit about coroutines before we actually write one.

A coroutine is like a function that has the ability to pause execution and continue where it left off after a period of time. By default, a coroutine is resumed on the frame after we start to use yield, but it is also possible to introduce a time delay using the WaitForSeconds function to specify how long you want to wait before it's called again.

5. Next, use the following script for the ShowContinue function:

```
        public IEnumerator ShowContinue(Button contButton)
        {
            while (true)
            {
                var btnText =
                    contButton.GetComponentInChildren
                        < TMPPro.TMP_Text>();

                /* Check if we haven't reached the next
```

```
        reward time yet (if one exists) */
var rewardTime =
    UnityAdController.nextRewardTime;

bool validTime = rewardTime.HasValue;
bool timePassed = true;

if (validTime)
{
    timePassed =
        DateTime.Now > rewardTime.Value;
}

if (!timePassed)
{
    /* Unable to click on the button */
    contButton.interactable = false;

    /* Get the time remaining until we get
       to the next reward time */
    TimeSpan remaining =
        rewardTime.Value - DateTime.Now;

    /* Get the time left in the following
       format 99:99 */
    var countdownText =
        string.Format("{0:D2}:{1:D2}",
            remaining.Minutes,
                remaining.Seconds);

    /* Set our button's text to reflect
       the new time */
    btnText.text = countdownText;

    /* Come back after 1 second and check
       again */
    yield return new WaitForSeconds(1f);
}
else
{
    /* It's valid to click the button now
    */
    contButton.interactable = true;
```

```
                    /* If player clicks on button we want
                       to play ad and then continue */
                    contButton.onClick.AddListener(
                        UnityAdController.ShowRewardAd);
                    UnityAdController.obstacle = this;

                    /* Change text to its original version
                    */
                    btnText.text = "Continue (Play Ad)";

                    /* We can now leave the coroutine */
                    break;
                }
            }
        }
```

This coroutine will do a number of things, starting off by entering a `while (true)` loop. Now, usually, this is a very bad thing, as it would cause an infinite loop, but we break out of the loop if we have no reward time set or if we've passed the time set in the `nextRewardTime` variable. If not, we will figure out how much time is left before that time has passed and will change the button's text to display it. We then use the `WaitForSeconds` function to pause execution and come back after 1 second has passed.

> **Important note**
>
> If you're interested in learning more about the behind-the-scenes aspects of how coroutines work, Oliver Booth wrote a neat article on it at `https://blog.oliverbooth.dev/2021/04/27/how-do-unitys-coroutines-actually-work/`.

6. Save all of our scripts and dive back into Unity and play the game:

Figure 7.10 – Delay screen working correctly

Upon restarting the game once, you'll see that if we try to do so again, we are brought to a delay screen. After the time gets down to 0, the player will then be able to continue once again.

> **Important note**
>
> For additional information on the best practices for rewarded ads such as this, check out `https://docs.unity.com/ads/MonetizationStrategy.html`.

Summary

With that, we've got a good foundation of how to add ads to our game. Hopefully, you can see how easy it is to implement and can think of new ways to engage players to have the best experience possible. Over the course of this chapter, we discovered how to set up Unity Ads. We then saw how we could create simple ads and learned how to react to the player's actions by implementing the `IUnityAdsShowListener` interface. Afterward, we saw how we can add rewards for players using opt-in advertisements in the game, and we added a cooldown to the system to make the game less annoying for players. With these newly acquired skills, you should be able to add advertisements and gain additional revenue from your own games that you create in the future.

> **Important note**
>
> By default, ads should be in test mode. It is against Unity Ads' terms of service to distribute live ads to beta testers. If they were to click on or install any of the advertised games, their activity would be monetized and the automated fraud system would flag the game for fraud and disable it.
>
> To disable test mode, you can go to the Analytics Monetization Dashboard by going to **Services | Ads | Configure** and then clicking on **Go to Dashboard**. (If you need to, select **Set Meditation Partner** and **I only plan to use Unity ads**.)
>
> From your project, select **Settings**. Scroll down to the **Test mode** section and modify the **Apple App Store** or **Google Play Store** properties as you wish.

While this is a valid way to monetize our games, we will dive into another more popular form of in-game monetization in the next chapter: in-app purchases.

8
Integrating Social Media into Our Project

We now have all of the foundational things needed to get our game out into the world; it's mechanically working and we've set up all of the monetization. Having all of the features that we have added to our project is great, but if no one is playing your game, there's no reason to have them.

Word-of-mouth marketing is the most reliable way to get others to try your game. Providing people with opportunities to share the game helps others discover the project, and it's something that we should really try to do because marketing and getting your game out there is one of the hardest things to do as an indie developer.

In this chapter, you will learn some of the different ways to integrate social media into your projects. We will start off by adding something to share – a score. Afterward, we will see how we can share the score on Twitter. Then, we will see how we can connect our game to Facebook and use content from Facebook within our game itself.

This chapter will be split into a number of topics. It will contain a simple step-by-step process from beginning to end. The following is the outline of our tasks:

- Adding a scoring system
- Sharing high scores via Twitter
- Downloading and installing Facebook's SDK
- Logging in to our game via Facebook
- Displaying a Facebook name and profile picture

Technical requirements

This book utilizes Unity 2022.1.0b16 and Unity Hub 3.3.1, but the steps should work with minimal changes in future versions of the editor. If you would like to download the exact version used in this book and there is a new version out, you can visit Unity's download archive at `https://unity3d.com/get-unity/download/archive`. You can also find the system requirements for Unity at `https://docs.unity3d.com/2022.1/Documentation/Manual/system-requirements.html` in the **Unity Editor system requirements** section. To deploy your project, you will need an Android or iOS device.

Unlike previous chapters, the use of the Facebook SDK requires both iOS and Android build support for your Unity version installed, so make sure that both are added before importing the package or you will have errors.

You can find the code files present in this chapter on GitHub at `https://github.com/PacktPublishing/Unity-2022-Mobile-Game-Development-3rd-Edition/tree/main/Chapter08`.

Adding a scoring system

In order to provide an incentive for players to share our game with others, we need to provide a compelling reason to do so. Some people are very competitive and wish to be the best at playing a game, challenging others to do better than them. To help with that, we can allow our players to share a score value via social media. However, to do that, we'll first need to have a scoring system. Thankfully, it's not too difficult to do that, so let's add that real quick using the following steps:

1. Start off by opening the `Gameplay.scene` file located in the `Assets/Scenes` folder of the project. To show our players what their score is, we'll need to have some way to display it on the screen. In our case, the easiest way would be with a text object.

2. From the **Hierarchy** window, select the **On Screen Controls** object that is the child of the **Canvas** object. Afterward, right-click on the **On Screen Controls** object and select **UI | Text – Text Mesh Pro**, as shown in the following screenshot:

Figure 8.1– Adding a text object to the screen

This will make the **Text** object a child of the **Panel** object, which in turn will automatically resize itself to fit within a notch if there is one in the devices.

3. Rename this object Score Text and use the **Anchors Preset** menu at the top, holding down *Shift + Alt* to set the pivot and position as well.

4. Afterward, let's set the **RectTransform** component's **Height** property on the object to 60 to ensure that we have space to hold the score when we increase the size.

5. Next, in **TextMeshPro - Text** component, change the **Text** property to 0 and set **Alignment** to centered both horizontally and vertically. Afterward, set **Font Size** to 45 so that it's easy to see.

6. To improve its readability, change **Material Preset** to **LiberationSans SDF – Outline** and let's change **Vertex Color** to black.

    Afterward, scroll down to the text material section (**LiberationSans SDF Material**) and click on the check next to the **Outline** section. Change the **Color** to white and then increase the **Thickness** to 1. Notice that it seems to fill both the inside and outside of the text. To fix this, in the **Face** section, change the **Dilate** value to 1.

Figure 8.2: Adjusting the properties of the text outline

7. Next, open up the `PlayerBehaviour` script and add the following line at the top of the file:

```
using TMPro; //TextMeshProUGUI
```

8. Next, add the following code inside the class:

```
[Header("Object References")]
public TextMeshProUGUI scoreText;

private float score = 0;
public float Score
{
    get
    {
        return score;
    }
    set
    {
        score = value;

        /* Check if scoreText has been assigned */
        if (scoreText == null)
        {

            Debug.LogError("Score Text is not set. " +
                "Please go to the Inspector and assign
                    it");
```

```
            /* If not assigned, don't try to update
               it. */
            return;
        }

        /* Update the text to display the whole number
           portion of the score */
        scoreText.text = string.Format("{0:0}",
            score);
    }
}
```

We first have a reference to the `scoreText` object, which we will need to set in the **Inspector**. This is of the `TextMeshProUGUI` class, which contains properties relating to the text displayed on the object.

This makes use of C#'s `get`/`set` functions, which are implicit getters and setters. Basically, any time we get or set the `Score` variable, we will execute whatever is located between { }. In our case, any time we set the `Score` variable, it will update our text for us.

> **Tip**
>
> For more info on TextMeshPro, check out `https://docs.unity3d.com/Packages/com.unity.textmeshpro@3.0/manual/index.html#support--api-documentation`.

This has an advantage over what a number of my students do, which is to update the value of the text every frame, which doesn't need to happen. We only need to update the text when the value changes, which makes it perfect for us to use in this situation.

> **Note**
>
> For more information on the get/set accessors, check out `https://docs.microsoft.com/en-us/dotnet/csharp/programming-guide/classes-and-structs/using-properties`.

9. Then, update the `PlayerBehaviour` class to have the following highlighted changes:

```
// Start is called before the first frame update
public void Start()
{
    // Get access to our Rigidbody component
    rb = GetComponent<Rigidbody>();
```

```
        minSwipeDistancePixels = minSwipeDistance *
            Screen.dpi;

        joystick =
            GameObject.FindObjectOfType<MobileJoystick>();

        Score = 0;

    }


    /// <summary>
    /// FixedUpdate is a prime place to put physics calculations
    /// happening over a period of time.
    /// </summary>

    void FixedUpdate()
    {
        /* If the game is paused, don't do anything */
        if (PauseScreenBehaviour.paused)
        {
            return;
        }

        Score += Time.deltaTime;
        // Rest of Update here...
```

What we are doing here is resetting our score whenever the player is created and increasing the value while the game isn't paused.

10. Save the script and dive back into Unity.

11. Select the **Player** object and drag and drop our **Score Text** object into the **Score Text** variable on the **Player Behaviour** component:

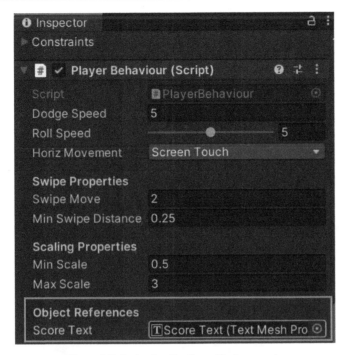

Figure 8.3: Assigning the Score Text property

12. Once the variable has been assigned, go ahead and play the game. The game's interface is shown in the following screenshot:

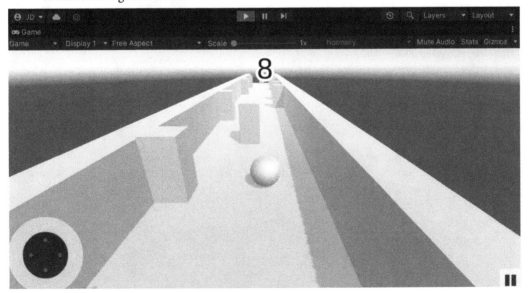

Figure 8.4: The score added to the game

Now, as you can see, we have a score for our game, which updates as we play. This will allow players to easily know what their competency with the game is and give them some information that they can share with others. Now that we have a scoring system, let's take a look at how we can share a high score using Twitter.

Sharing high scores via Twitter

Twitter is an online news and social networking service where users post and interact with each other through messages that they call *tweets*, which are limited to 280 characters. Many indie game developers use Twitter as a way to attract others to play their games.

Twitter is a great option to start off with because we can add it very easily to our project by simply opening a specific URL. Let's look at the steps to do just that:

1. Open the `PauseScreenBehaviour` script. Once inside, we will add the following code inside the `PlayerScreenBehaviour` class:

```
#region Share Score via Twitter

/// <summary>
/// Web address in order to create a tweet
/// </summary>
private const string tweetTextAddress = "http://twitter.com/
intent/tweet?text=";

/// <summary>
/// Where we want players to visit
/// </summary>
private string appStoreLink = "http://johnpdoran.com/";

[Tooltip("Reference to the player for the score")]
public PlayerBehaviour player;

/// <summary>
/// Will open Twitter with a prebuilt tweet. When called on iOS
/// or Android will open up Twitter app if installed
/// </summary>
public void TweetScore()
{
    /* Create contents of the tweet */
    string tweet = "I got " + string.Format("{0:0}",
        player.Score) + " points in Endless Roller!
            Can you do better?";
```

```
    /* Create the entire message */
    string message = tweet + "\n" + appStoreLink;

    /* Ensures string is URL friendly */
    string url =
        UnityEngine.Networking.UnityWebRequest
            .EscapeURL(message);

    /* Open the URL to create the tweet */
    Application.OpenURL(tweetTextAddress + url);



}

#endregion
```

First of all, we will use a number of new things. You'll note that the preceding block of code starts and ends with #region and #endregion, respectively. What this does is allow us to expand and collapse this portion of code inside Visual Studio. When we introduce longer code files, it can be convenient to be able to collapse or hide certain parts of your script so that you can focus only on the part of the file you're working on. Since this portion of code has nothing to do with the rest of the script, this is a good place for us to use it.

To open URLs inside Unity, we will need to make use of the Application.OpenURL function and the UnityWebRequest class.

> **Note**
>
> For more information on Twitter's Web Intents and the ways you can use them, check out https://dev.twitter.com/web/intents.

The UnityWebRequest class is typically used to load content at runtime, but it also has the EscapeURL function, which will convert a string into a format that web browsers are comfortable with. For instance, the newline character will not be displayed by itself.

> **Note**
>
> For more information on the EscapeURL function, check out https://docs.unity3d.com/ScriptReference/Networking.UnityWebRequest.EscapeURL.html.

Save the script and dive back into Unity. From the **Hierarchy** window, select the **Pause Screen Handler** object and then set the **Player** property in the **Inspector** tab to our `Player` object by dragging and dropping the **Player** game object from the **Hierarchy** window onto the **Player** property in the **Inspector** window:

Figure 8.5: Assigning the Player property

1. Now, we need to have a button for our **Game Over** screen to allow us to share our score.

2. Open up the **Canvas** object and toggle the **Game Over** object to **ON** by clicking on the checkmark beside its name in the **Inspector** window.

3. From there, expand the two **Panel** child objects and the **Game Over Contents** object. Select the **Main Menu Button** object and duplicate it by pressing *Ctrl + D*. Next, change the name to `Tweet Score Button` and also update the text in the child object to display `Tweet Score` as well.

4. Afterward, select the **Tweet Score** button object and scroll down to the **Button** component. From there, change the function we are calling to the **PauseScreenBehaviour | TweetScore** function:

Figure 8.6: Calling the TweetScore function

5. Select the **Game Over** object in the **Hierarchy** and disable it again. Next, save your scene and start the game.

6. Now when we fail the game, we can click on the **Tweet Score** button and our browser will open on our PC:

Figure 8.7: Result on PC

However, on our mobile devices, it will open up the Twitter app if it is installed:

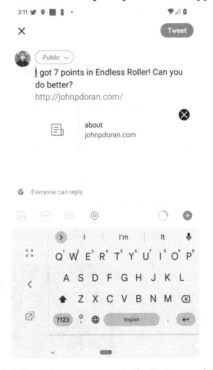

Figure 8.8: Tweeting our score via the Twitter mobile app

With that, you learned just how easy it is to share something using Twitter.

> **Note**
>
> For those who are interested in doing more than this with Twitter, it does have its own API for Unity, which will allow you to let users log in to your game using Twitter if you'd like to do that instead of Facebook, which we will do later on. If you're interested in looking into this, you can find more information at `https://dev.twitter.com/twitterkit/unity/overview`.

Of course, other social networks exist as well, some of which have their very own **software development kit** (**SDK**), which allows you to access the information that they have. In the next section, we will explore how to utilize this.

Downloading and installing Facebook's SDK

We couldn't have a chapter on social networking without mentioning Facebook. Facebook has its own SDK that can be used with Unity. This can allow us to use the information that Facebook already has, including the user's name and profile image, within our game experience. Let's look at the steps to incorporate them:

1. Open up your web browser and visit `https://developers.facebook.com/docs/unity/`:

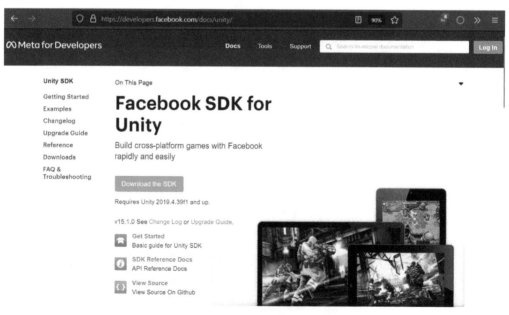

Figure 8.9: Facebook SDK for Unity page

2. Click on the **Download the SDK** button and wait for it to finish downloading. Once it is downloaded, unzip it and then open up the `facebook-unity-sdk-15.1.0` folder. Then, open up the `FacebookSDK` folder and you'll see a single file, `facebook-unity-sdk-15.1.0.unitypackage`.

    Unlike previous chapters, the use of the Facebook SDK requires both iOS and Android build support for your Unity version installed, so make sure that both are added before importing the package or you will have errors. To do so, in Unity Hub, go to the **Installs** section and, from the gear icon, select **Add Modules** and add the relevant items that weren't included before (if there are any).

3. Double-click on the `unitypackage` file, and you should have a window pop up, as shown here:

Figure 8.10: Unity package import dialog

    If this does not work, you can also go to **Assets | Import Package | Custom Package** and then find the folder that you unzipped the file to and open it that way.

4. Click on the **Import** button and wait for it to finish loading. From here, you'll get a popup noting the project may contain obsolete APIs. Go ahead and click on the **I Made a Backup. Go Ahead!** button and wait for it to finish.

5. Now, in order to use the Facebook API, we will first need to have a Facebook App ID, so let's do that next.

6. Go back to your web browser and go to `https://developers.facebook.com/` and click on the **Log In** button in the top-right corner of the screen. Once you log in to your Facebook account, you should see something similar to the following screenshot:

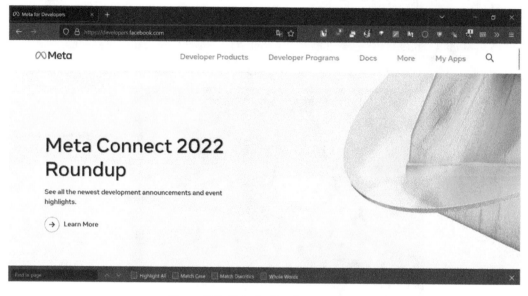

Figure 8.11: Meta for Developers menu

7. From the preceding page, click on the **Get Started** button in the top-right corner of the screen. From there, you'll be brought to a screen where you need to click **Next**, and then you'll be asked your role. Click on **Developer** and, on the next screen, click on the **Create First App** button.

8. Afterward, add a **Display Name** for your game (I used `Endless Roller`) and your **Contact E-mail**, and then select **Create App ID**.

9. Once you're brought to your app's page, click on the **Dashboard** option to the left of the default info for your game. Note the **App ID** and copy it by clicking on it or by highlighting it and then pressing *Ctrl + C*.

10. If you instead see a **My Apps** option, click on that and then click on the green **Create App** button on the right-hand side of the page. From the **Select an app type** menu, select **Gaming** and then select **Next**. In the **Add an app name** section, add a name (I used `Endless Roller`) and your contact e-mail, and then select **Create app**.

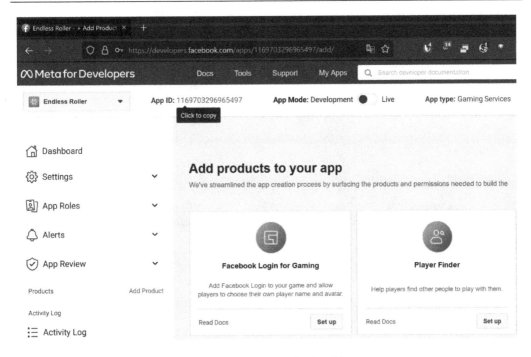

Figure 8.12: Getting the App ID

11. Return to Unity, and you may be asked to share some info with Google. Answer as you wish. Then, you'll have the option to enable Android auto-resolution. I set **Enable** and had to wait for it to resolve Android dependencies.

12. Afterward, you will note a new Facebook option in the top bar. Select it and then select **Edit Settings**. Once you're there, click on **Inspector** if you need to and you'll see several options. Set **Facebook App Id** to our created app's ID and then set the name to our game's name:

Figure 8.13: Adding the App Id to Facebook Settings

> **Tip**
>
> There is a possibility that you may get an error the next time that you try to export your game to Android due to changing the SDK location. If this is the case, close your Unity project and then go to the project folder and delete the `Temp` folder. Upon restarting the project, the error should go away.

13. Return to the Facebook Settings menu by going to **Facebook | Edit Settings....**

    Now, you'll notice that under **Android Build Facebook Settings**, there is a new error stating that OpenSSL is not found.

14. To fix this, we will first need to download OpenSSL by going to `http://slproweb.com/products/Win32OpenSSL.html`. From there, select the **EXE** link below the **Win64 OpenSSL v1.1.1u** option, as shown here:

> **Important note**
>
> For those on a Mac, you can follow the instructions given here in order to install OpenSSL and add it to your path: `https://developers.facebook.com/docs/facebook-login/android/advanced`.

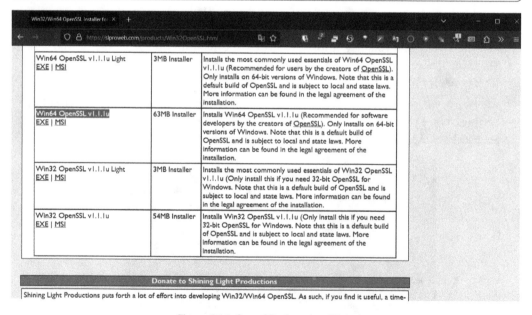

Figure 8.14: OpenSSL download link

Once it's downloaded, install the program with the default options, as shown in the following screenshot:

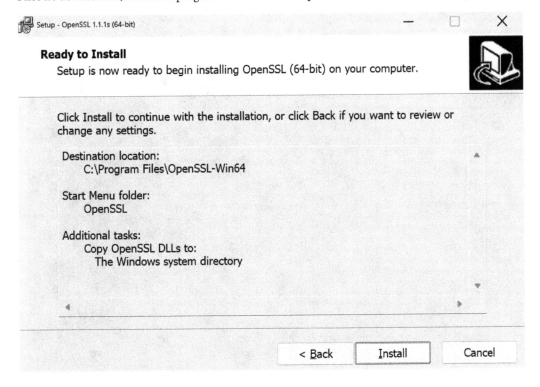

Figure 8.15: Installing OpenSSL

1. Once the installation is complete, you may uncheck the donation option and click on the **Finish** button.

2. We then need to add the location of OpenSSL to the path. To do this, press the Windows key on your

3. keyboard and start typing in env, and then select the **Edit the system environment variables**

4. option, as shown in the following screenshot:

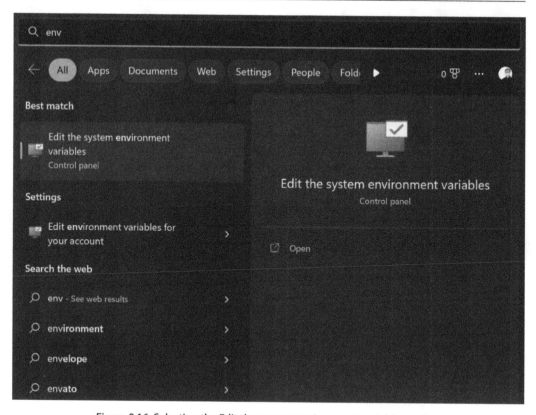

Figure 8.16: Selecting the Edit the system environment variables option

5. In the window that pops up, click the **Environment Variables...** option at the bottom right. Double-click on the **Path** option in the **System variables** section and then, from that menu, click on **New**. From there, put in the location of OpenSSL. For me, it was `C:\Program Files\OpenSSL-Win64\bin`:

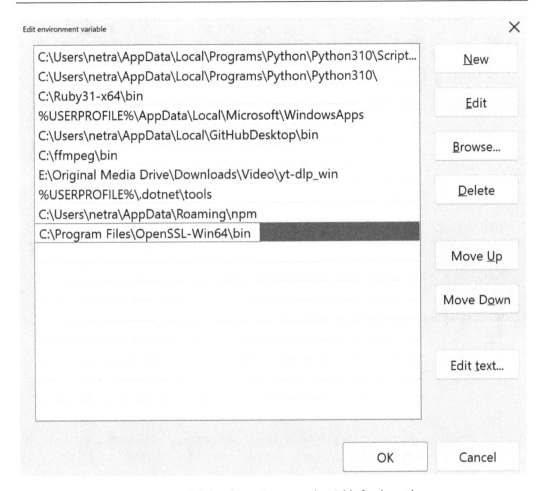

Figure 8.17: Editing the environmental variable for the path

6. Then, click on **New** one more time and add the path to the JDK tools. In my case, it was `C:\Program Files\Unity\Hub\Editor\2022.1.0b16\Editor\Data\PlaybackEngines\AndroidPlayer\OpenJDK\bin`.

7. Click on the **OK** button and then the **OK** button in the **Environmental Variables** window.

8. Once both options have been added, close your Unity project and restart your computer. Once Unity reopens, you may have to wait for the **Resolving Android Dependencies** menu to complete, but once it finishes, you should be able to see the **Facebook Settings (Facebook | Edit Settings)** menu working correctly and giving us a value under **Debug Android Key Hash [?]**:

Figure 8.18: Debug Android Key Hash

9. It is also required for calls to certain APIs to utilize a client token, so we will also get one of them. To do so, go back to your project's dashboard by going to **Facebook | Developers Page**.

10. Once the dashboard has loaded, go to **Settings | Advanced | Security | Client Token**. Copy the **Client token** value and then go back to the Unity Editor and paste it back into **Facebook Settings** in **Inspector**.

    This means that our setup of the Facebook SDK is complete!

11. Depending on the platform you wish to deploy to, go to the following websites and complete the tasks listed:

    *   For Android, check out `https://developers.facebook.com/docs/unity/getting-started/android`

    *   For iOS, check out `https://developers.facebook.com/docs/unity/getting-started/ios`

Now that we have set that up, we can start adding to it by first allowing our game to be logged in to using Facebook.

Logging in to our game via Facebook

One of the things we can do when using the Facebook API is to allow our users to log in to the game using their Facebook account. Then, we can use their name and image automatically within our project. The following steps show us how to achieve this:

1. Let's first open up our **Main Menu** level by going to the **Project** window, opening the `Assets/Scenes` folder, and then double-clicking on the `MainMenu` file.

2. From there, let's click on the **2D** button to go into 2D mode if you haven't done so previously. What we will do is replace the original menu and instead have a button for players to log in via Facebook, or play as a guest when the game starts.

3. Go to the **Hierarchy** window, select the **Canvas - Scale Physical** object, and expand it and the **Safe Area Holder** child. Select the **Panel** child and rename it `Menu Options`.

4. Then, select the **Menu Options** object in the **Hierarchy** window and duplicate it by pressing *Ctrl + D*. Then, rename the newly created `Facebook Login` object. Select the **Menu Options** game object again and then disable it by going to the **Inspector** tab and clicking on the checkmark beside its name:

Figure 8.19: Creating the Facebook Login menu

We will have the **Facebook Login** object turn the menu on when needed.

5. Next, open the **Facebook Login** options and remove the **Restore Button** and **Remove Ads Button** objects. Click on the **Play Button**, under **Rect Transform,** change the **Width** to 225, then right-click on the **Button** component, and then select the **Reset** option to remove its original **On Click ()** functionality.

6. Duplicate the **Play Button** object by pressing the *Ctrl + D* keys. Then, name those two buttons `Facebook Login Button` and `Continue as Guest Button`. Also, change the **Text** property of both of these buttons to `Facebook Login` and `Continue as Guest`:

Figure 8.20: Facebook Login Button setup

7. Now that we have the buttons working correctly, we need to write the script that will allow us to log in. Go to the `Scripts` folder and open our `MainMenuBehaviour` script. We will use the `List` class to hold the permissions we want in order to access Facebook and the content of the `FB` class in the Facebook SDK.

8. So, to do that, we'll first add the following to the top of the `MainMenuBehaviour` script:

    ```
    using UnityEngine;
    using UnityEngine.SceneManagement; // LoadScene
    using System.Collections.Generic; // List using Facebook.Unity;
    // FB
    ```

9. Then, add the following variables to the `MainMenuBehaviour` class:

    ```
    [Header("Object References")]
    public GameObject mainMenu;
    public GameObject facebookLogin;
    ```

10. Now, add the following code within the `MainMenuBehaviour` class:

```
#region Facebook
#endregion
```

Inside this region, we are going to add several different methods, starting with some methods dealing with initializing the Facebook APIs:

```
public void Awake()
{
    /* We only call FB Init once, so check if it
    /* has been called already */
    if (!FB.IsInitialized)
    {
        FB.Init(OnInitComplete, OnHideUnity);
    }
}
```

In this case, the `Awake` method calls the `FB.Init` function, which takes in two parameters, both of which are delegates, or functions to call whenever the initialization is complete and whenever the app is hidden or no longer the currently focused one. The definition of both those functions is as follows:

```
/// <summary>
/// Once initialized, will inform if logged in on Facebook
/// </summary>
private void OnInitComplete()
{
    if(FB.IsInitialized)
    {
        if (FB.IsLoggedIn)
        {
            print("Logged into Facebook");

            /* Close Login and open Main Menu */
            ShowMainMenu();
        }
    }
    else
    {
        print("Failed to init Facebook SDK; open as
            guest");
        ShowMainMenu();
    }

}
```

```
/// <summary>
/// Called whenever Unity loses focus
/// </summary>
/// <param name="active">If the game is currently
    active</param>
private void OnHideUnity(bool active)
{
    /* Set TimeScale based on if the game is
       paused */
    Time.timeScale = (active) ? 1 : 0;
}
```

In this case, we are going to print a message to the screen if we are logged in to Facebook and we will display the main menu. Likewise, if we ever lose focus of Unity, we are going to pause the game.

We have some other final functions that we need to add for our final implementation, which we will add next:

```
/// <summary>
/// Attempts to log in on Facebook
/// </summary>
public void FacebookLogin()
{
    List<string> permissions = new List<string>();

    /* Add permissions we want to have here */
    permissions.Add("public_profile");

    FB.LogInWithReadPermissions(permissions,
        FacebookCallback);
}


/// <summary>
/// Called once facebook has logged in, or not
/// </summary>
/// <param name="result">The result of our login request</param>
private void FacebookCallback(IResult result)
{
    if (result.Error == null)
    {
        OnInitComplete();
    }
    else
    {
        print(result.Error);
```

```
    }
}

public void ShowMainMenu()
{
    if (facebookLogin != null && mainMenu != null)
    {
        facebookLogin.SetActive(false);
        mainMenu.SetActive(true);
    }
}
```

In this case, we are accessing the player's public profile, which contains information such as their name and their profile picture.

> **Note**
>
> For all of the properties that we can get access to, check out `https://developers.` `facebook.com/docs/facebook-login/permissions#reference-public_` `profile`.

11. Save your script and go to the **Facebook Login** button and change the button's **OnClick()** action to now call your function by clicking on the + button and then dragging and dropping the **Main Menu** object in and then selecting **Main Menu Behaviour** | **Facebook Login** instead:

Figure 8.21: Calling the FacebookLogin function

12. Then, on the **Continue as Guest Button** under the **Button** component, go to the **On Click** () section and then click on the + button. Drag and drop the **Main Menu** object into the slot below the **Runtime Only** dropdown. Afterward, have the button call the `MainMenuBehaviour.` `ShowMainMenu` function.

Figure 8.22: Setup for Continue as Guest Button

13. Finally, we will need to set the variables we have created. Select the **Main Menu** object in the **Hierarchy** window and then set the **Main Menu** and **Facebook Login** properties:

Figure 8.23: Setting the Main Menu Behaviour properties

Ensure that the **Facebook Login** is set to the **panel** object holding both buttons.

14. Save your scene, start the game, and then click on the **Facebook Login** button:

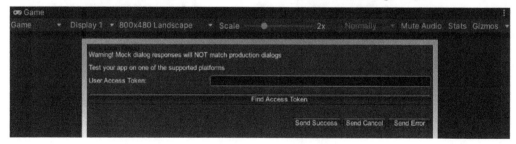

Figure 8.24: User Access Token Request Screen

Important note
To see everything properly within the editor, it's a good idea to maximize the **Game** tab, which you can do by right-clicking on the **Game** tab and selecting **Maximize** or by checking the **Maximize On Play** option on the toolbar.

Now, you should see a menu asking for a user access token, a value that every profile has and we can associate it with. We'll need to go to Facebook to get that, so that's what we'll do next.

1. Click on the **Find Access Token** page, and a web browser will open with a new page:

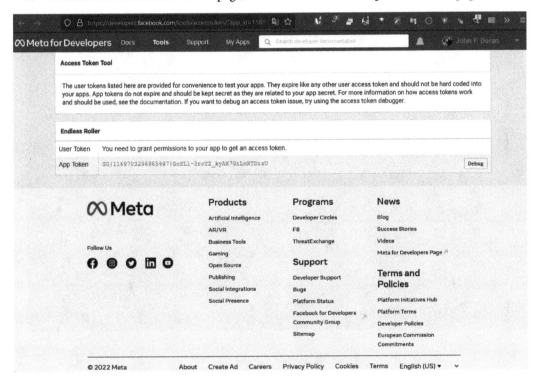

Figure 8.25: Access Token Tool page

2. You'll then need to click on the **need to grant permissions** link and then, on **Generate Access Token**, click **Continue** and you'll see a string of characters under **User Token**. Copy the string, paste it into the **User Access Token** property in Unity, and then click on the **Send Success** button.

> **Note**
>
> If you get an error when granting permissions stating **Future off- Facebook activity for this app is off**, that means that your Facebook settings do not allow your Facebook profile to be used outside of Facebook. In order to use Facebook to log in, your account must have Off-Facebook tracking enabled. To do so, you can go to `https://www.facebook.com/off_facebook_activity` and ensure the **Future off- Facebook Activity** value is set to ON to be able to log in. We will be allowing users to log in as a guest if you'd prefer not to be tracked.

Now, you'll note that the Console has printed that we've logged in to Facebook and that the menu closes when we've sent the key:

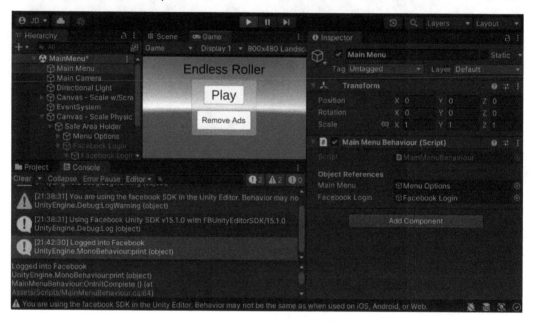

Figure 8.26: Logged in to Facebook

> **Note**
>
> For more information on user access tokens, check out `https://developers.facebook.com/docs/facebook-login/access-tokens/#usertokens`.

Now that we have the ability to log in to Facebook, we can now use the information that we get from Facebook in order to customize our game, which is what we will do next.

Displaying a Facebook name and profile picture

A good thing to do is to personalize our game to fit our players. So, with that, once the player logs in, we will welcome them and display their image on the screen by following these steps:

1. Go to the `MainMenuBehaviour` script once again. From there, we'll need to add a new `using` statement to display an image and change the text we need in order to use Unity's UI system and TextMeshPro:

    ```
    using UnityEngine.UI; // Image
    using TMPro; //TextMeshProUGUI
    ```

2. We will then need to add two new variables:

    ```
    [Tooltip("Will display the user's Facebook profile pic")]
    public Image profilePic;

    [Tooltip("The text object used to display the greeting")]
    public TextMeshProUGUI greeting;
    ```

    These variables will hold the information that we wish to display once we get it from Facebook.

3. Afterward, we will update the `ShowMainMenu` function and add some new functions to use:

    ```
    public void ShowMainMenu()
    {
        if (facebookLogin != null && mainMenu != null)
        {
            facebookLogin.SetActive(false);
            mainMenu.SetActive(true);

            if (FB.IsLoggedIn)
            {
                /* Get information from Facebook profile
                */
                FB.API("/me?fields=name",
                        HttpMethod.GET,
                        SetName);
                FB.API("/me/picture?width=256&height=256",
                        HttpMethod.GET,
                        SetProfilePic);
            }
        }
    }
    ```

The FB.API function makes a call to Facebook's Graph API to get data or take an action on the user's behalf and allows us to get the information that we have permission to as defined earlier. In our case, we are looking for the name and the profile picture of the user and calling the SetName and SetProfilePic functions, respectively, once we have obtained that data.

However, we currently do not have SetName and SetProfilePic functions, so we will go ahead and add them now.

4. Add the following additional code within the Facebook region of the script:

```
private void SetName(IResult result)
{
    if (result.Error != null)
    {
        print(result.Error); return;
    }

    string playerName =
        result.ResultDictionary["name"].ToString();

    if (greeting != null)
    {
        greeting.text = "Hello, " + playerName + "!";
        greeting.gameObject.SetActive(true);
    }


}

private void SetProfilePic(IGraphResult result)
{
    if (result.Error != null)
    {
        print(result.Error); return;
    }

    // Variable setup
    int texWidth = result.Texture.width;
    int texHeight = result.Texture.height;
    Rect rect = new Rect(0, 0, texWidth, texHeight);
    Vector2 pivot = Vector2.zero;
    Texture2D texture = result.Texture;

    // Create the profile pic
    Sprite fbImage = Sprite.Create(texture, rect,
        pivot);
```

```
if (profilePic != null)
{
    profilePic.sprite = fbImage;
    profilePic.gameObject.SetActive(true);
}
}
```

After getting the data, we will modify the image or string to display the new data that we retrieved.

> **Important note**
>
> For more information on the FB.API function, check out https://developers.facebook.com/docs/unity/reference/current/FB.API.

5. Now, we will need to actually create the text and image we want to display. Open up the **Canvas - Scale w/Screen** object in the **Hierarchy** tab and then rename the **Panel** child object Safe Area Holder. Then, right-click on the **Safe Area Holder** child object and select **UI | Panel**. Rename this object Welcome Profile:

Figure 8.27: Creating Welcome Profile

This will act as a container for all of our information for the player.

6. With the **Welcome Profile** object still selected, add a **Horizontal Layout Group** with **Padding** and **Spacing** both set to 10. From there, change **Child Alignment** to **Lower Center** and then check **Width** and **Height** under the **Control Child Size** property. Then, add a **Content Size Fitter** component and change the **Horizontal Fit** and **Vertical Fit** size to **Preferred Size**. Finally, in the **Anchor Presets** menu, hold down *Alt + Shift* and select **Bottom-center**.

7. Now, select the **Welcome Profile** object in the **Hierarchy** tab, right-click on it, and select **UI | Text - TextMeshPro**.

8. Rename the next **Text** object `Greeting`.

9. Then, adjust **Text** to `Welcome` and the size to something larger, such as `50`, change the **Vertex Color** to black, and then adjust **Alignment** to be centered vertically and horizontally:

Figure 8.28: Greeting Text setup

10. Likewise, let's next right-click on **Welcome Profile** again, and this time select **UI | Image**. You may notice that, by default, we are unable to set the image size due to the parent object having a **Horizontal Layout Group**. To override this default, select the image object and add a **Layout Element** component to it. From there, set **Min Width** and **Min Height** to `256`. Afterward, check the **Preferred Width** and **Preferred Height** properties as well and set them to `256` as well, because Facebook may give us images larger than this, and this will keep the images smaller. The **Layout Element (Script)** component is great for allowing you to override things that **LayoutGroups** will do by default and can be useful if you're not getting exactly what you want from the default behavior.

> **Note**
>
> For more information on the **Layout Element (Script)** component, check out `https://docs.unity3d.com/Manual/script-LayoutElement.html`.

11. Next, change the name of the **Image** object to `Profile Pic` and then reorder it so it is above the **Greeting** object in the **Hierarchy**:

Figure 8.29: Profile Pic setup

Reordering objects with a **Horizontal Layout Group** modifies their placement order.

If you change the resolution to a much smaller size, the image is drawn on top of our menu. This is possible due to both canvases being told that they have the same priority in being drawn, similar to how Z-fighting works for 2D games. To fix potential problems in the future, we will instead put the scaling canvas as the background element.

12. To do this, we will select **Canvas - Scale Physical**, and under the **Canvas** component, change **Sort Order** to 1.

13. Now, dive back into the **Main Menu** object and set the **Greeting** and **Profile Pic** properties in the **MainMenuBehaviour** component.

14. Finally, since we don't want them visible when the game starts, let's turn off **Greeting** and our **Profile Pic** object as well.

15. Save our game, and then start it up again by going through the appropriate login information:

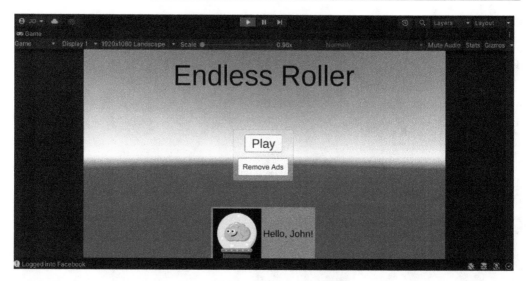

Figure 8.30: Logged into Facebook

As you can see, we are logged in and you can see my name, but I have a profile pic that isn't quite my actual profile pic. This is because it is using my gaming profile. If we want to use my actual Facebook profile pic, we have to add another permission to our app:

1. Back in Graph API Explorer, go back to the **Permissions** section and, under **Add a Permission**, click on the dropdown and select **gaming_user_picture**.

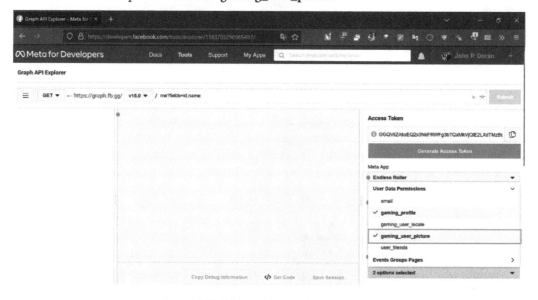

Figure 8.31: Adding the user picture option

2. From there, click on **Generate Access Token** again and get a new access token that share your actual profile information. Note that the user will have to choose to share this info with you.

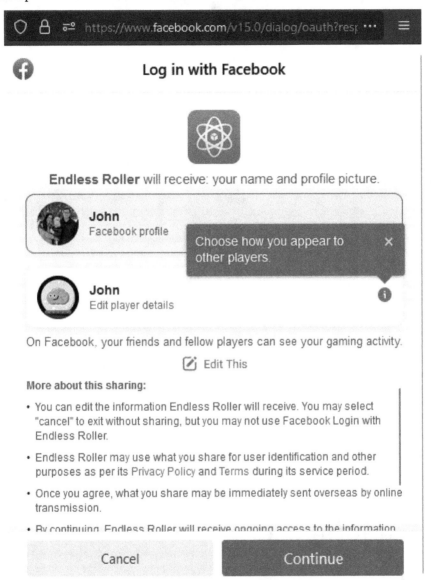

Figure 8.32: Choose how you log in to Facebook

Now use your new access token and try to run the game.

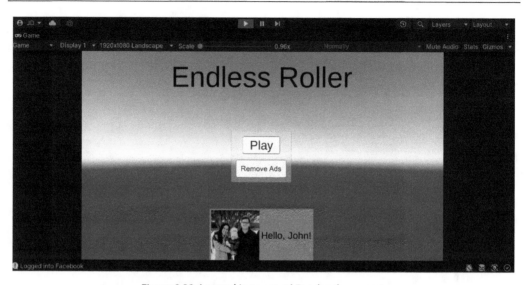

Figure 8.33: Logged in to actual Facebook account

As you can see in the preceding screenshot, I retrieved my actual Facebook info once I logged in.

Facebook is still an incredibly useful platform for game developers and can help personalize a user's gameplay experience. This can be easily expanded to utilize several other pieces of data that Facebook has and share content with all of your user's friends.

For those that are just looking for the ability to have the ability to sign in to your game to authenticate players for specific platforms, there are several other options available that you can use. For details on that, check out `https://docs.unity.com/authentication/ SettingupExternalIdentityProviders.html`.

Summary

In this chapter, we were introduced to some of the potential ways that we can share our game with others, as well as personalizing our game experiences and utilizing the functionality that social media provides us with. We started off by adding a simple score system and then allowed users to share their scores via Twitter. We then set up the Facebook SDK, making it so that we can log in to it to play our game and retrieve information about our users, which we can use to customize their gameplay experience.

Now that we have people playing our game, we want them to keep coming back and playing over time. One of the easiest ways to do this is through the use of notifications, which we will look at in the next chapter.

Part 3:
Game Feel/Polish

In this part of the book, we will focus on adding polish to your game to enhance the overall player experience. By the end of this part, you will have all the tools and knowledge necessary to take your game to the next level by polishing it and the player experience.

This part has the following chapters:

- *Chapter 9, Keeping Players Involved with Notifications*
- *Chapter 10, Using Unity Analytics*
- *Chapter 11, Remote Config*
- *Chapter 12, Improving Game Feel*
- *Chapter 13, Building a Release Copy of Our Game*
- *Chapter 14, Submitting Games to App Stores*
- *Chapter 15, Augmented Reality*

9

Keeping Players Involved with Notifications

One of the best ways to keep users coming back to your game is through the use of push notifications. This allows you to stay in contact with your users even when they're not using your game. Used wisely, this can keep users playing your game for a long period of time. Using notifications too often or poorly will cause users to mute your app's notifications, which is not an ideal situation.

In this chapter, we will explore how to create notifications for both Android and iOS devices. We will then learn how to schedule notifications to keep players returning to the game later on, as well as ways that we can customize them.

The chapter is split into a number of topics. It contains a simple, step-by-step process from beginning to end. Here is the outline of our tasks:

- Setting up notifications
- Scheduling notifications ahead of time
- Customizing notification presentation
- Canceling notifications

Technical requirements

This book utilizes Unity 2022.1.0b16 and Unity Hub 3.3.1, but the steps should work with minimal changes in future versions of the editor. If you would like to download the exact version used in this book, and there is a new version out, you can visit Unity's download archive at `https://unity3d.com/get-unity/download/archive`. You can also find the system requirements for Unity at `https://docs.unity3d.com/2022.1/Documentation/Manual/system-requirements.html` in the *Unity Editor system requirements* section. To deploy your project, you will need an Android or iOS device.

You can find the code files present in this chapter on GitHub at `https://github.com/`
`PacktPublishing/Unity-2022-Mobile-Game-Development-3rd-Edition/tree/`
`main/Chapter09`.

Setting up notifications

Before we can start adding notifications to our project, we will need to add a special preview package
that Unity makes available. Follow the steps given here:

1. From the Unity Editor, go to **Window | Package Manager**.

2. From there, if the top-left section does not say **Packages: Unity Registry**, click on the **In Project**
    drop-down menu from the toolbar of the **Packages** menu and select **Unity Registry**.

3. Scroll down the available options until you reach **Mobile Notifications** and select it. Once
    there, click on the arrow to the side of it and select **See All Versions** and then select the latest
    version (in my case, it was **Version 2.0.2**). From there, click the **Install** button and you'll see
    the following screenshot:

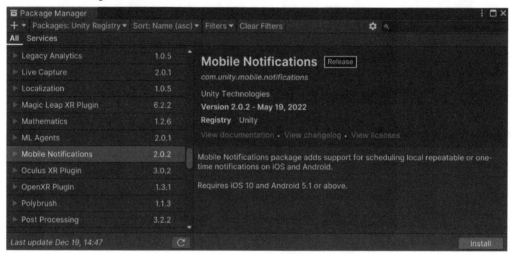

Figure 9.1: Installing the Mobile Notifications package

> **Note**
>
> It's important to note that this package requires your game to use Android 5.1 (API level 22)
> and iOS 10 or above in order to function properly.

We will also be using a cross-platform wrapper, also written by Unity, in order to get notifications working quickly and remove the requirement of writing platform-specific code.

4. After this, open up the **Samples** section and then click on the **Import** button next to the **Notification Samples** button.

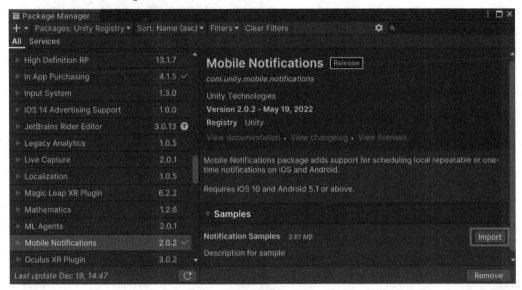

Figure 9.2: Importing the notification samples

This project, created by Unity, is used to show how you can use Unity's Mobile Notifications API in some real-world examples. We are using it for the cross-platform wrapper, which will allow us to create a notification once, and it will work on both Android and iOS without us doing any additional work.

5. After installing this, you may close the **Package Manager** window. To ensure that we can export our project, we need to ensure that our project has the correct Minimum API level.

6. Next, go to the **Project Settings** menu by going to **Edit | Project Settings**. From there, go to the **Player** options and under **Other Settings** scroll down to **Minimum API Level** and verify that it is set to the version specified in the Mobile Notifications package (in this case, **Android 5.1 'Lollipop' (API level 22)**) or higher. Afterward, you can close the **Project Settings** window:

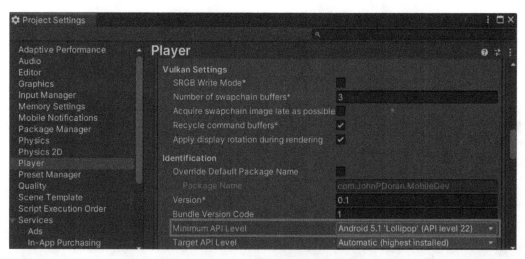

Figure 9.3: Ensuring the Minimum API Level is set correctly

You should see that there are a number of folders that are part of the project. The files that we care about are located in the `Assets\Samples\Mobile Notifications\2.0.2\ Notification Samples\Scripts` folder. See the following screenshot:

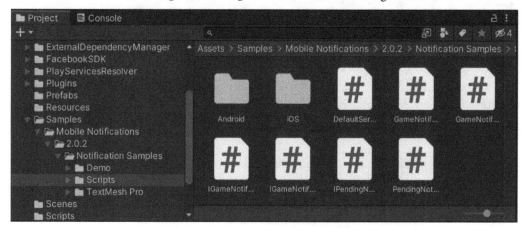

Figure 9.4: The Notification Samples Scripts folder

This gives us the code needed – in particular, the `GameNotificationManager` class – to be added to our script. At this point, we could move these scripts into a subfolder of our `Scripts` folder and delete the other files or keep the files where they are.

To begin displaying notifications on our screen, we first need to add a new object to our level that will contain the Game Notifications Manager:

1. Open the **MainMenu** scene if it isn't already open. From there, create a new game object by going to **GameObject | Create Empty**.

2. From the **Inspector** window, change the name of the object to `Notifications Manager` and, for the sake of neatness, reset the **Transform** component's **Position** property by right-clicking on the **Transform** component and selecting the **Reset Position** option.

3. Afterward, attach the **Game Notifications Manager** component to the **Notifications Manager** object by clicking on the **Add Component** button and then typing in `gamen`, and then selecting **Game Notifications Manager** from the list. It should look something like the following screenshot:

Figure 9.5: Adding the Game Notifications Manager

After the component has been placed, we can do the setup needed to create our first notification. Due to the implementation of the `GameNotificationsManager` class, we will need to have another script to send the notifications, which we will call `NotificationsController`.

4. From the **Project** window, open the `Assets/Scripts` folder and create a new C# script called `NotificationsController`. Double-click on the newly created file to open up your code editor of choice.

5. Next, add the following code for the class:

```
using UnityEngine;
using NotificationSamples; /* GameNotificationManager */

public class NotificationsController : MonoBehaviour
{
    private GameNotificationsManager notificationsManager;

    // Start is called before the first frame update
    private void Start()
    {
        /* Get access to the notifications manager */
        notificationsManager =
```

```
                    GetComponent<GameNotificationsManager>();


        /* Create a channel to use (required for Android)
        */
        var channel = new
            GameNotificationChannel("channel0",
                "Default Channel",
                    "Generic Notifications");

        /* Initialize the manager so it can be used. */
        notificationsManager.Initialize(channel);
    }


}
```

In the preceding code, we are first getting access to the GameNotificationsManager class through the component. Since we are attaching this script to the same game object that contains this script, we can use the GetComponent function. Afterward, we create a channel to post our notifications on. Lastly, we initialize the GameNotificationsManager component using the channel.

6.   Save your script and go back to the Unity Editor. From the **Inspector** window, attach the **Notifications Controller** script to the **Notifications Manager** object, as shown in the following screenshot:

Figure 9.6: Adding the Notifications Manager

Now that we have the setup taken care of, let's see how we can actually schedule a notification to happen.

Scheduling notifications ahead of time

One of the most common forms of creating a notification is asking players to come back and play the game at a later time. This encourages users to continue playing our game and to come back multiple times. We can do this by setting a delivery time in the future using the following steps:

1. Open up the NotificationsController script and add the following function to it:

    ```
    public void ShowNotification(string title, string body,
    DateTime deliveryTime)
    {
        IGameNotification notification =
            notificationsManager.CreateNotification();

        if (notification != null)
        {
            notification.Title = title;
            notification.Body = body;
            notification.DeliveryTime = deliveryTime;
        notificationsManager.ScheduleNotification(
            notification);
        }
    }
    ```

    This function takes in three parameters – the title, the body, and the time at which to send the notification.

2. This function requires the use of the System namespace for the DateTime class, so at the top of the NotificationsController file, add the following line:

    ```
    using System; /* DateTime */
    ```

3. Creating the function doesn't do anything, so for the sake of testing that everything has been set up correctly, let's call the function within our Start function by adding the following highlighted code:

    ```
    // Start is called before the first frame update
    private void Start()
    {
        /* Get access to the notifications manager */
        notificationsManager =
            GetComponent<GameNotificationsManager>();
    ```

```
/* Create a channel to use for it (required for
   Android) */
var channel = new
   GameNotificationChannel("channel0",
       "Default Channel",
           "Generic Notifications");

/* Initialize the manager so it can be used. */
notificationsManager.Initialize(channel);

/* Create sample notification to happen in 5
   seconds */
var notifText = "Come back and try to beat your
   score!!";
var notifTime = DateTime.Now.AddSeconds(5);

ShowNotification("Endless Runner", notifText,
   notifTime);

}
```

In this example, we are passing in "Endless Runner" as the title, "Come back!" as the body, and for the third parameter, we are getting the current time by using DateTime.Now and then asking to add 5 seconds by using the AddSeconds method, passing in 5.

4. Save the script and return to the Unity Editor.

5. Unfortunately, you won't be able to test whether notifications work on your PC. We'll have to export the game to see whether it works correctly.

6. Export your game to your device and start the game. As you can see, our notifications are working correctly!

Figure 9.7: Our default notification working properly

> **Important note**
>
> By default, the **Game Notifications Manager** component has **Mode** set to **Queue Clear and Reschedule**, which will make it so that you will be unable to see notifications if the game is open. If you would like to see the notifications always, change the mode to **NoQueue**.

7. Generally, these kinds of notifications should be sent a day after the player has last played. We can do that by modifying the function to the following:

```
// Start is called before the first frame update
private void Start()
{
    /* Get access to the notifications manager */
    notificationsManager =
    GetComponent<GameNotificationsManager>();


    /* Create a channel to use (required for
        Android) */
    var channel = new
        GameNotificationChannel("channel0",
            "Default Channel",
                "Generic Notifications");

    /* Initialize the manager so it can be used.
    */
    notificationsManager.Initialize(channel);

    /* Create sample notification to happen in 5
        seconds */
    var notifText = "Come back and try to beat
        your score!!";
    var notifTime = DateTime.Now.AddDays(1);

    ShowNotification("Endless Runner", notifText,
        notifTime);

}
```

This will make it so that when we reach a level, we will display the notification after a day, but this will also happen every time we go to the main menu. To prevent this, we can add a `static bool` variable that will turn on when adding the notification. In Unity, when a variable is marked as `static`, it will be consistent throughout the running of the program. To add this variable, follow the steps given here:

1. Update the script to add the following code highlighted in bold:

```
private static bool addedReminder = false;

// Start is called before the first frame update
private void Start()
{
    /* Get access to the notifications manager */
    notificationsManager =
    GetComponent<GameNotificationsManager>();


    /* Create a channel to use (required for
       Android) */
    var channel = new
        GameNotificationChannel("channel0",
            "Default Channel",
                "Generic Notifications");

    /* Initialize the manager so it can be used.
    */
    notificationsManager.Initialize(channel);

    /* Check if the notification hasn't been added
       yet */
    if (!addedReminder)
    {
        /* Create sample notification to happen
           later */
        var notifText = "Come back and try to beat
            your score!!";
        var notifTime = DateTime.Now.AddDays(1);

        ShowNotification("Endless Runner",
            notifText, notifTime);
```

```
        /* Cannot be added again until the user
           quits game */
        addedReminder = true;
    }

}
```

2. Save your script. Now, when we play the game, we will only see the notification once every time we play the game!

This shows us how we can create notifications within our script, but right now, the notifications are kind of plain. Thankfully, it's possible to customize notifications, which is what we'll be working on next.

> **Note**
>
> If you'd like to look into how to send notifications from outside of Unity to your app through tools such as Google Firebase, check out `https://firebase.google.com/products/cloud-messaging`.

Customizing notifications

Unity includes some default visuals to be used with notifications, but generally, replacing the content with our own will help our game stand out and be more visually appealing to players. In order to have custom icons for Android notifications, you are required to have a small icon with at least 48 x 48 pixels, and have only white pixels with a transparent backdrop. The large icon must be at least 192 x 192 and can have whatever colors we'd like. You can create images of your own, or use the images named `Hi-ResIcon.png` and `Small-ResIcon.png` provided in the example code for this book in the `Chapter 08\Assets\Sprites` folder of the GitHub repository. Follow the steps given here for customization:

1. From the **Project** window, select the images you are planning to use for the small and large icons.

2. With the images selected, go to the **Inspector** window and check the **Alpha Is Transparency** property.

3. Finally, open up the **Advanced** options and check the **Read/Write** properties. Click on the **Apply** button so the changes happen.

    You can see the options in the **Inspector** window in the following screenshot:

Figure 9.8: Setting the properties needed for the notification icons

At this point, our images are ready and we can start to put them into our notifications. To do this, we will need to go to the **Project Settings** menu:

1. Open the **Project Settings** menu by going to **Edit | Project Settings**.

2. From there, go to the **Mobile Notifications** settings option.

3. From the menu, you'll see two options – iOS and Android. We will want to use the default properties for the iOS options so we will first select **Android** if it isn't selected already.

4. Check the **Reschedule Notifications on Device Restart** option. This will make it so that if someone plays the game again, they will no longer get the notification we created earlier. This will help the user not get annoyed at us spamming them too often.

5. Next, under **Notification Icons**, click on the plus (+) icon. Drag and drop the small icon image into the first **Texture 2D** option. Next, click on the plus (+) icon again and then change **Type** to **Large**. Afterward, assign your large icon to the Texture 2D spot:

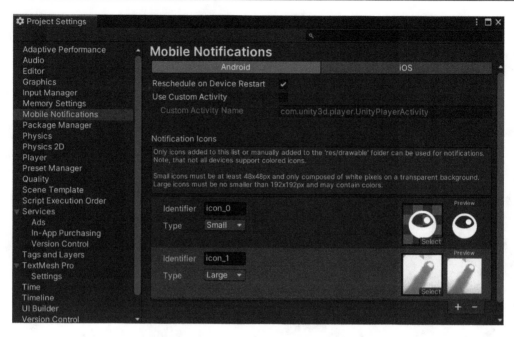

Figure 9.9: Setting up Mobile Notification Icons

6.   Then, go back to the `NotificationsController` script and update the `ShowNoti-`
     `fication` function to use our new icons:

```
public void ShowNotification(string title, string body, DateTime
deliveryTime)
{
    IGameNotification notification =
    notificationsManager.CreateNotification();

    if (notification != null)
    {
        notification.Title = title;
        notification.Body = body;
        notification.DeliveryTime = deliveryTime;
        notification.SmallIcon = "icon_0";
        notification.LargeIcon = "icon_1";


        notificationsManager.ScheduleNotification(
            notification);
    }
}
```

7. Save your script and return to the Unity Editor. Export your game to Android and you should see the icons update. Now, the notification will show the small icon from the toolbar, as shown in the following screenshot:

Figure 9.10: Small notification icon being shown

And it will use both icons when accessing the notification itself! This can be seen in the following screenshot:

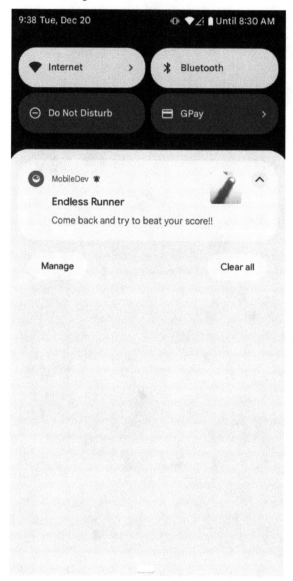

Figure 9.11: Seeing the notification from the notifications bar with both icons

It is also possible to modify other properties, such as the badge number used in iOS, by using a line such as the following:

```
notification.BadgeNumber = 5;
```

> **Important note**
>
> For more information on how you can customize your notifications, check out `https://docs.unity3d.com/Packages/com.unity.mobile.notifications@1.0/manual/index.html`.

This allows us to have our notifications look just the way we want them to with as much polish as we would like them to have. Now that we have our notifications customized the way that we want them, it might be pertinent for us to discuss how we can cancel notifications that we no longer wish to have happen.

Canceling notifications

There are several reasons why we may want to cancel notifications. This could be due to the fact that, during play, the player has made a decision that has caused something to no longer be relevant.

For this example, let's create a sample notification that we will cancel before it has a chance to happen. But for us to cancel a notification, we must have a way of knowing which notification is which. Thankfully, the Notifications Manager has a property called an `Id` that each notification has. We can set the notification ourselves by hand or Unity will generate it for us. In our case, we will use the automatically generated one:

1. Open up the `NotificationsController` script and go to the `ShowNotification` function. Update it to the following:

```
public int? ShowNotification(string title, string body, DateTime
deliveryTime)
{
    IGameNotification notification =
    notificationsManager.CreateNotification();

    if (notification != null)
    {
        notification.Title = title;
        notification.Body = body;
        notification.DeliveryTime = deliveryTime;
        notification.SmallIcon = "icon_0";
        notification.LargeIcon = "icon_1";


        var pendingNotif =
            notificationsManager.ScheduleNotification(
                notification);

        return pendingNotif.Notification.Id;
```

```
    }

    return null;
}
```

Note that our return type for this function has changed from `void` to `int?` and the question mark is not a typo. This is something called a **nullable type**. Nullable types are instances of the `System.Nullable` struct, which is basically a special type that allows us to have a variable that can consist of having any value of the type associated with it, but also can be assigned to `null` as well. That means that this value can either be set or not. Some platforms, such as PCs, don't have support for notifications with the system so, in those cases, they've chosen to use `null` instead of something like *negative one*.

2. Now that we've updated our script, let's now show an example of how we can cancel a notification. Go to the `Start` function and update it to the following:

```
// Start is called before the first frame update
private void Start()
{
    /* Get access to the notifications manager */
    notificationsManager =
    GetComponent<GameNotificationsManager>();


    /* Create a channel to use (required for Android)
    */
    var channel = new
        GameNotificationChannel("channel0",
            "Default Channel",
                "Generic Notifications");

    /* Initialize the manager so it can be used. */
    notificationsManager.Initialize(channel);

    /* Check if the notification hasn't been added yet
    */
    if (!addedReminder)
    {

        /* Create sample notification to happen in 5
            seconds */
        var notifText = "Come back and try to beat
            your score!!";
```

```
// After 5 seconds
var notifTime = DateTime.Now.AddSeconds(5);

// After 1 day
//notifTime = DateTime.Now.AddDays(1);
ShowNotification("Endless Runner", notifText,
    notifTime);

// Example of canceling a notification
var id = ShowNotification("Test", "Should Not
    Happen", notifTime);

if(id.HasValue)
{
    notificationsManager.CancelNotification(
        id.Value);
}

/* Cannot be added again until the user quits
    game */
addedReminder = true;
        }

    }
```

3. Save your script and build your game. If you open up the project on your Android or IOS device, you should be able to see that the verification that we have set to not be canceled plays as normal. But the one that we canceled does not happen.

> Tip
> You can also cancel all notifications at once by simply calling the `CancelAllNotifications` function from the `GameNotificationManager` class. For more information on canceling notifications, check out `https://docs.unity3d.com/Packages/com.unity.mobile.notifications@1.0/manual/index.html`.

Summary

At this point, we have seen how we can make use of Unity's Mobile Notifications package to create notifications for our players. We've learned how to schedule them to take place in the future as well as how to customize these notifications to have our own distinct visual style!

We now have everything in place for players to play and come back to our game, but we are only relying on what we created. In addition to that, we may want to see what our players are doing while playing our games. Then, we can use that information to improve and/or tweak our game.

In the next chapter, we will take a look at how we can do this using tools from Unity Analytics.

10
Using Unity Analytics

Making a game is a wonderful experience and a lot of hard work, but when designing projects, you have to rely on your experience and gut feelings in order to make it as awesome as possible. Often, in the game industry, we will use playtesting – a process where select people play a game and give feedback, and then we use the feedback we receive to improve the project.

This playtesting is most often done in person; however, by creating games for mobile, a lot of people will be playing your game after release, and most of them will have an internet connection. With this combination of people playing the game and also being online, we can send data about how the game is being played to ourselves. This will still allow us to do playtesting with a large variety of people. Being able to look at our data will allow us to check whether the choices that are made to change the game are the right ones, and we will be able to make adjustments to our games on the fly.

This data could be about something as simple as where players tend to die in the game or things such as how often they come back to play, the daily average time they spend playing, the number of users we have at a time, how long people play the game before stopping, and what choices they made. Over the course of this chapter, we will learn how to become able to learn what our users are doing through the use of Unity's Gaming Services platform and built-in Analytics system.

This chapter will cover a number of topics. The chapter itself is a simple step-by-step process from beginning to end. Here is an outline of our tasks:

- Setting up Unity Analytics
- Tracking custom events
- Working with the Funnel Analyzer
- Tweaking properties with Remote Config

Technical requirements

This book utilizes Unity 2022.1.0b16 and Unity Hub 3.3.1, but the steps should work with minimal changes in future versions of the editor. If you would like to download the exact version used in this book, and there is a new version out, you can visit Unity's download archive at `https://unity3d.com/get-unity/download/archive`. You can also find the system requirements for Unity at `https://docs.unity3d.com/2022.1/Documentation/Manual/system-requirements.html` in the *Unity Editor system requirements* section. To deploy your project, you will need an Android or iOS device.

You can find the code files present in this chapter on GitHub at `https://github.com/PacktPublishing/Unity-2022-Mobile-Game-Development-3rd-Edition/tree/main/Chapter10`.

Setting up Analytics

Although we activated the Analytics option from Unity Gaming Services in order to use Unity's Ads system in *Chapter 7 Advertising Using Unity Ads*, we didn't really dig deep into the system itself. Let's finish the setup for that now using the following steps:

1. To start, we need to install the Unity Analytics package in our project. We can do so by returning to the Unity Editor and opening the package manager, by going to **Window | Package Manager**.

2. There is a bug with the version of Unity this book was written for, with the Analytics package not showing up by default; instead, Unity shows the legacy Analytics Library package. However, it is possible to add the new package by clicking on the + button at the top left and then selecting the **Add Package by Name** option. From there, type in `com.unity.services.analytics`. If all goes well, you should be able to see that the Analytics package has been installed correctly by checking the **Package Manager** window:

Figure 10.1: Analytics attached

The next step is to initialize the SDK and ensure that consent is given by our users to log events that they cause to happen. To do this, we will need to write some code.

3. From the **Project** window, go to the `Assets/Scripts` folder and create a new C# script, naming it `AnalyticsManager`.

4. Double-click on the newly added script to open it with the code editor of your choice, and use the following code:

```csharp
using System.Collections.Generic; /* List */
using Unity.Services.Analytics; /* AnalyticsService,
ConsentCheckException */
using Unity.Services.Core; /* UnityServices */
using UnityEngine;

public class AnalyticsManager : MonoBehaviour
{
    // Start is called before the first frame update
    async void Start()
    {
        try
        {
            await UnityServices.InitializeAsync();
            List<string> consentIdentifiers = await
                AnalyticsService.Instance
                    .CheckForRequiredConsents();
        }
        catch (ConsentCheckException)
        {
            /* Something went wrong */
        }
    }
}
```

5. Save the script and return to the Unity Editor.

This is the minimum amount of code that is required for us to be able to initialize the SDK, as well as for us to be able to send events to Unity Gaming Services.

Note that several keywords here haven't been utilized previously. For instance, our `Start` function has `async` before the return type. Likewise, there's also `await` before two function calls. Here, we're utilizing something called asynchronous programming. The `await` keyword allows us to wait for the `async` method until it returns a value. So, the main application thread stops there until it receives a return value. If we did not use the `await` keyword, the next function would be called immediately afterward, and since we need the result to be figured out before we can continue, that's why we're utilizing it. The `async` keyword enables the `await` keyword. So, any method using `await` must be marked `async`.

> **Note**
>
> For more info on `async` and `await`, check out the official MSDN docs at `https://learn.microsoft.com/en-us/dotnet/csharp/programming-guide/concepts/async/`.

In addition, note that we have a `try` and `catch` block. When we use `try` and then a block of code, we are noting that there is a possibility that the code that we are putting inside of there has a chance of failure. For example, it's possible that there could be an exception that is thrown. If an exception of type `ConsentCheckException` is caught during the execution of the `try` block, it means something went wrong with the consent check.

If that were to happen normally, Unity would throw an error to the console. The code within the `catch` block handles this exceptional situation. The `catch` block is where, instead of throwing an error to the console and causing issues in the game, this is a way for us to attempt to remedy the situation instead. In our case, we would want to handle how we would run our game without using Unity Services, which would likely mean that we just wouldn't log events.

> **Note**
>
> For more info on `try` and `catch`, check out the official MSDN docs at `https://learn.microsoft.com/en-us/dotnet/csharp/language-reference/keywords/try-catch`.

Of course, just having this code doesn't do anything. We have to actually run it. So to do that, we're going to need to add the script to an object. And for ease of use, we're going to create a new object to attach this to.

6. Back in the Unity Editor, create an empty game object by going to **Game Object | Create Empty**.
    Rename the object `Analytics Manager`, reset its position, and then add the Analytics
    Manager script to that object.

Figure 10.2: The Analytics Manager setup

As long as **Analytics** is enabled, the Editor sends an App Start event to the Analytics service
when we press the **Play** button to start the game:

The nice thing about this is that we can ensure that this feature works correctly without having
to export our game. However, this message is not shown to us by default. We can enable logging
to the Editor console to allow us some extra visibility while we are experimenting by enabling
a scripting define symbol.

7. Go to **Edit | Project Settings**, and from there, go to the **Player** option. From **Other Settings**,
    go to the **Script Compilation** section, and from there, go to **Scripting Define Symbols**. From
    there, we're going to click on the + button to add an entry and then add the following keyword
    – `UNITY_ANALYTICS_EVENT_LOGS`. Once completed, hit the **Apply** button and wait for
    it to finish compiling scripts.

> **Tip**
> If, for some reason, your scripting define symbols disappear on the Android platform, switching
> to the PC settings and putting the value in first seems to correct the issue.

8. Save the project and run the game. If all goes well, you should see the events appear in the
    Console window:

Figure 10.3: The console receiving our default events

Now that we have this working, we can go check to see if the events are happening via the game side.

9.   From the top bar of Unity go to **Services | General Settings**. From there go to **Analytics – Gaming Services** and then click on **Go to Dashboard**. Once there click on the **Event Browser** button, you should see the most recent 100 events that Unity has received:

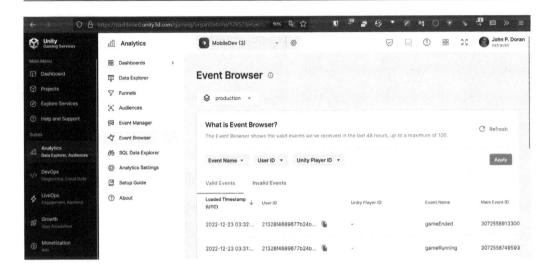

Figure 10.4: The Event Browser page

Now that we have Unity Analytics set up, let's start creating our own custom events to track!

Tracking custom events

Unity Analytics does a number of different things automatically to make it easy to work with. However, as a game designer, you may often want to check whether certain aspects of a game are being used or whether players are reaching certain pieces of content. To keep track of this, we can make use of the **custom events** system.

Custom events are pieces of data that users send to the cloud as they play a game. Each custom event can have its own parameters, which will allow us to filter the data that we send when it is generated. We will discuss how you can send information over the cloud through the use of code.

Sending basic CustomEvents

The first kind of event we are going to send is just an event name. This can be used for something such as tracking the number of times people access a certain place or checking whether something invalid appears to be happening. To make it easy to trigger and track for testing purposes, we will cause an event to happen each time a game is paused. Let's look at the steps:

1. Open the `PauseScreenBehaviour` script and add the following `using` statement to the top of the script:

    ```
    using Unity.Services.Analytics; /* AnalyticsService */
    ```

    This namespace contains all of the functions used by Unity's Analytics system.

2. Update the `SetPauseMenu` function to include the following highlighted code:

```
/// <summary>
/// Will turn our pause menu on or off
/// </summary>
/// <param name="isPaused">is the game currently paused</param>
public void SetPauseMenu(bool isPaused)
{
    paused = isPaused;

    /* If the game is paused, timeScale is 0,
       otherwise 1 */
    Time.timeScale = (paused) ? 0 : 1;

    pauseMenu.SetActive(paused);
    onScreenControls.SetActive(!paused);

    /* Send custom gamePaused event */
    if (paused && (AnalyticsService.Instance != null))
    {
        AnalyticsService.Instance.CustomData(
            "gamePaused");
        AnalyticsService.Instance.Flush();
    }
}
```

This code will call the `AnalyticsService.Instance.CustomData` function when pauseMenu has been turned on. The first parameter of `AnalyticsService.Instance.CustomData` is a string, which is the name that you wish the event to have. This name will be used within Unity Analytics. Events are automatically sent every 60 seconds if there's an internet connection available. However, if you want to immediately upload all recorded events to the server, there's also the `AnalyticsService.Instance.Flush` function, which will immediately upload the events when called.

3. Save the script and then return to the Unity Editor. Once there, play the game and then pause it. As you can see, the event was sent over the cloud successfully!

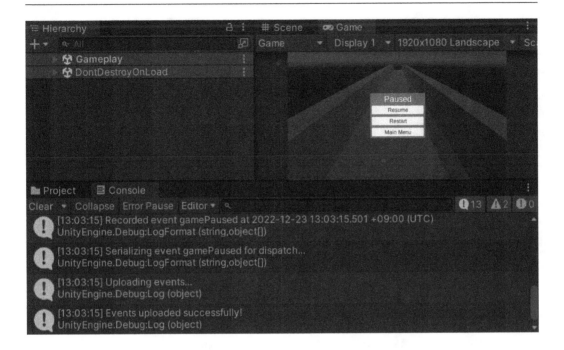

Figure 10.5: Paused events uploaded successfully

Previously, Unity Analytics used to accept any event that you were to send it. However, with this new system, you have to actually define the event in the dashboard ahead of time, or it will ignore the information. So, we are going to need to go to the dashboard and define this event as well before we start seeing it trigger in the Event Manager.

As mentioned before, it can take quite some time before information shows up on the Unity dashboard, but it's a good idea at this point to see where this information can be received later on.

4.   From the **Dashboard**, go to **Analytics**, and then select **Event Manager**.

This is the place where you can see the custom events and parameters that have been received from the game.

5.   From there, select **Add New**, and then select **Custom Event**.

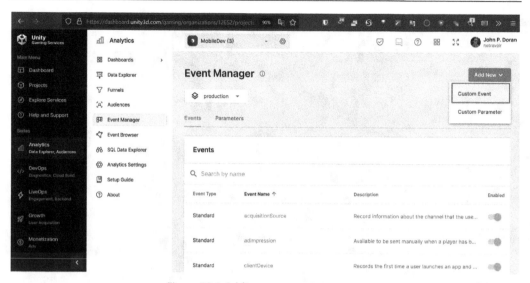

Figure 10.6: Adding a new custom event

6. Name the custom event `gamePaused`, spelled exactly the same as we've done here, for the string that we've been passing into the `CustomData` function in the `SetPauseMenu` function. We'll also add an event description of the event for our future reference. Afterward, click on the **Create** button, and the event should be ready for us to work with.

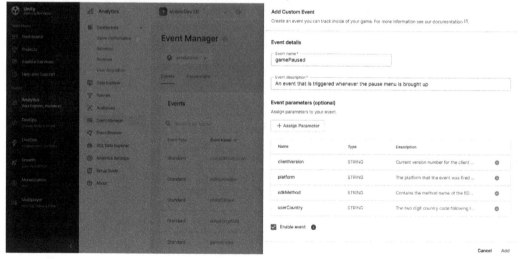

Figure 10.7: Setting Custom Event Details

7. Lastly, scroll down to the event and double check that the **Enabled** option is turned on; otherwise, the events will only show up in the **Invalid Events** area of the event browser.

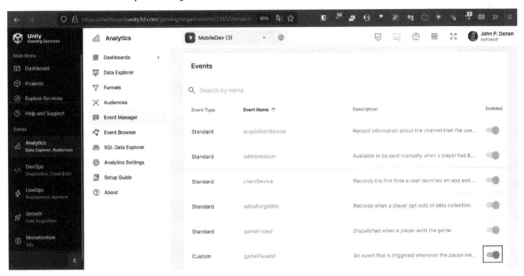

Figure 10.8: Enabling the event

8. Go back to the Unity Editor and play your game again, triggering the `gamePaused` event so that it will show up correctly.

9. Wait 15 minutes or so, go back to the event browser, and hit the **Refresh** button. If all goes well, you should see the `gamePaused` event there! To make it easier to see, you can also click on the **Event Name** dropdown, select `gamePaused`, and then hit the **Apply** button to isolate the event browser to only show those events.

   If not, it may take some time before the events are updated in the event browser, but they should show up eventually.

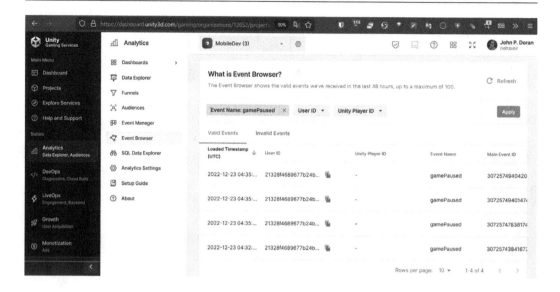

Figure 10.9: Our simple custom events in the event browser

10. Next, click on the **Data Explorer** option.

In the **Data Explorer** tab, you'll see two buttons for **Metric** and **Event**. We can also use this menu to observe whenever the gamePaused event is called.

> **Tip**
>
> If you have just created the event, it may take up to 12 hours for the information to be received. Go ahead and check back later if that's the case. In the past, I've had to wait up to even 48 hours for the data, so do not be alarmed if it takes a while for it to show up, although I have not had this issue with the newest iteration of Unity Gaming Services.

11. Click on the + button to the left of **Add Event** to add a custom event to this graph. Then, select the **Add Event** dropdown and then **gamePaused**. Since we have just made the event, we won't see it on previous dates in Analytics, but we can see it a little easier if we click on the **Column Chart** button to change how the data is displayed:

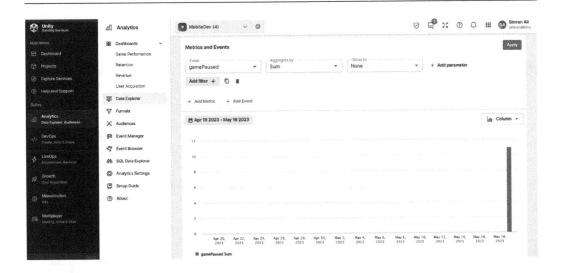

Figure 10.10: Add Event

Now, when we scroll down, we can see that **Data Explorer** now shows how often the gamePaused event has been called!

Sending custom events with properties

One additional thing that we may want to track is how far players get before they lose. Let's take a look at how to do that now:

1. In the Dashboard, first, go to the Event Manager. Click on **Add New** and select **Custom Event**. For **Event name**, type in gameOver, and then fill in the **Event description** field with something like Records when the players causes a game over event to occur. Afterward, click on the **Create** button.

2. From there, you'll be brought to a page for the event. Click on the **Assign Parameter** button, and from there, under the **Parameter** dropdown, select **Add New Parameter**.

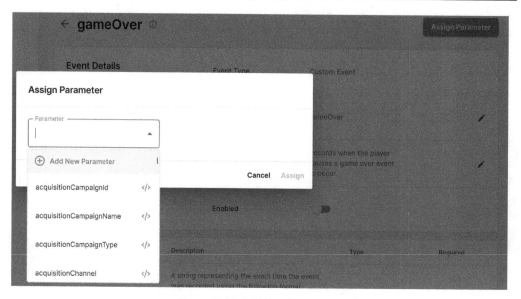

Figure 10.11: Add New Parameter

3. For the parameter name, type in `score`, and then fill in a description for the parameter. For the parameter type, select **Float**, and then click the **Create** button.

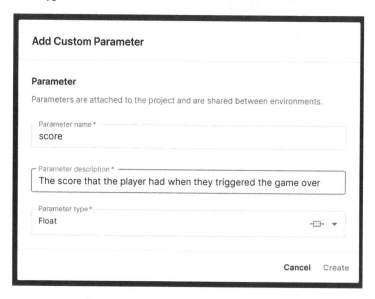

Figure 10.12: Adding a custom parameter

4. Create a new event called `gameOver` and a custom parameter, which we will call `score` and will be a float. Then, click on the **Create** button, select `score`, and then click **Assign**.

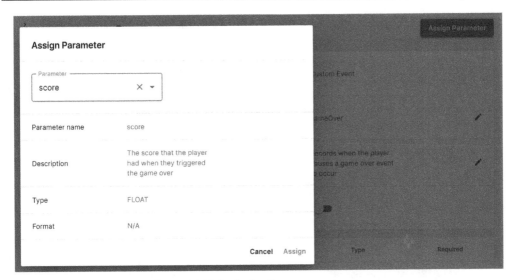

Figure 10.13: Assigning the score parameter

5. Finally, click on the **Enabled** toggle so that the gameOver event will be saved when it occurs. Unity will ask whether you're sure you want to enable the event; click on the **Enable** button to ensure that it will happen.

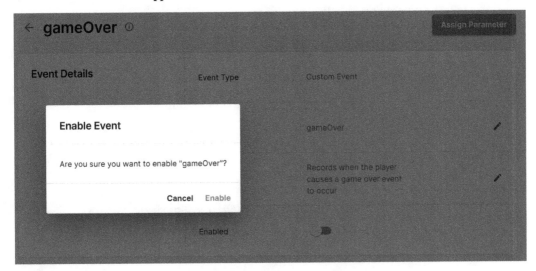

Figure 10.14: Enabling the event

6. Now, return to the Unity Editor. First, we will need to open up the ObstacleBehaviour script to modify what happens when the game ends.

7. To utilize Unity Analytics with parameters, at the top of the file, we will add the following `using` declarations:

```
using Unity.Services.Analytics; /* AnalyticsService */
using System.Collections.Generic; /* Dictionary */
```

The top option is obvious, but we are also adding `System.Collections.Generic` in order to get access to the `Dictionary` class, which we will use in the next piece of code.

8. Next, we will update the `OnCollisionEnter` function to the following:

```
private void OnCollisionEnter(Collision collision)
{
    var go = collision.gameObject;
    var playerBehaviour =
        go.GetComponent<PlayerBehaviour>();

    // First check if we collided with the player
    if (playerBehaviour)
    {
        // Destroy the player
        //Destroy(collision.gameObject);

        // Destroy (Hide) the player
        player = go;
        player.SetActive(false);

        /* If Unity Analytics doesn't exist will throw
           an exception */
        try
        {
            /* Define Custom Parameters */
            var eventData = new Dictionary<string,
                object>
            {
                { "score", playerBehaviour.Score }
            };

            AnalyticsService.Instance.CustomData("game
                Over", eventData);
            AnalyticsService.Instance.Flush();
        }
```

```
catch(ServicesInitializationException e)
{
    /* Displays the exception but doesn't
       break * the game */
    Debug.LogWarning(e.Message);
}



    /* Call the function ResetGame after waitTime
       has passed */
    Invoke("ResetGame", waitTime);
    }
}
```

We've done a number of things within this script. To start off with, we have rewritten our check that the player uses the component as a variable now, so we don't have to call `GetComponent` again for the same thing. Aside from that, the main addition is the calling of the `AnalyticsService.Instance.CustomData` function with a second parameter. The second parameter (which is optional) is a dictionary, which we haven't discussed yet.

A **dictionary** is a class that represents a pair of keys and values. The key is an identifier of some sort, which allows us to have a reference to obtain the value. This is most often used with the `string` class as the key type so that you can refer to some other data type.

> **Note**
>
> For more information on dictionaries, check out `http://csharp.net-informations.com/collection/dictionary.htm`.

We've wrapped this code in a `try` and `catch` block because if `AnalyticsService.Instance` is called and it is `null`, the code written by Unity will throw an exception. This will cause the game to break and no longer work. The game currently works fine if we start the game from the title screen, but if we start the game from the gameplay scene, it will no longer work correctly due to Analytics not being initialized. This time, instead of doing nothing like the previous example, I added a line to actually print out the message that the error gives us as a warning. It's always a good idea to have our code be as robust as possible, so that's why we added this check.

9. Save the script and return to the Unity Editor.

10. Play the game and lose it. Note in the **Console** window that you are now sending a gameOver event:

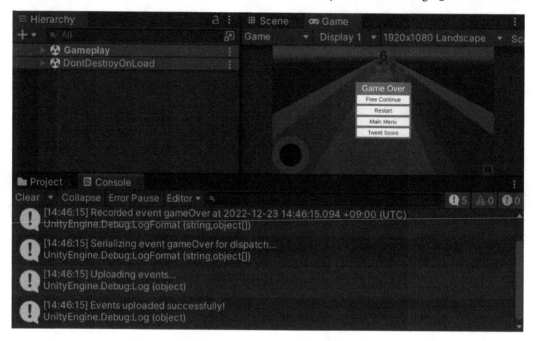

Figure 10.15: A Game Over event being dispatched

You can also dive into the dashboard to see the information as well, but Unity says it may take up to 6 hours before it becomes visible, although I usually see it within 15 minutes or so. You will see the messages instantly in the **Console** window, but they don't populate in Analytics until the backend calculations have been processed at Unity's end, due to all of the events it receives.

11. After you've waited, go to the **Analytics** tab and click on the **Dashboard** button once again. Then, go to the event browser and access the gameOver events.

12. To be able to see the value of the score parameter we created on the far right, click on the button that looks like <> to access the JSON event content for the particular event. Note that we can see the value of our score here:

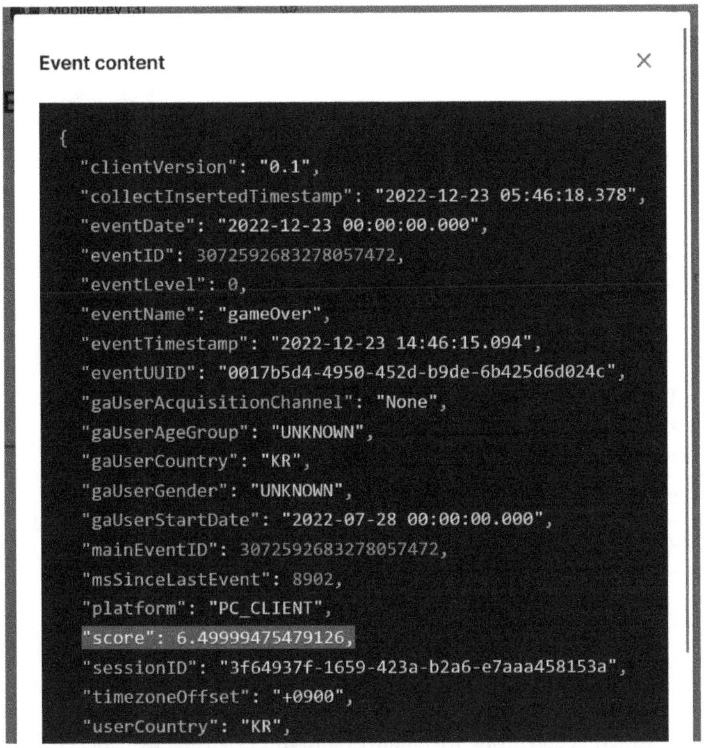

Figure 10.16: The score value in the event content

And with that, we now know how to access events!

This information is formatted in the manner of a JSON file. **JSON** stands for **JavaScript Object Notation** and is a format that is used to read/write text. The JSON file type is commonly used to transmit data and even save files. It's nice for programmers because it works with a key-pair system, such as the `Dictionary` class that we used previously.

One of the limitations of the event browser is the fact that we are only able to see the most recent 100 events. As our project becomes more and more popular, it is likely that we're going to have more and more events. With that in mind, we will likely want to have some way to be able to interpret that information. One of the ways that we can use do this is through the SQL Data Explorer. This allows us to access all the events that are created, but we have to utilize **Structured Query Language (SQL)**, which is a domain-specific language that was created to manage data held within a database.

13. Click on the **SQL Data Explorer** button to open the menu. Note that the **Query** field contains some default text.

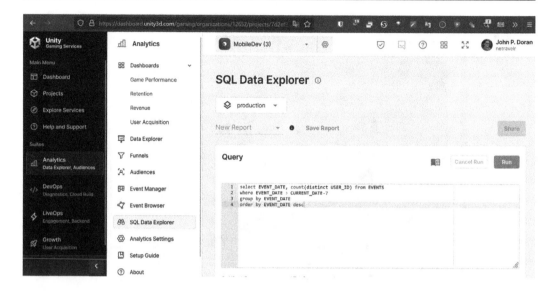

Figure 10.17: SQL Data Explorer

14. Hit the **Run** button to see the default result and how it works. Once the query finishes, you'll be able to create a chart using the data it interpreted from this query.

15. To get a feel for how this can work with chart data, under **Chart Setup**, set **X-axis column** to **EVENT_DATE** and **Y-axis 1 column** to **COUNT(DISTINCT USER_ID)**, and then click the **Apply** button.

Figure 10.18: Chart Setup

This will allow you to create a chart in a similar manner to what we saw earlier with the Data Explorer, but this gives us more fine-tuned control if we want to use the power of SQL.

There are entire books out there about SQL for those that are interested in exploring it further, but in our case, we want to extract the score values from our custom events. Therefore, instead of a chart, we want to create a table so that, in addition to writing some custom queries, we can also see how to export the data as well.

16. In the **Query** field, replace the code with the following:

```
SELECT EVENT_JSON:score::FLOAT
FROM EVENTS
WHERE EVENT_NAME = 'gameOver'
```

This code is going to go through every single event and check whether the name of the event is gameOver. If so, it will isolate the score property from it. This will allow us to create a list of all of the score properties from the entire project.

17. Hit the **Run** button and wait for it to execute. Once done, you'll see the **Share** button on the top has turned blue and you can press it. Once selected, click on the **Export as CSV file** option.

CSV stands for **comma-separated values**. This is a file type that uses commas to separate each of the different values that are designated within the file, but if you open the file with Google Sheets or Excel, the program will be able to parse the file to resemble a nice table.

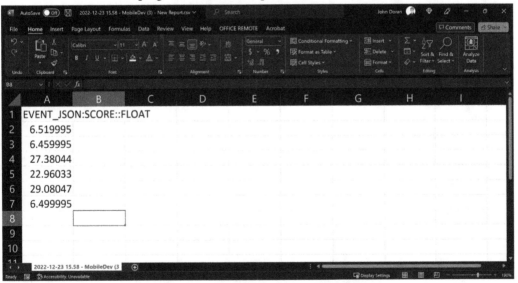

Figure 10.19: The table of score values in Microsoft Excel

This gives us a way to see all the various different score values that our players have achieved as they played the game. This can help us see whether people are doing well or really poorly, and allow us to cater the game however we'd like.

Use a snippet like the following:

```
SELECT EVENT_JSON
FROM EVENTS
WHERE EVENT_NAME = 'gameOver'
```

The preceding code would make it so that instead of the first event just showing 6.5199995, we would have each of the slots consist of the entirety of the JSON data that we discussed earlier – in this case, the following:

```
"{
  ""clientVersion"": ""0.1"",
  ""collectInsertedTimestamp"": ""2022-12-23
    05:36:22.379"",
  ""eventDate"": ""2022-12-23 00:00:00.000"",
  ""eventID"": 3072590187314819072,
  ""eventLevel"": 0,
  ""eventName"": ""gameOver"",
  ""eventTimestamp"": ""2022-12-23 14:36:19.072"",
  ""eventUUID"": ""0d924683-5667-4455-b899-722bfeae93cd"",
  ""gaUserAcquisitionChannel"": ""None"",
  ""gaUserAgeGroup"": ""UNKNOWN"",
  ""gaUserCountry"": ""KR"",
  ""gaUserGender"": ""UNKNOWN"",
  ""gaUserStartDate"": ""2022-07-28 00:00:00.000"",
  ""mainEventID"": 3072590187314819072,
  ""msSinceLastEvent"": 12124,
  ""platform"": ""PC_CLIENT"",
  ""score"": 6.51999473571777,
  ""sessionID"": ""0ce65df8-9696-40e8-ae44-924417e0d406"",
  ""timezoneOffset"": ""+0900"",
  ""userCountry"": ""KR"",
  ""userID"": ""21328f4689677b24baf59487ae951228""
}"
```

By adding `:score::FLOAT`, we get the `score` variable from the JSON data and tell the computer to interpret it as a floating-point value.

For those that are interested in exploring SQL more, I suggest checking out the Unity Gaming Service's example cookbook at `https://github.com/Unity-Technologies/UGS-SQL-Cookbook`, which contains a collection of common SQL queries and best practices for use with Unity Analytics.

This, of course, is just a simple example, so I would suggest that you create custom events for whenever a user reaches an important milestone – for example, when they level up or when they make an **In-App Purchase (IAP)**.

Now that we know how to create different types of events, let's see how we can actually track events and learn more about what our players are doing, utilizing the Funnel Analyzer tool.

Working with funnels

One of the many things we'd like to know about our players is how they are actually playing a game – for instance, are users skipping our tutorial? To keep track of how players proceed through a series of events, we have funnels. Funnels help us to identify where player drop-off happens in our game.

If you happen to see a large number of people not getting to a certain step, you can assume that something that happened in the preceding step causes people to stop playing our game.

> **Note**
>
> For more information on how funnels work as well as why you'd want to use them, check out https://data36.com/funnel-analysis/.

Funnels are based on the concept of custom events, which we used in the *Sending custom events with properties* section of this chapter. We can use the Funnels tool (previously known as the Funnel Analyzer) to look at the data sent via these funnels, which we can then use to make educated decisions on what changes should be made to the game. Follow the steps given here to add the tool:

1. From the dashboard, go to **Analytics** and select **Funnels**:

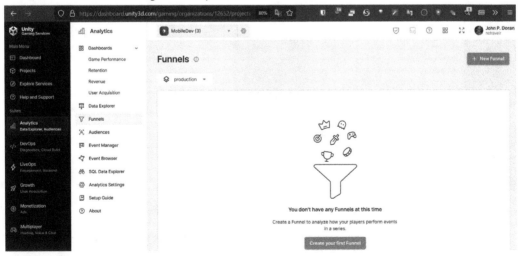

Figure 10.20: The Funnels page

Right now, there are no funnels set up, so we should create one.

2. Click on the **+ New Funnel** button and fill in the details, as shown in the following screenshot. Then, scroll all the way down and click on the **Apply** button:

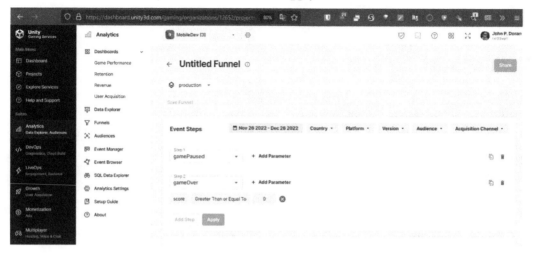

Figure 10.21: Funnels setup

If you've played the game already, you can see the results from the events that have already triggered:

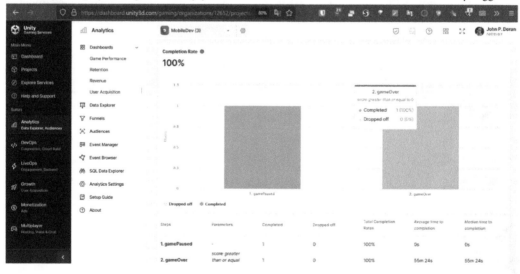

Figure 10.22: The event trigger results

In our case, we have played the game and lost, so we currently have a 100% completion rate.

3. Scroll up to the top page and click on the **Save Funnel** button. Give the funnel a name, describe what it is you're creating, and then hit the **Save** button.

Figure 10.23: The funnel setup

You should be able to select that funnel, and it will provide information on all the times it has been called.

The concepts used here can easily be expanded upon in other ways as well, such as keeping track of how often users watch ads or make purchases in the game and what causes them to do so.

> **Note**
>
> Funnels are great when a game is working correctly, but if the game crashes, it's also possible to get analytics from that as well from Unity Cloud Diagnostics. For information on that as well as how to set it up, check out https://docs.unity.com/cloud-diagnostics/en/manual/CrashandExceptionReporting/SettingupCrashandExceptionReporting.

Summary

In this chapter, we explored a number of ways that we can make use of Unity's Analytics tool to make our games better, from how to understand what our players are doing to learning how to adjust our game based on that feedback, without users having to download an entirely new copy of our game.

Specifically, we learned how to set up the Unity Analytics section of the Unity Editor, and then we saw how we can make use of code to create events to be sent to the cloud for us to look at. With the given data, we learned how we could make use of funnels and the Funnel Analyzer to learn more about our players.

Now that we have seen how to create events, let's see one of the other main benefits of utilizing Unity Gaming Services – being able to change projects using the Remote Config feature, which we will learn more about in the next chapter.

11

Remote Config

Getting a new build of your game exported can take quite a bit of time. It takes time to actually make the changes in the Unity Editor, and then you have to export the game and upload a new version on each of the app stores you are targeting. Then, you have to spend time waiting for them to approve the app and for everyone to actually download it.

One of the things I talk to my students about is creating projects that can be easily changed without having to open the Unity Editor. This can be done using data-driven development practices – such as building levels or encounters using text files, AssetBundles, or Unity's **Remote Config** (previously **Remote Settings**) menu – allowing us to instantly modify variables in copies of the game that are already out.

In this chapter, we're going to see just how easy it is to set up Unity's Remote Config system, and how we can utilize it for a simple example, by changing the difficulty of our game by changing the speed at which the player moves.

The chapter itself is a simple step-by-step process from beginning to end. Here is an outline of our tasks:

- Remote Config setup
- Integrating Game Overrides into gameplay

Technical requirements

This book utilizes Unity 2022.1.0b16 and Unity Hub 3.3.1, but the steps should work with minimal changes in future versions of the editor. If you would like to download the exact version used in this book, you can visit Unity's download archive at `https://unity3d.com/get-unity/download/archive`. You can also find the system requirements for Unity at `https://docs.unity3d.com/2022.1/Documentation/Manual/system-requirements.html` in the **Unity Editor system requirements** section. To deploy your project, you will need an Android or iOS device.

You can find the code files present in this chapter on GitHub at `https://github.com/PacktPublishing/Unity-2022-Mobile-Game-Development-3rd-Edition/tree/main/Chapter11`.

Remote Config setup

In order for us to use Remote Config, the first thing we're going to need to do is add the Remote Config package to our project. So, let's take a look at how we can do that using the following steps:

1. From the Unity Editor, open the **Services** window of the Package Manager (shown in the top-right part of the next screenshot) by either clicking on the cloud button at the top left of the screen or going to **Window | General | Services**.

Figure 11.1: The location of the Services button

If all goes well, you should see something like the following screenshot:

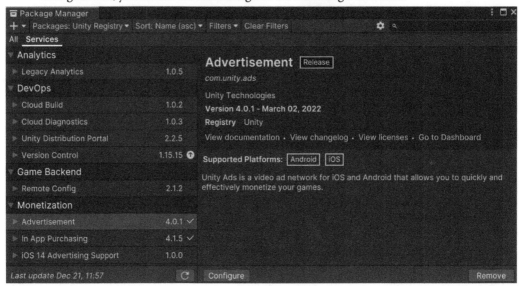

Figure 11.2: Package Manager | Services

2. From there, scroll down and click on the **Remote Config** package, and then click on the **Install** button at the bottom right. If all went well, you should see something like the following screenshot:

Figure 11.3: The Remote Config packages installed

3. Close out of the Package Manager and open the **Remote Config** window by going to **Window | Remote Config**. This will open a separate window that I will then drag and drop next to the Console for ease of use. If all goes well, your editor should look similar to the following:

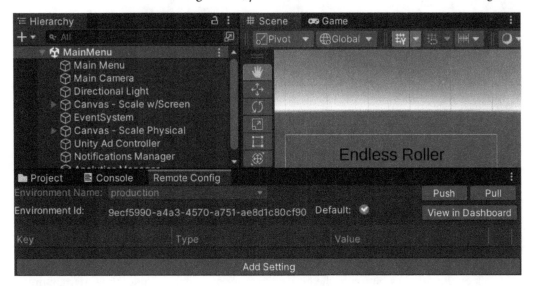

Figure 11.4: The Remote Config window added

And with that, the Remote Config package is installed correctly!

Just like how in the previous chapter we needed to create a connection between Unity Gaming Services and our project in order to use Unity Analytics, we will also need to do the same thing to tweak Remote Config values.

Creating key-value pairs

The first thing we will need to do is create the variables that we would like to change:

1. From the Unity Editor, if the **Remote Config** window is open, click on the **View in Dashboard** option.

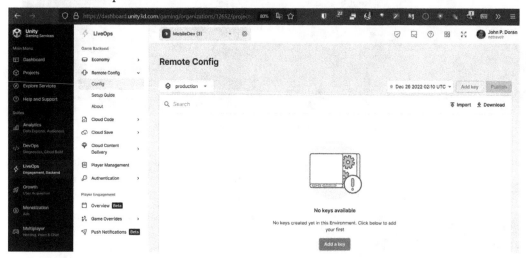

Figure 11.5: The Remote Config page

Alternatively, for those on the Unity dashboard website, you can click on **LiveOps**. Once there, on the left-hand side, open up the **Remote Config** section, and then click on the **Config** tab located under it.

This section is the location where we can set and modify the values. Just like working with dictionaries, the settings are key-value pairs, and while there is currently only one configuration now, production, it is possible to create many other environments. Generally, there are two configurations that can be used – **Release** or **Development**. The **Release** configuration is used by computers and devices running regular builds of your game. **Development** is the mode used by playing the game in the Unity Editor, as well as any builds created with the **Development Build** property set to True from the **Build Settings** window.

2. Click on the **Add key** button in the top-right corner of the table. Under the **Enter a name** property, type RollSpeed. Under the **Choose a type** dropdown, select **Float**. Lastly, put **5** in the **Float Value** field. Finally, click on the **Add** button:

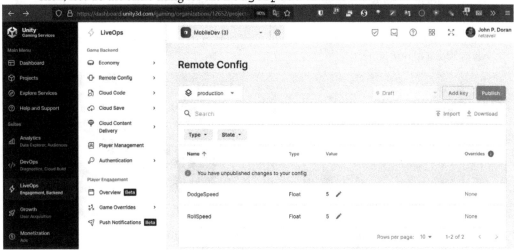

Add a key

Dec 26 2022 02:10 UTC ▾   Add key   Publish

☝ Import   ⬇ Download

Enter a name
RollSpeed

Choose a type
Float   ▾

Float value
5   ⌃⌄

Cancel   Add

Figure 11.6: Adding a key

Then, let's do the same thing for the `DodgeSpeed` variable with a value of **5**:

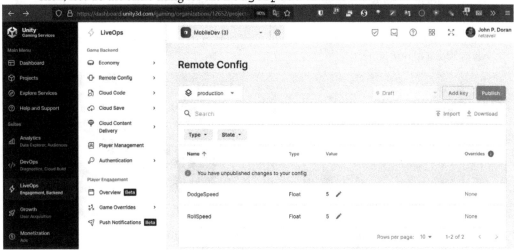

Figure 11.7: The DodgeSpeed and RollSpeed keys added

3.   It's important to note that this doesn't actually make a change. In fact, you'll see a note above the values saying that there are unpublished changes. Note how there is a big blue button that says **Publish**. Click on that to deploy the changes. It'll present a window asking whether you want to confirm the changes:

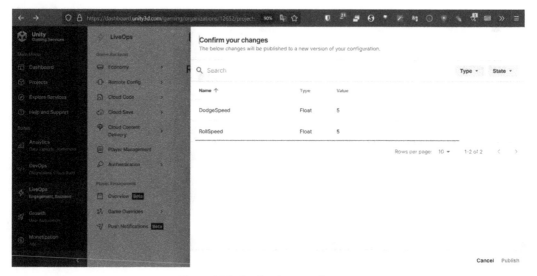

Figure 11.8: Confirming our change.

4. Now that we have some values to grab, let's take a look at how we can actually do that. Head back into the Unity Editor.

5. In the **Remote Config** window, click on the **Pull** button. If all went well, you should see the values added to our project:

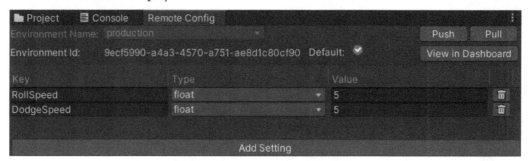

Figure 11.9: The values added to our Remote Config after a pull

It's a good habit to pull every time that you are about to make changes to your remote configs from your project, ensuring that you always have the latest version of your properties possible. And with that, we've now seen how we can create different key-value pairs to add to our project.

Integrating Game Overrides into gameplay

Now that we can see how to get those values and how the system works, let's see how we can actually integrate it with our project and have it affect gameplay:

1. Open up the gameplay scene if it isn't open already, and create a new GameObject by going to **GameObject | Create Empty**. Name the new object `Remote Config Manager` and reset its position.

2. Then, from the **Project** window, go to the `Assets\Scripts` folder and create a new C# script called `RemoteConfigManager`.

3. Attach the newly created `RemoteConfigManager` component to the `RemoteConfigManager` object we created in *step 1*. If all went well, your project should look similar to the following screenshot.

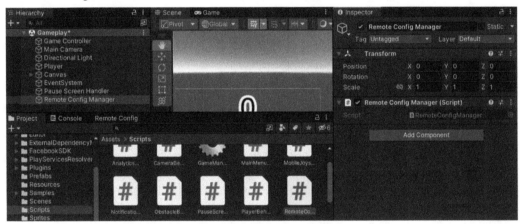

Figure 11.10: Adding RemoteConfigManager

4. Back in the **Project** window, double-click on the `RemoteConfigManager` script to open it with the script editor of your choice and replace its script with the following:

```
using UnityEngine;
using Unity.RemoteConfig; /* ConfigManager */

public class RemoteConfigManager : MonoBehaviour
{
    public PlayerBehaviour playerBehaviour;

    public struct userAttributes { }

    public struct appAttributes { }
```

```
    private void Awake()
    {
        ConfigManager.FetchCompleted +=
            ApplyRemoteSettings;
        ConfigManager.FetchConfigs<userAttributes,
            appAttributes>(new userAttributes(),
                new appAttributes());
    }

    private void ApplyRemoteSettings(ConfigResponse
        configResponse)
    {
        /* Check if new settings have been loaded */
        if (configResponse.requestOrigin ==
            ConfigOrigin.Remote)
        {
            /* There are, so values should be updated
            */
            playerBehaviour.UpdateRemoteConfigValues();
        }
    }
}
```

In the Awake function, we utilize the ConfigManager.FetchConfigs method in order to get the app configuration settings from the remote server. Upon completing the fetch operation successfully, the ConfigManager.FetchCompleted event is triggered. In this case, we added an ApplyRemoteSettings function, which should also be called when that event triggers, which we then implement.

That method takes in a ConfigResponse struct that represents the response of a RemoteConfig fetch. Of note is the requestOrigin property, which is an enum representing the origin point of the last retrieved configuration settings. It can be one of three options:

- Cached: The config settings loaded in our current session are cached from a previous session, so no new configuration settings are loaded

- Default: There are no configuration settings that are loaded in the current session

- Remote: There are new configuration settings that were loaded from the remote server in the current session

In our case, we only need to do something if the value is Remote. If this is the case, that means that there are new settings that have been loaded, which means that we need to update the values that are currently loaded.

5. Then, we need to go to the `PlayerBehaviour` script and add the following to the top section with the rest of the `using` statements:

```
using Unity.RemoteConfig; /* ConfigManager */
```

6. Afterward, we need to add the `UpdateRemoteConfigValues` function to the `PlayerBehaviour` class because it currently doesn't exist; otherwise, we will get a compiler error:

```
/// <summary>
/// Will update each value for this component we are using with
/// Remote Config
/// </summary>
public void UpdateRemoteConfigValues()
{
    /* Get the value from the cloud and set the value
       to use */
    float newRollSpeed =
        ConfigManager.appConfig.GetFloat("RollSpeed");
    Debug.Log("Update RollSpeed to: " + newRollSpeed);
    rollSpeed = newRollSpeed;

    /* Get the value from the cloud and set the value
       to use */
    float newDodgeSpeed =
        ConfigManager.appConfig.GetFloat("DodgeSpeed");
    Debug.Log("Update DodgeSpeed to: " +
        newRollSpeed);
    dodgeSpeed = newDodgeSpeed;
}
```

In this case, we are using the `appConfig` property of `ConfigManager`, which is the `RuntimeConfig` object, allowing us to access the current values as they are currently set from the cloud for our environment(s). Then, we set the current values of our `rollSpeed` and `dodgeSpeed` variables to the values that we retrieved from the cloud.

For more information on the `ConfigManager` class, check out the following: `https://docs.unity3d.com/Packages/com.unity.remote-config@0.3/api/Unity.RemoteConfig.ConfigManager.htm`

7. Save both scripts and return to the Unity Editor. Then, go to the **Hierarchy** window, select **Remote Config Manager**, and from the **Inspector** window, assign the **Player Behaviour** value to the **Player** object.

Figure 11.11: Adding Player Behaviour

8. Upon playing the game, you should be able to see in the **Console** window our Debug.Log statement being called, telling us that the value is being updated to whatever we placed in **Remote Config**:

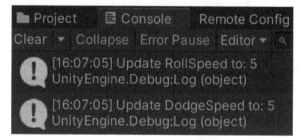

Figure 11.12: Values are updating correctly

9. Since the dodgeSpeed and rollSpeed variables are now being set via the UpdateRemoteConfigValues function, we can now hide them from the **Inspector** window. Replace their declarations in the PlayerBehaviour script so that the class looks as follows:

```
/// <summary>
/// How fast the ball moves left/right
/// </summary>
[HideInInspector]
public float dodgeSpeed = 5;

/// <summary>
/// How fast the ball moves forwards automatically
/// </summary>
```

```
[HideInInspector]
public float rollSpeed = 5;
```

Here, we've modified the two properties, adding the [HideInInspector] tag, which will hide the item in the **Inspector** window. We've also changed the variables to use XML comments instead of tooltips, since they are no longer being displayed in the **Inspector** window.

10. Save the script and select the **Player** object. From there, go to the **Inspector** window and note that the properties are no longer visible in the **PlayerBehaviour** component:

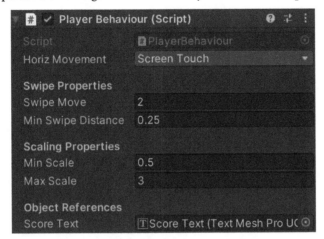

Figure 11.13: Values are hidden in the Inspector window

Now, the values will be set through the **Remote Config** component, and users won't be confused about why their values are being replaced by what's in **Player Behaviour**.

Being able to tweak these values while the game is live can be incredibly useful and allows you to share changes to the game without requiring your users to download a new version!

Summary

In this chapter, we learned how we can use **Remote Config** to make adjustments to our games on the fly.

> **Important note**
>
> There's a lot more that you can do with Remote Settings. You can learn more about **Remote Config** and how to use it to work with non-default parameters at https://docs.unity3d.com/Manual/UnityAnalyticsRemoteSettingsComponent.html.

With this, we have all of the implementation details of our game complete, but our game right now is pretty bare. In the next chapter, we will look into ways to make our game more polished, using features such as particle systems and screen shake.

12
Improving Game Feel

We now have a basic game, but it's just that... basic. In this chapter, you will learn some of the secrets of game developers to take the basic prototype of their game and turn it into something with a lot of polish that feels satisfying to play, which is known as improving the game feel of the project.

Also known as *juiciness*, or making our games juicy, in some corners of the game industry, **game feel** is a kind of catch-all term for all the things that we do in a game to make it pleasing for its users to interact with. This is something that is done with most mobile games that are out there today, and lacking this kind of interactivity will make others believe our project is lacking in polish.

In this chapter, you will learn some of the different ways that you can integrate several of these features into your projects. We will start off by learning how to make use of animations. We will then see how we can use Unity's material system in order to add visual appeal to our objects. We will then improve the overall visual quality of our game through the use of postprocessing effects. Lastly, we will use one of the most powerful tools in a game developer's toybox, the particle system, to improve feedback when the player moves in the environment.

This chapter covers a number of topics. It goes through a simple step-by-step process from beginning to end. Here is an outline of the tasks we will cover:

- Animation using LeanTween
- Adding tweens to the pause menu
- Working with materials
- Using postprocessing effects
- Adding particle effects

Technical requirements

This book utilizes Unity 2022.1.0b16 and Unity Hub 3.3.1, but the steps should work with minimal changes in future versions of the editor. If you would like to download the exact version used in this book, and there is a new version out, you can visit Unity's download archive at `https://unity3d.com/get-unity/download/archive`. You can also find the system requirements for Unity at `https://docs.unity3d.com/2022.1/Documentation/Manual/system-requirements.html` in the **Unity Editor system requirements** section. To deploy your project, you will need an Android or iOS device.

You can find the code files present in this chapter on GitHub at `https://github.com/PacktPublishing/Unity-2022-Mobile-Game-Development-3rd-Edition/tree/main/Chapter12`.

Animation using LeanTween

Currently, our game's menus are completely static. This is functional but does not make players excited about playing our game. To make the game seem more alive, we should animate our menus. Being able to use Unity's built-in animation system is great, and it can be quite useful if you want to modify many different properties at once. If you don't need precise control, say, if you're only modifying a single property or you want to animate something purely via code, you can also make use of a tweening library.

Tweening, short for "in-betweening," is a common technique used in animation and game development to create smooth transitions between two states or values over a specified duration. It involves interpolating or transitioning a property or set of properties from one value to another gradually.

If it is given a start and an end, the library will take care of all the work in the middle to get that property to that endpoint within the time and speed you specify. By using tweens, developers can easily add fluid and visually appealing animations to their applications without having to manually handle the interpolation calculations and animation loops. Tweening libraries provide convenient APIs and functionalities to create and control tweens in a straightforward and efficient manner.

One of my favorite tweening libraries is Dented Pixel's *LeanTween*, which is open source, usable for free in commercial and non-commercial projects, optimized for mobile devices, and used in many games, including Pokémon Go. In the following sections, we will first install and set up LeanTween and then see how we can use it to animate our title screen UI menus.

LeanTween setup

LeanTween allows us to spin, shake, punch, move, fade, and tweak objects in many different ways with only one line of code per task. It also gives us the ability to fire custom events during the start, middle, and end of the animations, allowing us to effectively do whatever we want to create an animation in a way that is incredibly powerful once you get familiar with it.

Now that we know we want to add tweens to our project, let's start off by actually adding the LeanTween engine to our project. Implement the following steps:

1. Open up the **Asset Store** tab by going to `https://assetstore.unity.com/` in your web browser of choice. Once there, at the top of the search bar, type in `LeanTween` and then press *Enter*.

2. From there, you'll be brought to a list of items, with the first one being **LeanTween**; select it and you will be brought to LeanTween's product page:

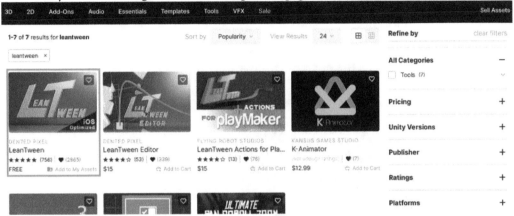

Figure 12.1: Asset Store search

3. Once on the project page, click on button that either says **Add to My Assets** or **Open In Unity** depending on if you have the package or not. At this point you may need to log into your Unity account. Once added, from the **Package Manager**, go ahead and from the asset page click on the **Import** button.

Figure 12.2: Package Manager

Important note

The packages in the Package Manager here will likely look different than yours as they are ones that I have personally purchased from the Asset Store.

4. You should see an **Import Unity Package** window pop up. From there, you can check or uncheck whatever files you want to keep. We will just use the contents of the Framework folder here; however, the others may be useful to you, so feel free to use them yourself.

5. Once you've finished selecting what you want, click on the **Import** button:

Figure 12.3: Import Unity Package dialog

6. We don't need the Package Manager anymore, so go ahead and close it. You'll notice that now we have the files we have selected inside our **Project** tab, in the Assets/LeanTween/ Framework folder:

Figure 12.4: LeanTween imported

With that, we have set up LeanTween.

Now that we have a tweening system in place, let's see how we can actually use it!

Creating a simple tween

Made popular in animation before transitioning to game development, the process of tweening (or *inbetweening*) is where, given a starting and ending value, the computer will generate the intermediate frames between the two states, giving the appearance of the beginning value evolving smoothly into the second value. A tween is the information that we have to provide in order to start the tweening process.

Now that we have LeanTween included in our project, we can use it inside our code. To do that, perform the following steps:

1. From the Unity Editor, open the **MainMenu** level by going to the **Project** window and double-clicking on the **MainMenu** scene.

2. Now, move to the `Scripts` folder and open `MainMenuBehaviour` by double-clicking on it.

3. We will add the following new function, which we will use to have the object move from the left side of the screen to the center:

```
/// <summary>
/// Will move an object from the left side of the screen
/// to the center
```

```
/// </summary>
/// <param name="obj">The UI element we would like to
/// move</param>
public void SlideMenuIn(GameObject obj)
{
    obj.SetActive(true);

    var rt = obj.GetComponent<RectTransform>();

    if (rt)
    {
        /* Set the object's position offscreen */
        var pos = rt.position;
        pos.x = -Screen.width / 2;
        rt.position = pos;

        /* Move the object to the center of the screen
           (x of 0 is centered) */
        LeanTween.moveX(rt, 0, 1.5f);
    }
}
```

Before we move anything using LeanTween, we will first set the position of our object (the `obj` parameter) off screen by setting the x position. It's important to note that when dealing with UI elements in Unity, by default, we are dealing with screen space, which, as you can recall from *Chapter 3, Mobile Input/Touch Controls*, means that we are moving in terms of pixels.

From here, we'll see that we are calling the `moveX` function from LeanTween. The version we are using takes in three parameters, the first being the `RectTransform` object we wish to move and the second being the x position to move it to. Based on how we set up the anchors and pivots, a position of 0 on the *x* axis is actually centered, so we pass in 0. Lastly, we have the amount of time (in seconds) in which we want the transition to happen.

4. Now that we have this function, let's actually call it. Change the `Start` function of the `MainMenuBehaviour` script so that it now looks as follows:

```
protected virtual void Start()
{
    /* Initialize the showAds variable */
    bool showAds =
        (PlayerPrefs.GetInt("Show Ads", 1) == 1);
    UnityAdController.showAds = showAds;

    /* Slide in the login menu if it exists */
    if (facebookLogin != null)
```

```
    {
        SlideMenuIn(facebookLogin);
    }


    /* Unpause the game if needed */
    Time.timeScale = 1;


}
```

The first thing we do is bring the Facebook login menu to the screen by calling the `SlideMenuIn` function, which in turn will tween the menu to the center of the screen. LeanTween, by default, makes use of the game's `Time.timeScale` property to scale movement. When we leave the game from the pause menu and go back to the main menu, the game will still be paused. This ensures that the game will be unpaused by the time we want to slide this menu in. When we start building the pause menu, we'll see how we can make our tweens work even when the game is paused.

If you play the game now, you'll notice that the Facebook login screen will now move from off screen back into the center of the screen.

Right now, the object moves in a fairly static manner. One of the ways we can add life to this tween is by giving it some additional features, such as `easeType`.

5. Add the following highlighted code to the `SlideMenuIn` function:

```
/// <summary>
/// Will move an object from the left side of the screen
/// to the center
/// </summary>
/// <param name="obj">The UI element we would like to
/// move</param>
public void SlideMenuIn(GameObject obj)
{
    obj.SetActive(true);

    var rt = obj.GetComponent<RectTransform>();

    if (rt)
    {
        /* Set the object's position offscreen */
        var pos = rt.position;
        pos.x = -Screen.width / 2;
        rt.position = pos;

        /* Move the object to the center of the screen
           (x of 0 is centered) */
```

```
        LeanTween.moveX(rt, 0,
            1.5f).setEase(LeanTweenType.easeInOutExpo);
    }
}
```

What is happening here is that the `LeanTween.moveX` function returns an object of the `LTDescr` type, which is actually a reference to the tween that was created. To that tween, we can add additional parameters by calling additional functions onto the tween. In fact, an alternate way to write this is the following:

```
// Move the object to the center of the screen (x of 0 is
// centered)
var tween = LeanTween.moveX(rt, 0, 1.5f);
tween.setEase(LeanTweenType.easeInOutExpo);
```

However, most of the examples in LeanTween's documentation use the former method, chaining a number of different events to happen at once.

> **Important note**
>
> To see what some of the other commonly used methods are besides `easeType` in LeanTween, check out `https://tedliou.com/archives/leantween-ui-animation/`.

6. Finally, we will add the ability for the current menu to slide off screen when we select a button to go to another menu:

```
/// <summary>
/// Will move an object to the right offscreen
/// </summary>
/// <param name="obj">The UI element we would like to
/// move </param>
public void SlideMenuOut(GameObject obj)
{
    var rt = obj.GetComponent<RectTransform>();

    if (rt)
    {
        var tween = LeanTween.moveX(rt,
            Screen.width / 2, 0.5f);

        tween.setEase(LeanTweenType.easeOutQuad);

        tween.setOnComplete(() =>
        {
            obj.SetActive(false);
```

```
        });
    }
}
```

Note that this is similar to the previously written function, except now we are also using another function called setOnComplete, which can take in either a function or an expression lambda, which works basically as a function without a name and is often used in **Language-Integrated Query (LINQ)**. In this case, because I wanted to have access to obj, I used a lambda. What this will do is after the object is off screen, it will automatically turn off; but we have the potential to do anything. This can be incredibly powerful, as we can do anything that we'd normally be able to do via code.

Important note

For more information on lambda expressions, check out https://docs.microsoft.com/
en-us/dotnet/csharp/programming-guide/statements-expressions-
operators/lambda-expressions.

---

7. Then, we will need to update the ShowMainMenu function to actually display the menus:

```
public void ShowMainMenu()
{
    if (facebookLogin != null && mainMenu != null)
    {
        SlideMenuIn(mainMenu);
        SlideMenuOut(facebookLogin);

        // No longer needed as menus will be animating
        //facebookLogin.SetActive(false);
        //mainMenu.SetActive(true);


        if (FB.IsLoggedIn)
        {
            /* Get information from Facebook profile
            */
            FB.API("/me?fields=name",
                    HttpMethod.GET,
                    SetName);
            FB.API("/me/picture?width=256&height=256",
                    HttpMethod.GET,
                    SetProfilePic);
        }
    }
}
```

8.   Save the script and dive back into the game:

Figure 12.5: Menus sliding in and out

As you can see, the menus will now fly in and out when on the main menu.

With the preceding example, you should be able to see just how easy it is to add motion to our projects and how it can improve the overall quality of the game, making it more enjoyable to interact with.

Adding tweens to the pause menu

Now that we have finished the main menu, let's continue adding tweens to the pause menu:

1.   Go ahead and open up our **Gameplay** scene. Update the `PauseScreenBehaviour` script to have the following implementation of `SetPauseMenu`:

```
/// <summary>
/// Will turn our pause menu on or off
/// </summary>
/// <param name="isPaused">is the game currently
/// paused</param>
public void SetPauseMenu(bool isPaused)
{
    paused = isPaused;

    /* If the game is paused, timeScale is 0,
       otherwise 1 */
    Time.timeScale = (paused) ? 0 : 1;

    // No longer needed
    //pauseMenu.SetActive(paused);
```

```
        if (paused)
        {
            SlideMenuIn(pauseMenu);
        }
        else
        {
            SlideMenuOut(pauseMenu);
        }


        onScreenControls.SetActive(!paused);

        /* Send custom gamePaused event */
        if (paused && (AnalyticsService.Instance != null))
        {
            AnalyticsService.Instance.CustomData(
                "game Paused");
            AnalyticsService.Instance.Flush();
        }
    }
}
```

Note that because `PauseMenuBehaviour` inherits from `MainMenuBehaviour`, it can also call the `SlideMenuIn` and `SlideMenuOut` functions, respectively, as long as they are marked as `protected` or `public`.

Now, if we run the game, nothing will appear to happen when we hit the pause menu. This is because—as I mentioned previously—tweens are scaled by `Time.timeScale`, which we just changed. To fix this, we can make use of another LeanTween function, called `setIgnoreTimeScale`, which we will set to `true` in both functions we wrote previously in the `MainMenuBehaviour` script. Go back to the `MainMenuBehaviour` script and add the following highlighted code to the `SlideMenuIn` method:

```
/// <summary>
/// Will move an object from the left side of the screen
/// to the center
/// </summary>
/// <param name="obj">The UI element we would like to
/// move</param>
public void SlideMenuIn(GameObject obj)
{
    obj.SetActive(true);

    var rt = obj.GetComponent<RectTransform>();
```

```
        if (rt)
        {
            /* Set the object's position offscreen */
            var pos = rt.position;
            pos.x = -Screen.width / 2;
            rt.position = pos;

            /* Move the object to the center of the screen
                (x of 0 is centered) */
            var tween = LeanTween.moveX(rt, 0, 1.5f);
            tween.setEase(LeanTweenType.easeInOutExpo);
            tween.setIgnoreTimeScale(true);
        }
    }
```

2. Add the highlighted code to the `SlideMenuOut` method:

```
/// <summary>
/// Will move an object to the right offscreen
/// </summary>
/// <param name="obj">The UI element we would like to
/// move </param>
public void SlideMenuOut(GameObject obj)
{
    var rt = obj.GetComponent<RectTransform>();

    if (rt)
    {
        var tween = LeanTween.moveX(rt,
            Screen.width / 2, 0.5f);

        tween.setEase(LeanTweenType.easeOutQuad);
        tween.setIgnoreTimeScale(true);

        tween.setOnComplete(() =>
        {
            obj.SetActive(false);
        });
    }
}
```

3. Save both scripts and dive into the Editor to try it out:

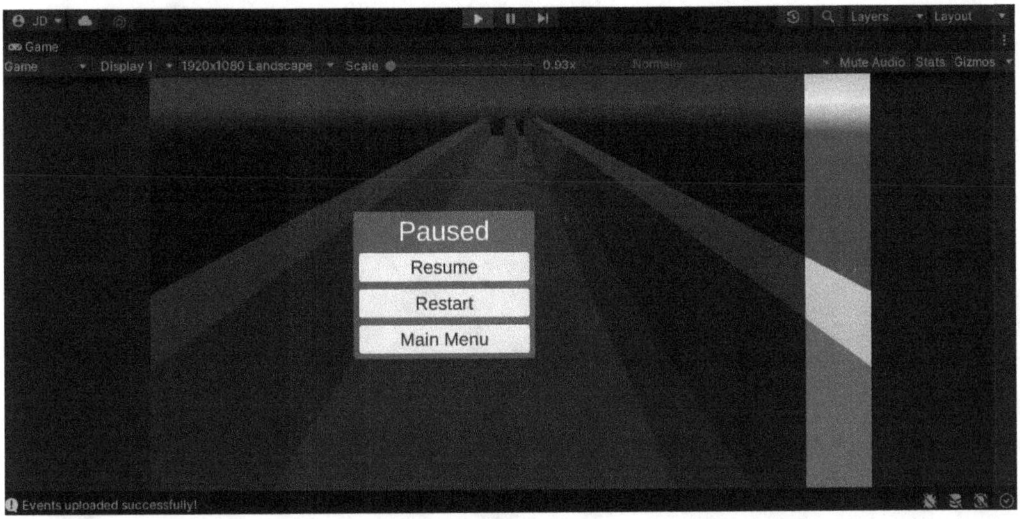

Figure 12.6: Screen flying in

Perfect! We now have the screen flying in just like we wanted it to.

In the previous two sections, we learned how to create tweening events and how to apply them to different scenarios. In the next section, we will see another way that we can improve the visuals of our project through the use of materials.

Working with materials

Previously, we have always used the default material for everything in our project. This has worked out well for us, but it may be a good idea for us to talk a little bit about creating custom ones to improve the visuals of our player. Materials are instructions on how to draw 3D objects within Unity. They consist of a shader and properties that the shader uses. A **shader** is a script that instructs the material on how to draw things on the object.

Shaders are a huge subject that entire books have been written on, so we can't dive too much into them here, but we can talk about working with one that is included in Unity, the **Standard Shader**. Implement the following steps:

1. First, open the **Gameplay** scene. Then, let's create a new folder in the **Project** window called Materials:

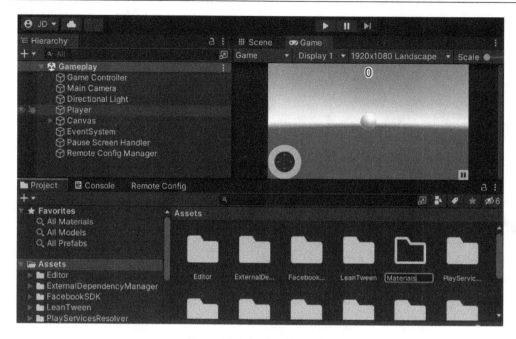

Figure 12.7: Adding Materials

2.   Open up the Materials folder we just created, and then once inside, create a new material by right-clicking within the folder and then selecting **Create** | **Material**:

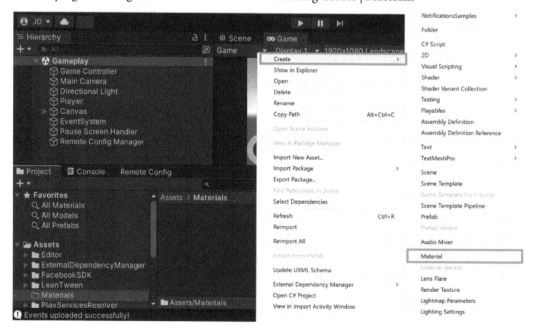

Figure 12.8: Creating a material

3. Name this new material Ball. In the **Inspector** window, you'll be brought to the **Shader** menu with the properties for the **Standard** shader. Change the **Albedo** to a gray color. Then, set the **Metallic** property to 0.9 and the **Smoothness** property to 0.8.

4. Now, go to the **Scene** view and drag and drop the **Ball** material onto our player object.

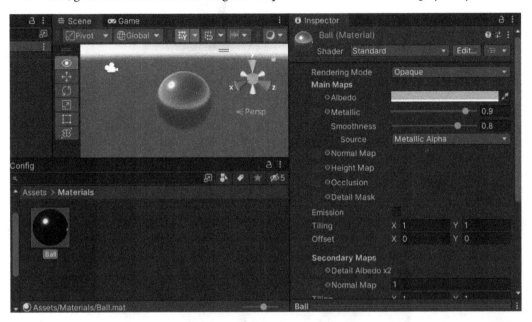

Figure 12.9: Setting material properties

The albedo property acts as a diffuse map setting the base color of an object, though you can also apply a texture to use an image file to change how it looks. The **Metallic** parameter of a material determines how *metal-like* the surface is. The more metallic a surface is, the more it reflects its environment. The **Smoothness** property determines how smooth the surface is; a higher smoothness will have light bounce off it uniformly, making the reflections clearer.

Important note

For more information on the standard shader and its parameters, check out https://docs.unity3d.com/Manual/StandardShaderMaterialParameters.html.

Using materials is only one of the ways that we can improve the visual quality of our project. In fact, one of the most drastic ways that we can modify our project's visuals is through the use of postprocessing effects, which we will be looking at next.

Using postprocessing effects

One of the ways that we can improve the visual quality of our game with little effort is by using postprocessing effects (previously called **Image Effects**). Postprocessing is the process of applying filters and other effects to what the camera will draw (the image buffer) before it is displayed on screen.

Unity includes a number of effects in its freely available postprocessing stack. Unity's postprocessing stack is a set of visual effects that can be applied to the rendered images in a game or application to enhance the overall visual quality. These effects can include things like color grading, depth of field, motion blur, ambient occlusion, and more. By using the postprocessing stack, developers can easily add these effects to their games without having to create them from scratch.

The term "stack" is used to emphasize that these effects are designed to be used together, in a layered manner, to achieve a desired visual style or aesthetic. By providing a pre-built collection of effects as a stack, Unity simplifies the process of implementing advanced visual effects for developers, allowing them to focus more on the creative aspects of their projects. So, let's go ahead and add it using the following steps:

1. Open up the Package Manager again by going to **Window** | **Package Manager**. From there, go to the **Packages** dropdown from the top left and set it to **Unity Registry**. Afterward, scroll down until you see the **Post Processing** option and select it:

Figure 12.10: Post Processing

2. Once selected, click on the **Install** button and wait for it to complete.

3. Switch to the **Scene** window and then, from the **Hierarchy** window, select our **Main Camera** object, select **Add Component** in the **Inspector** window, and type in Post Process. Then, move your mouse over the **Post-process Layer** selection and click to add the script to your project.

The **Post-process Layer** component handles the blending of postprocessing volumes and what the postprocessing should be based on.

4. Under the **Post-process Layer** component, change **Layer** to **Everything**. This will make it so everything in our scene will be used in terms of blending between volumes.

5. We will next need to add the **Post-process Volume** component to our **Main Camera** game object. Do this by clicking on the **Add Component** button and then selecting the **Post-process Volume** option.

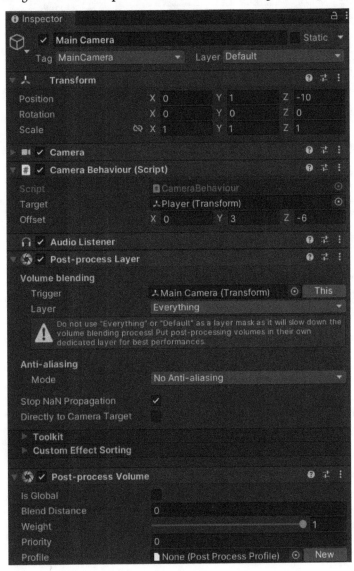

Figure 12.11: Adding the volume

Note that this component requires a profile. We can go ahead and add that next.

6. We can create a new postprocessing profile by right-clicking on the **Project** window, opening the `Assets` folder, selecting **Create | Post-processing Profile**, and then naming it `MobilePostProcessing`:

Image 12.12: Adding a postprocessing profile

7. Go back to the **Main Camera** object and attach this object to the **Profile** property of the **Post-process Volume** component. Afterward, go to the **Post-process Volume** component and then check the **Is Global** property box.

    This will make it so the volume we have created will always be visible on our player's screen no matter where their camera is positioned in the world.

8. Because `Post-processing Profile` is a separate file, we can make changes to it while playing the game without worrying about losing our changes. With that in mind, start the game and pause it once gameplay has started.

    Now, there's a large number of possible effects that can be added to modify how the game looks.

Important note

Note that for each element that we add to the profile you add, the frame rate of the devices we are trying to run our game on will be decreased. Keep testing your device with these options and note how it works.

---

9. Next, under the **Post-process Volume** component section, you'll see a section called **Overrides**. Click on the **Add effect...** button and then select **Unity | Vignette**. Click on the arrow to the left of the name to open up the potential options. From there, check the **Intensity** property and increase it to 0.45:

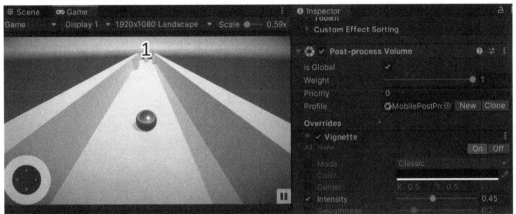

Figure 12.13: Adding Vignette

Note how there now seems to be a blackened edge or border around the game.

> **Tip**
>
> If the UI menu disappears, switching from the **Scene** view back to the **Game** view seems to fix this issue.

10. Next, enable **Smoothness** and set it to 0.35 to make it even darker by clicking on the top right of the section to expand it:

Figure 12.14: Enabling Smoothness

Vignetting is the term used for the darkening and/or desaturating toward the edges of an image compared to the center. I like to use this when I want to have players focus on the center of the screen.

11. Click on the **Add effect...** button again and this time, select **Unity | Grain**.

Check and set **Intensity** to 0.15 and you'll note that the screen has become fuzzier. While it's not a great idea if it is set too large, note that decreasing **Size** to 0.3 and unchecking **Colored** will help with the appearance of things:

Figure 12.15: Grain

If you've been to a movie theater that still uses film, you may have noticed how there were little specks in the filmstock that were visible over the course of the film. The **Grain** effect in Unity simulates this film grain, causing the effect to become more pronounced the more the movie is played. This is often used in horror games to obscure the player's vision.

12. Another property to add is **Unity | Bloom**, which makes bright things even brighter. Enable the property and then set **Intensity** to 10. From there, set **Soft Knee** to 0.6 to help brighten things up:

Figure 12.16: Bloom

The **Bloom** effect attempts to mimic the imaging artifacts of real-world cameras, where things in areas with light will glow along the edges, thus overwhelming the camera.

13. Lastly, stop the game, then go back to the **Post-process Layer** component and, under **Anti-aliasing**, change **Mode** to **Fast Approximate Anti-aliasing (FXAA)** and then check **Fast Mode**:

Figure 12.17: Anti-aliasing

Aliasing is an effect where lines appear jagged on the screen. This happens if the screen on the device we are trying to play our game on doesn't have a high enough resolution to display properly.

Anti-aliasing attempts to reduce that effect by combining colors near these lines to remove its prominence, at the cost of it appearing blurrier.

> **Important note**
>
> For more information on postprocessing in Unity, check out `https://docs.unity3d.com/Packages/com.unity.postprocessing@3.2/manual/index.html`.

There are a number of other properties to look into and adapt to get your project looking just the way you want. Explore them and find what works well for the vision you are looking to achieve!

The game itself currently works, but it could use some more polish. One of the things we can do to increase the polish of the game is to make use of particle systems, which is what we can look at next.

Adding particle effects

Typically used for effects that are natural or organic, such as fire, smoke, and sparks, particle systems create objects that are designed to be as low cost as possible, called particles. Due to this, we can spawn many of the particles at once with a minimal performance cost. One of the easiest types of particle systems to create is a trail to follow our player, so let's add one of those now using the following steps:

1. Select **Player** in the **Hierarchy** window, and then right-click and select **Effects | Particle System**.

    This will make this system a child of the player, which will be good for what we are going to do.

2. In the **Particle System** component, change **Start Speed** to 0 and **Simulation Space** to **World**. Then, change **Start Color** to a color that stands out, such as purple.

3. Open up the **Shape** section by clicking on it. Change **Shape** to **Sphere** and set **Radius** to 0 (it will automatically change to 0.0001).

    This is a step in the right direction. The purple particles are now following the player, as shown in the screenshot:

Figure 12.18: Particle trail

However, there are still a number of things we can do to improve this. Instead of just a single color, we can change it so that it randomly alternates between two colors.

4. To do that, go to the right side of **Start Color**, and you'll see a little downward-facing arrow. Click on that and then select **Random Between Two Colors**. Then, change the color to one of two purple colors for some randomness.

5. Then, next to **Start Size**, click on the right arrow, select **Random Between Two Constants**, and then set the values between 0.5 and 1.2.

6. With that, set the **Start Speed** property to be a random value from 0 to 0.2.

7. Then, open up the **Emission** section and set the **Rate over Time** property to 100:

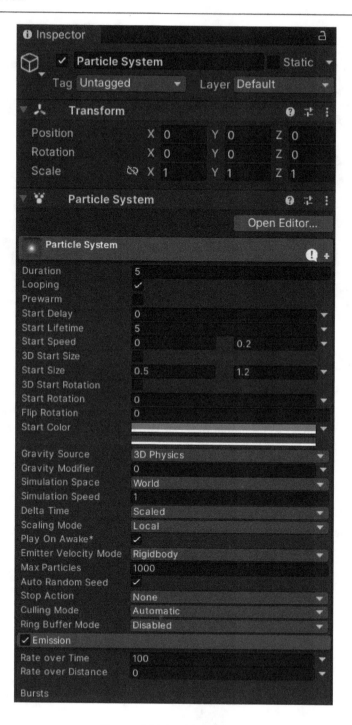

Figure 12.19: Particle settings

8. Save the game and play:

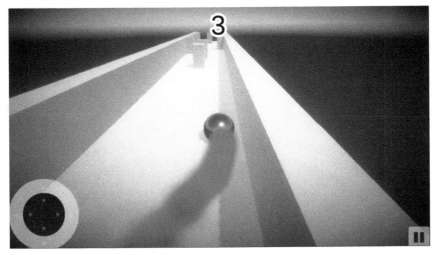

Figure 12.20: Final particle trail

> **Tip**
>
> If you're interested in exploring more details on things that can be done to polish projects, you can check out another of my Unity books, *Unity 5.x Game Development Blueprints*, also available from Packt, which also dives into game polish.

As you can see, the particle system looks great on both our PC and mobile devices.

Of course, there are many other areas that can be improved through the use of particle systems. Perhaps whenever the player hits a wall, we can display some sparks; when we swipe, we could play another effect; when the player pauses the game, we could have something falling on the screen. The possibilities are endless!

Summary

We have now improved our game by a huge amount by only doing a few simple things. We first animated our menus with a few lines of code using tweens from LeanTween and saw how a few lines of code can improve the visual quality of our UI in a number of ways. We next saw how to create materials to improve the visual quality of our ball and then used some postprocessing effects to polish the contents of our screen. Finally, we discussed how to use particle effects to create a nice trail following our player.

With these concepts, you now have the skills to dramatically improve the feel of your game projects so that players actually enjoy interacting with your game.

By this point, our game is finally ready for the big leagues. In the next chapter, we will explore how to build our games in order to get our game onto the Apple App Store and Google Play.

13

Building a Release Copy of Our Game

Building a release copy of our game is a crucial step in the process of submitting our game to the app stores. This step involves creating a version of our game that is stable and ready for us to release to the public.

In this chapter, we will walk you through the steps required to build a release copy of your game for both iOS and Android devices. We will cover some extra steps that need to be taken in order in order for our project to work. We will also provide tips and best practices to ensure that your release copy is of the highest quality and free from bugs and other issues. So, let's dive in and get started on creating a release copy of your game. This chapter will be split into a number of topics. It will contain a simple step-by-step process from beginning to end. Here is the outline of our tasks:

- Generating release builds for app stores

Technical requirements

This book utilizes Unity 2022.1.0b16 and Unity Hub 3.3.1, but the steps should work with minimal changes in future versions of the editor. If you would like to download the exact version used in this book, and there is a new version out, you can visit Unity's download archive at `https://unity3d.com/get-unity/download/archive`. You can also find the system requirements for Unity at `https://docs.unity3d.com/2022.1/Documentation/Manual/system-requirements.html` in the **Unity Editor system requirements** section. To deploy your project, you will need an Android or iOS device.

You can find the code files present in this chapter on GitHub at `https://github.com/PacktPublishing/Unity-2022-Mobile-Game-Development-3rd-Edition/tree/main/Chapter13%20and%2014`.

Generating release builds for app stores

We exported copies of our game previously in *Chapter 2, Project Setup for Android and iOS Development*, but there are some additional steps that we should do before actually releasing the game on an app store:

1. The first step will be to confirm you are currently ready to deploy your project to the mobile platform of choice. You can check this by going into the **Build Settings** menu by navigating to **File | Build Settings**.

2. From there, you should see the Unity logo to the right of the **Android** or **iOS** selection depending on the platform you wish to build for. If it is not at the correct platform, select that platform you wish to build to and then click the **Switch Platform** button and wait for it to finish reimporting the assets for the project:

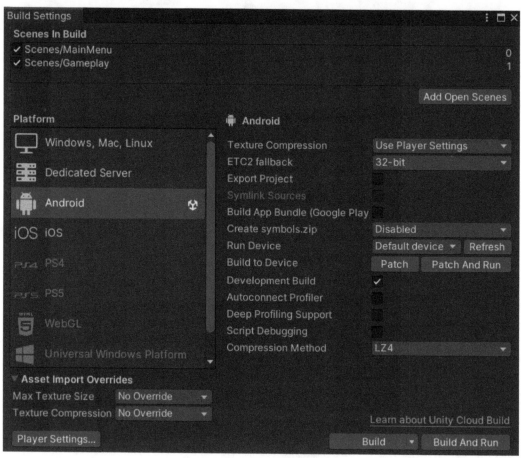

Figure 13.1 – The Build Settings menu

3. After confirming whether we are building for **Android** or **iOS**, open up the **Player** settings menu by clicking on the **Player Settings...** button from the menu or by going to **Edit | Project Settings | Player**.

4. If you haven't done so already, set the **Company Name** and **Product Name** values to your own values. In my case, I used JohnPDoran and Endless Roller, respectively.

5. You'll then see a **Default Icon** item. Drag and drop the Hi-ResIcon image from the Assets folder and then drag and drop it into the **Default Icon** slot. This will cause the **Icon** section of the Android settings to automatically scale the image to fit whatever device you are targeting:

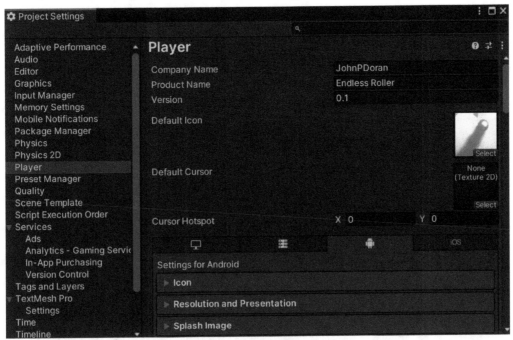

Figure 13.2 – Setting the Default Icon image

Of course, you can also use your own image, and you can use transparency if you would like to.

6. Under the **Resolution and Presentation** section, you can enable or disable different rotations and aspect ratios as desired. We adjusted the game to fit these, but this may be useful to know about as you work on your own projects or if you wish to restrict users to one experience or another.

7. The **Splash Image** option can be used to display your own logo in addition to Unity's if you have Unity Personal. If you have a Unity Pro license, you may disable it entirely if you wish here by unchecking the **Show Splash Screen** option.

8. Confirm under **Other Settings** that the **Package Name** property is not set to the default values. The general method of naming is com.CompanyName.GameName.

9. Next, open up **Publishing Settings**. This is where we will enter information about who our game's publisher is (in this case, I'm assuming it's you). Whenever you build a game for Android, you need a **Keystore**, which allows you to sign off the game, approving it for the build process. Click on the **Keystore Manager** button. From there, you'll be brought to a menu.

10. From the menu, click on the **Keystore...** drop-down menu and then select **Create New | Anywhere...**, and choose a location for this file.

11. Keep in mind where this is going to be located, as you will be using it in the future to create new versions of your game

12. Then, you'll need to set a value in the **Password** field that you will need to know as you'll be using it repeatedly. Afterward, in the **Confirm password** textbox, you should enter the same thing as you did before.

13. From there, under the **New Key Values** section, you'll need to add the same information as before—the password with confirmation and then your name and other information. You can see what I put down in the following screenshot. Once finished, click on the **Add Key** button:

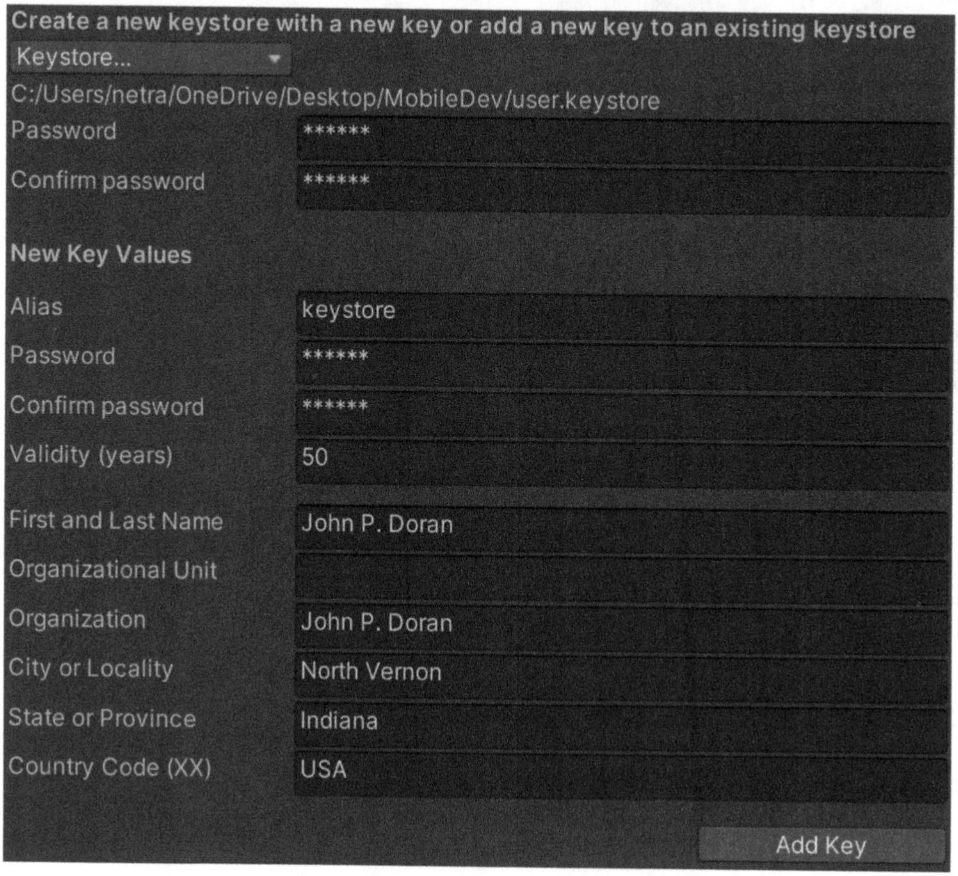

Figure 13.3 – Creating a keystore

14. You'll have a popup asking whether you'd like to set the new keystore as your **Project Keystore** and **Project Key** values. Click on **Yes**.

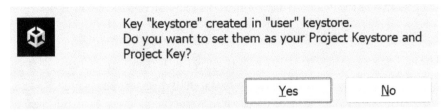

Key "keystore" created in "user" keystore.
Do you want to set them as your Project Keystore and Project Key?

| Yes | No |

Figure 13.4 – Confirmation window

You should then see this screen:

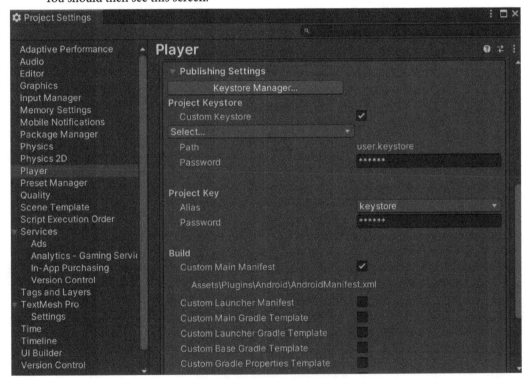

Figure 13.5 – Keystore assigned

At this point, you should be finished for those working on iOS, but for those wishing to target Google Play, there are some additional tasks we will need to complete.

Google Play requires a newer version of their Billing Library to be used so we will need to update the Unity **In App Purchase (IAP)** package.

15. From the Unity Editor, go to the `Assets` folder, right-click, and select **Show in Explorer** to go to the location of your project. From there, enter the `Packages` folder and open the `manifest.json` file in a text editor of your choice. Next, find the following line:

```
"com.unity.purchasing": "4.1.5",
```

16. Update it to `"com.unity.purchasing": "4.4.1",`.

17. Save the file and return to the Unity Editor, and it should update the package. However, this will also introduce a bug to our previous code that will cause the ads to not display correctly on our devices. So, with that in mind, open up the `UnityAdController` script and add the following code to the class:

```
public bool rewardCalled = false;

// To account for a bug in Unity Advertisements 4.0.1
// with Google
// Play we have to add a way for UnityAdsShowComplete
// to be
// called by ourselves as well if it isn't called by
// Unity
IEnumerator RewardRoutine(string placementId)
{
    rewardCalled = false;

    yield return new WaitForSecondsRealtime(0.25f);

    while (Advertisement.isShowing)
    {
        yield return null;
    }

    Debug.Log("Done");

    // If reward wasn't called yet, call it
    if(!rewardCalled)
    {
        OnUnityAdsShowComplete(placementId,
            UnityAdsShowCompletionState.COMPLETED);
    }
}
```

18. Then, update the `ShowAd` function to the following:

```
/// <summary>
/// Will load and display an ad on the screen
```

```
/// </summary>
public void ShowAd()
{
    // Add fix for Unity Ads bug
    StartCoroutine(RewardRoutine(GetAdID()));

    // Display it after it is loaded
    Advertisement.Show(GetAdID(), instance);
}
```

19. We are also required to load our ads now ahead of time, so update the `Start` function to the following:

```
/// <summary>
/// Unity Ads must be initialized, or else ads will
/// not work properly
/// </summary>
private void Start()
{
    /* No need to initialize if it already is done */
    if (!Advertisement.isInitialized || instance ==
        null)
    {
        instance = this;
        // Use the functions provided by this to allow
        // custom
        Advertisement.Initialize(gameId, testMode);

        // Load an Ad to play
        Advertisement.Load(GetAdID());
    }
}
```

20. On that same line of thinking, `OnUnityAdsShowComplete` now needs to be updated to only happen once, so we add a check to see whether the reward was given yet. Also, after the ad has been completed, we load a new ad:

```
/// <summary>
/// This callback method handles logic for the ad
/// finishing.
/// </summary>
/// <param name="placementId">The identifier for
/// the Ad Unit showing the content</param>
/// <param name="showCompletionState">Indicates
/// the final state of the ad (whether the ad was
```

```
/// skipped or completed).</param>
public void OnUnityAdsShowComplete(string
    placementId, UnityAdsShowCompletionState
        showCompletionState)
{

    if(!rewardCalled)
    {
        if (obstacle != null &&
            showCompletionState ==
            UnityAdsShowCompletionState.COMPLETED)
        {
            obstacle.Continue();
        }

        /* Unpause game when ad is over */
        PauseScreenBehaviour.paused = false;
        Time.timeScale = 1f;

        rewardCalled = true;

        // Load an Ad to play
        Advertisement.Load(GetAdID());
    }
}
```

Google Play also stipulates that ads cannot be played at the beginning of a level, so we will need to adjust our scripts for that. Open up the PauseScreenBehaviour.cs file and adjust the Start function:

```
protected override void Start()
{
    /* Initialize Ads if needed */
    base.Start();


    //if (!UnityAdController.showAds)
    //{
    //    /* If not showing ads, just start the game
    //    */
    //    SetPauseMenu(false);
    //}

    // Can no longer show ads at the Start of the game
    SetPauseMenu(false);
```

```
    }
```

21. Then go to `MainMenuBehaviour` and update the `LoadLevel` script:

```
/// <summary>
/// Will load a new scene upon being called
/// </summary>
/// <param name="levelName">The name of the level we
/// want to go to</param>
public void LoadLevel(string levelName)
{
    /* Can no longer show an ad upon starting gameplay
    */

    try
    {
        if (UnityAdController.showAds && levelName !=
            "Gameplay")
        {
            /* Show an ad */
            UnityAdController.instance.ShowAd();
        }
        else
        {
            Time.timeScale = 1f;
        }
    }
    catch { }

    SceneManager.LoadScene(levelName);
}
```

22. Save all of the scripts we've worked on and return to the Unity Editor.

In the editor, return to the **Gameplay** level and select the **Resume** button. From there, go to the **On Click** event and ensure that the **Show Pause** button has a **Set Active** to true event. This way, when we click the **Resume** button, we will be able to pause the game again:

Figure 13.6 – Turning on the pause menu

23. We will also want to make sure that Unity Gaming Services is always initialized. One way to do this is by going to **Services | In-App Purchasing | IAP Catalog** and checking the **Automatically initialize Unity Gaming Services** property. Otherwise, we may get a bug with the Codeless IAP that we added earlier:

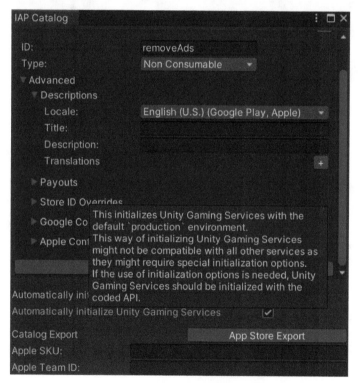

Figure 13.7 – Automatically initializing Unity Gaming Services

The Google Play Store also now requires new apps to be an **Android App Bundle** (**AAB**) instead of an **Android Application Package** (**APK**), so we will need to configure the application to be an AAB instead.

> **Note**
>
> For more information on why this change, check out https://android-developers.
> googleblog.com/2021/06/the-future-of-android-app-bundles-is.html.

24. Under **Publishing Settings**, enable **Split Application Binary**.

25. I also set **Target API Level** to API level 31 as that is what Google Play is asking applications to currently target though it may be a larger number in the future. This may cause Unity to ask you to download an update to your Android **software development kit** (**SDK**) when you make a build.

26. In addition, Google Play requires us to support ARM64, so to do that, under **Configuration**, change **Scripting Backend** to **IL2CPP** to enable the option and afterward check the **ARM64** option.

27. Next, go to **File** | **Build Settings** and enable **Build App Bundle (Google Play)**. Also, make sure to uncheck **Development Build** if it is checked; Google Play currently does not support development builds:

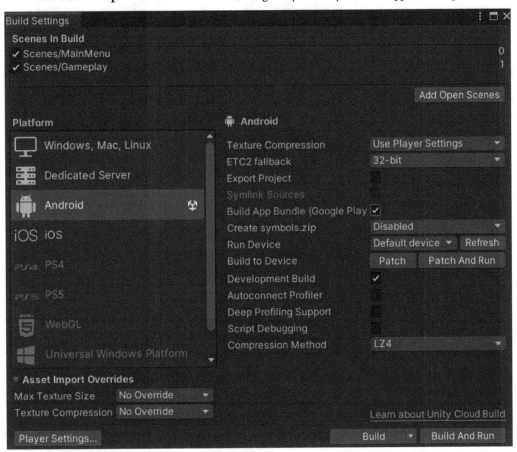

Figure 13.8 – Build App Bundle

28. Lastly, we also will need to disable debugging from the `AndroidManifest` file. From the Unity Editor, go to the **Assets** window, go to the `Plugins\Android` folder, and open the `AndroidManifest.xml` file. From there, search for the `android:debuggable="true"` line and change `"true"` to `"false"` and save the file.

The app manifest is something that every Android project must have, which tells Android all of the different components that the app has as well as all the permissions that the applications need to have in order for the project to have to work. For security reasons, you need to disable debugging before an application can be published in Google Play.

29. Go back to the **Build Settings** menu and then hit the **Build** button and give your project a name.

30. If all goes well, you should see the file get created as a `.aab` file, which can then be uploaded to the Google Play Store!

Summary

It is exciting to see all the hard work come together in a finished product that is ready to be shared with the world. The process of building a release copy of your game and updating the build settings is an important step toward making your game ready for distribution.

However, the ultimate goal of any game development project is to release the game to the public and have it played by as many people as possible. This is where the process of submitting your game to the app stores comes into play. In the next chapter, we will delve into the details of how to successfully submit your game to both the Google Play Store and the iOS App Store.

14
Submitting Games to App Stores

Over the course of this book, we have gone over many aspects of building games for mobile devices. The last step in our game development journey is actually releasing the game out into the wild and having people actually play it. All of those long hours of hard work have now come together into something that the masses will be able to enjoy.

When doing this, there are a number of things to keep in mind, and this is exactly what we will be discussing next.

In this chapter, we will go over the process of submitting your game to the Google Play Store or iOS App Store, with tips and tricks to help the process go smoother. By the end of this chapter, you will know exactly how to create developer accounts for both stores, as well as how to submit your game to the respective stores.

This chapter will be split into a number of topics. It will contain a simple step-by-step process from beginning to end. Here is the outline of our tasks:

- Putting your game on the Google Play Store
- Putting your game on the Apple iOS App Store

Technical requirements

This book utilizes Unity 2022.1.0b16 and Unity Hub 3.3.1, but the steps should work with minimal changes in future versions of the editor. If you want to download the exact version used in this book, and there is a new version out, you can visit Unity's download archive at `https://unity3d.com/get-unity/download/archive`. You can also find the system requirements for Unity at `https://docs.unity3d.com/2022.1/Documentation/Manual/system-requirements.html` in the **Unity Editor system requirements** section. To deploy your project, you will need an Android or iOS device.

You can find the code files present in this chapter on GitHub at `https://github.com/PacktPublishing/Unity-2022-Mobile-Game-Development-3rd-Edition/tree/main/Chapter13%20and%2014`.

Putting your game on the Google Play Store

Now that your game is built, you will need to actually put it up on Google's Play Store. To put games up on the Google Play Store, you are required to pay a one-time $25 dollar fee. This may or may not seem like a large amount of money, but it is much cheaper than the iOS App Store and is a one-time fee, so for those who are a bit more budget-conscious, you may wish to dive into Google first and make some profit before moving on to Apple's store. We will first look at the Google Play Console before filling out all of the details needed in order to submit our game to the store. We will also discuss how to mark our game as a beta version to get feedback from others before making the final submission.

Setting up the Google Play Console

The first step is to gain access to the Google Play Console. This allows you to publish an Android app on Google Play as well as Google Play Game Services if want. Implement the following steps:

1. Open up your web browser and go to `https://play.google.com/console/about/`. This is the **Google Play Console** page, which allows you to add apps to the Google Play store.

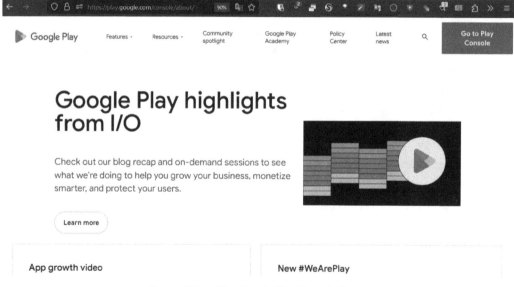

Figure 14.1 –– The Google Play Console Page

2. If you aren't signed in to your Google account, you'll need to sign in; otherwise, you will need to sign up as a developer:

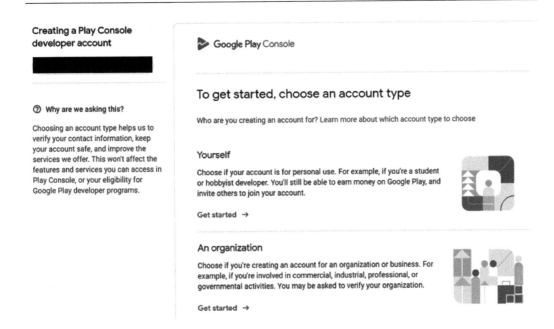

14.2 – Creating a Play Console developer account

3. You'll pick an account type, and then you'll need to fill out information related to your developer account and information related to the apps that you will be publishing.

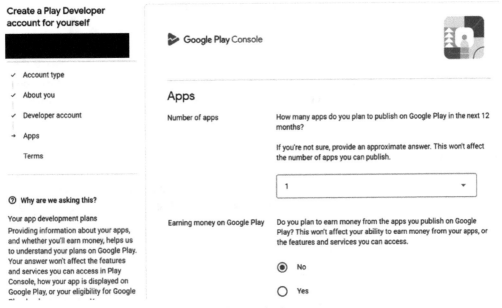

Figure 14.3 – Adding info about your apps

4. Next will come a page where you'll have to accept the terms and click on **Create account and pay**. Afterwards you'll put in your credit or debit card info in order to complete the purchase.

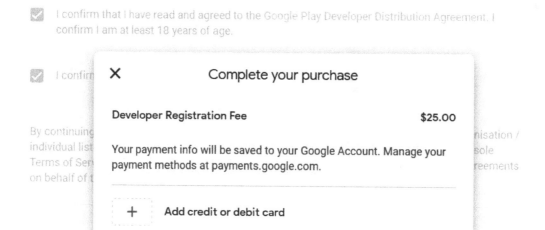

Figure 14.4 – Completing payment for the developer registration fee

5. If all goes well, you'll be brought to the Google Play Console.

Once you have an account, you can now start the process of actually publishing a game to the Google Play store. To start that process, we will need to add a project to our account, which is what we will be doing next.

Publishing an app on Google Play

The process of publishing an app to Google Play involves filling out a number of different fields with information about your game, as well as art assets for screenshots. To do this, implement the following steps:

1. From the **All apps** page, click on the **Create app** button.

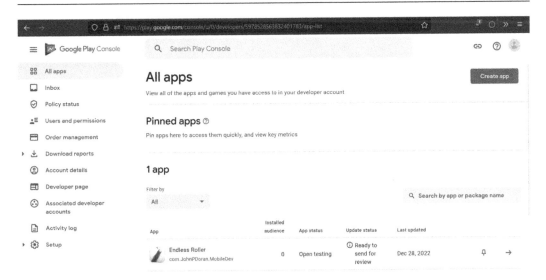

Figure 14.5 – The All apps page

2. You'll be brought to a page where you need to select the app name and default language of your game. You'll then need to select whether it's an app or a game. We'll choose **Game**.

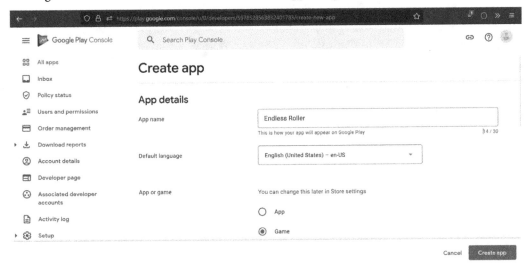

Figure 14.6 – The Create app menu

3. Scroll down, and you'll see three declarations that you'll need to read through and check whether they're relevant, and then, click on the **Create app** button:

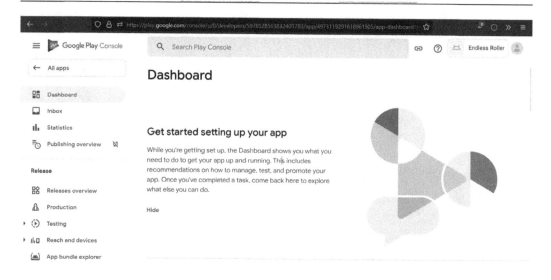

Figure 14.7 – The app dashboard

The dashboard page shows details of all of the latest steps that are required in order to get your app up and running. The first section includes building a test version of your game so that others can give you feedback before the final release.

Scroll down to the **Start testing now** section. From there, select the **Select testers** option.

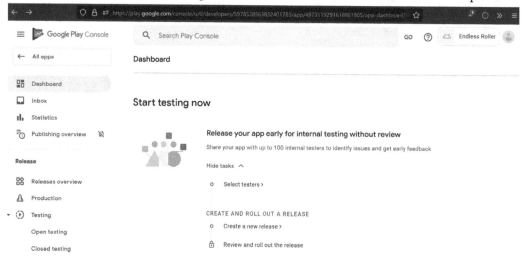

Figure 14.8 – Start testing now

4. This will open the Internal testing page, which can also be accessed by going to **Testing |
    Internal testing** via the **Release** section of the dashboard. From there, scroll down, and under
    Testers, you'll see an option for you to create an e-mail list of testers for your game by clicking
    the **Create email list** button.

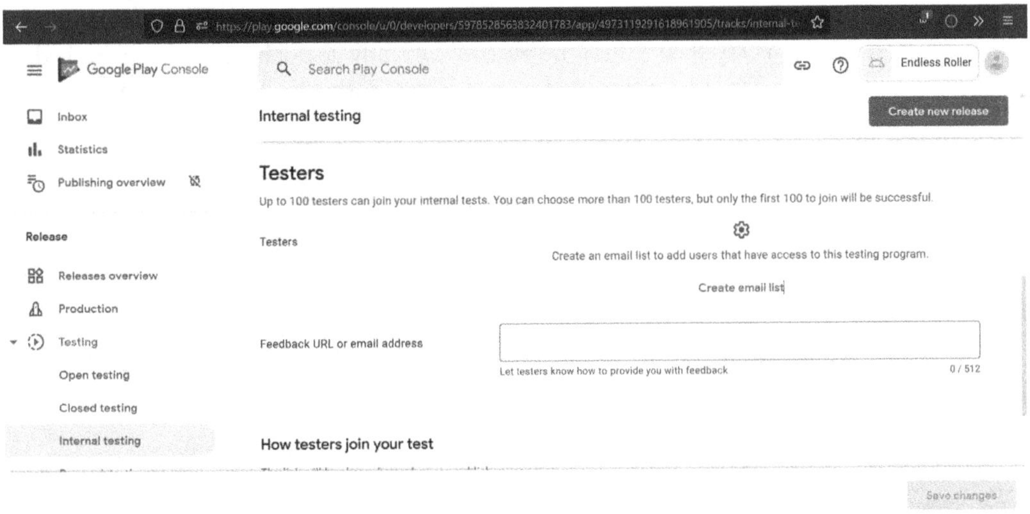

Figure 14.9 – The Internal testing menu

This will bring up a window, where you can fill out a list name and then add the email addresses
of those you want to test your game, by typing in the values yourself, separated by commas, or
by using a CSV file, as we discussed previously.

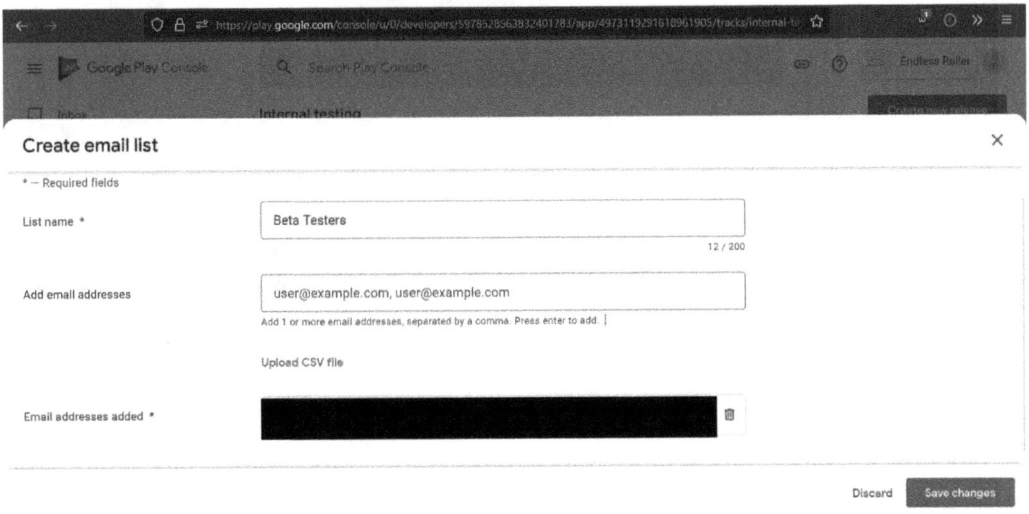

Figure 14.10 – Creating an email list

5. Once finished, hit the **Save changes** button, and you will be asked to confirm the saved changes. Note that this email list will be available to use across all apps in your developer account. Hit **Create**, and you should move back to the previous section.

6. From there, for **Feedback URL or email address**, fill in your email address or website. Afterward, click on the **Save changes** button. Note that the **How testers join your test** section currently has the **Copy link** button grayed out. This is because we currently do not have the app published; however, that will be fixed once we create a release, which is what we will be doing next.

7. At the top right, hit the **Create new release** button. This will bring you to the **Create internal testing release** page. From there, scroll down until you get to the **App bundles** section, and then drag and drop your `.aab` file into the **drop app bundles here to upload** section.

8. Below that, you'll be able to provide a release name and release notes about this particular version of the game. Once you've finished filling out those details, go ahead and hit the **Save as Draft** button, and then hit **Next**.

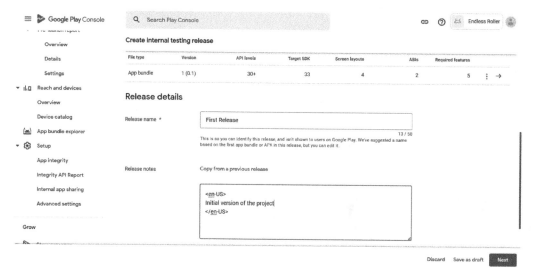

Figure 14.11 – Filling out Release details

You'll see some information and any errors, warnings, and messages about your project. Read through them if needed, and assuming there are no errors, you should be able to click on the **Save** button to allow others to try out your project!

Figure 14.12 – Reviewing the release

9. Return to the dashboard by clicking on the **Dashboard** button. Upon returning to the main page, you'll see that the next section is **Set up your app**:

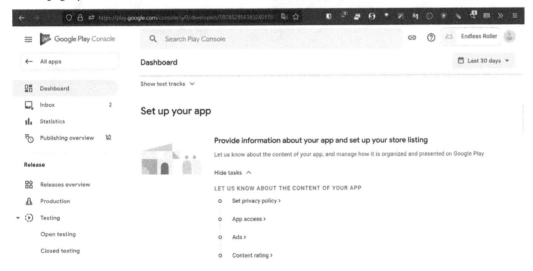

Figure 14.13 – Set up your app

We will need to go through each of these sections and complete them in order to set up the store listing.

10. First, click on the **Set privacy policy** option and provide a link to a privacy policy you want to use. In the past, people have used a link that Unity themselves recommended for those using Unity Analytics and Ads (`https://unity3d.com/legal/privacy-policy`), but Google has recently changed their policy, and now your organization or app's name needs to be included in the policy.

    The safest option is to hire a lawyer to draft a privacy policy for your app, but if you wish you create your own privacy policy, this site can help you create the materials: `https://letsmakeagame.net/game-privacy-policy-generator/`. In my case, I checked the **Facebook** and **Unity** options in the included links to the privacy policy of the **Third Party Services** section, and then I filled in the needed data. Once completed, hit the **Generate** button, and you'll have the boilerplate data needed for your own privacy policy to then host on your own web page.

11. Next, go to **App access**, then select **All functionality is available without special access**, and press **Save**.

12. Under **Ads**, select **Yes, my app contains ads**, and select **Save**.

13. Go to **Content ratings**, select **Start new questionnaire**, and answer the questions based on your game.

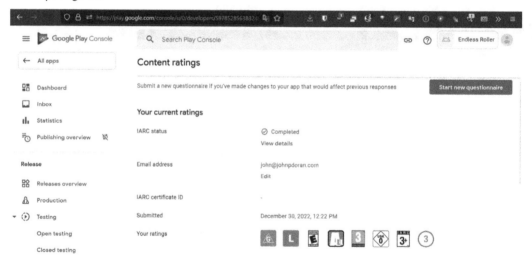

Figure 14.14 – Content ratings

14. Next, you'll answer questions about your target audience and content. Note that if you say your audience contains children aged 13 and under, there are several other questions that you will need to answer. Previously, we said the game wasn't, so I checked the other ages above

    In the next sections, you'll confirm that your game is not a news app or a COVID-19 contact tracing or status app.

15. Next, in the **Data Safety** section, you'll need to go through each of the pages and answer the given questions.

    For the data safety requirements for the different areas of Unity Gaming Services, you can use the following link: `https://docs.unity.com/ugs-overview/GoogleDataSafety.html`. In our project, we use In-App Purchasing, Ads Monetization, Remote Config, and Analytics. We will need to go through all three of these options and ensure that we pick the correct options for each. Note that just because something is shared one way by one product doesn't mean it is shared another way by another.

16. In the **Data Collection and security** section, I answered **Yes, Yes, My app does not allow users to create an account**, and **No**.

17. Under **Data Types**, check the **Approximate location** option.

18. Under **Personal Info**, check **User IDs**. Analytics can track more, but we will not enable them.

19. Under **Financial Info**, check **Purchase History**.

20. Finally, under **Device or other IDs,** check **Device or other IDs**. Then, click the **Next** button.

21. For each of these values, we will need to click on the arrow to answer questions about them. For **User IDs**, mark that the property is **Collected** and **Shared**, that it is **not processed ephemerally**, **Data collection is required**, and its purpose for collection and sharing is for **App functionality**. Then, hit the **Save** button.

22. For **Purchase history**, check that is it **Collected** and **Shared**, that it is **not processed ephemerally**, **Data collection is required**, and its purpose for collection and sharing is for **App functionality**. Then, hit the **Save** button.

23. For **Approximate location**, check that is it **Collected** and **Shared**, that it is **not processed ephemerally**, **Data collection is required**, and its purpose for collection and sharing is for **App functionality**. Then hit the **Save** button.

24. For **Device or other IDs**, check that it is **Collected**, check the **Yes, this collected data is processed ephemerally** and **Data collection is required (users can't turn off this data collection)** options, and then confirm that the data is collected for **App functionality**. Afterward, hit the **Save** button. Then, you should be able to hit the **Next** button.

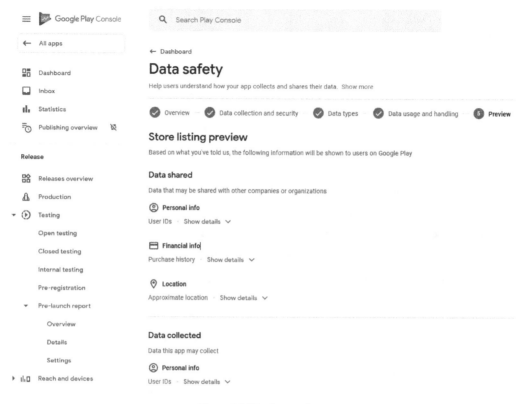

Figure 14.15 – Data safety

25. If everything looks good, go ahead and hit the **Save** button, and you can then return to the dashboard.

26. Next, select the **Government** apps section, answer **No**, and hit **Save**.

27. Then, in the **Manage how your app is organized and presented** section, click on the **Select an app category and provide contact details** option.

28. From here, you'd select whether the game is an app or a game; **Game** was preselected for me. Then, you can select a category (I picked Arcade). You can then use tags to help describe the content of your game. This is a way to help people define your app and one way that can help people to discover the project through certain keywords, so think about the things that make your game unique and ensure to include them here. Under each tag, there is a question mark that you can click on to get info about them, helping you if you're unsure what they are. In the end, I settled for Arcade, Casual, Hyper-casual, Runner. When you're done, hit **Apply**.

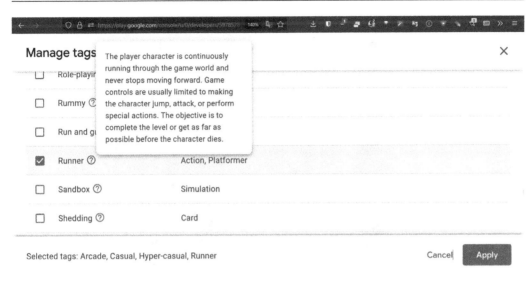

Figure 14.16 – Manage tags

29. Then, fill out your store listing contact details. Note that the information is shown to users on Google Play, so I wouldn't add your personal phone number. Once finished, hit the **Save** button and return to the dashboard **Dashboard**.

30. Finally, click on the **Set up your store listing** option. Scrolling down, you'll then be brought to a section where you'll need to fill in information about your game, starting with a short description and then a more detailed full description:

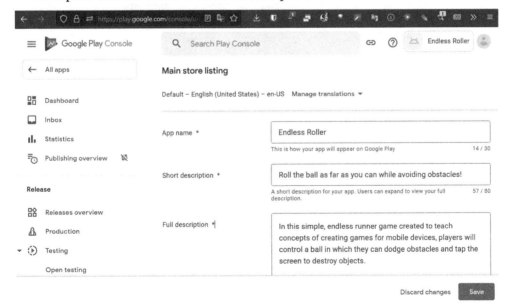

Figure 14.17 – Creating a main store listing

31. You'll then need to provide graphical assets to be used to display your game. You are required to have at least two screenshots and then some additional icons and graphics:

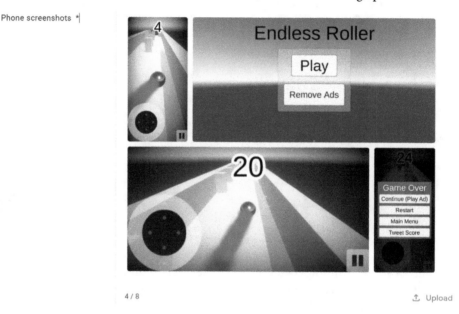

Figure 14.18 – Adding phone screenshots

32. You'll then need to include some more images for icons and other featured graphics. The ones with an asterisk (*) are required. You can find some pre-created ones in the example code with this book, but I suggest that you create your own once you've customized this game to your liking:

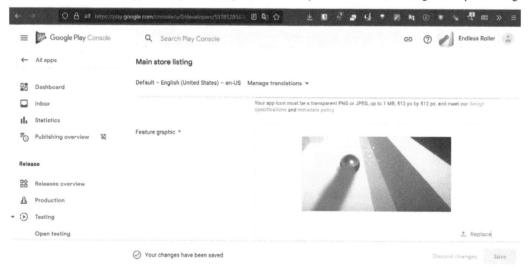

Figure 14.19 – Finishing the main store listing

33. When you're finished, hit the **Save** button and return to the dashboard.

34. At this point, you've been through most of the hurdles of the Google Play development process. You can now choose to go to the **Release your app** section and jump to the **Publish your app on Google Play** section, create a new build and roll out the release to the world, or go through an alpha and beta phase of your project first to get valuable feedback and iterate on your project to make a better first impression. Either way, the process will be the same as what you did in the previous steps, aside from selecting what countries and regions you want the project to be available in and what you want to charge for the game.

With these steps finished, we can now start the process of publishing on Apple's iOS App Store, which we will be doing next.

Putting your game on the Apple iOS App Store

Just like the Google Play store, there is an additional fee to put your game on the App Store. Unlike the Google Play store, the fee is $99 plus tax every year. However, a lot of people believe that having their titles on iOS devices is worth the extra cost. In this section, we will go through the process of getting our game on the App Store. We will start by setting up your Apple Developer account and creating a provisioning profile. Afterward, we'll utilize the iTunes Connect tool to actually add the app to the store and utilize Xcode to make an archive, with which we can upload the project to the App Store so that it can finally be reviewed for submission.

Apple Developer setup and creating a provisioning profile

In order to deploy an app onto an iOS device, you are required to use a Mac computer, but before we move on to the iTunes store, we first need to have all of the certificates and permissions figured out in advance.

Implement the following steps:

1. On a Mac computer, go to `developer.apple.com`:

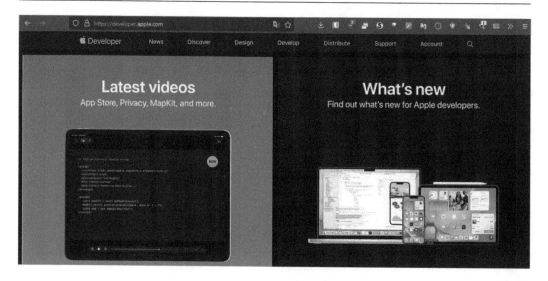

Figure 14.20 – The Apple Developer site

2. From there, click on the **Account** button at the top right of the screen, fill in your Apple ID and password, and then press *Enter* to sign in:

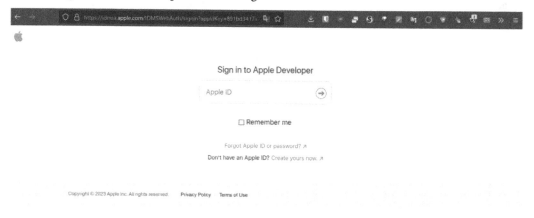

Figure 14.21 – Sign in to Apple Developer

If you have a two-factor identification method set up, you may need to verify that you are indeed yourself.

3. From there, click on **Accounts**. Now, at this point, you will need to make the payment for the $99 annual fee. This process should be fairly straightforward, and once you have finished doing that, you will arrive on a page similar to the following:

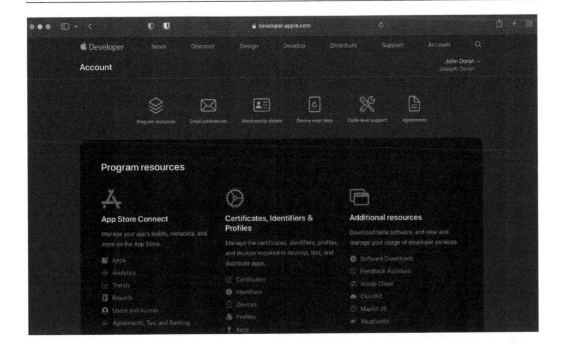

Figure 14.22 – The Apple Developer Account Page

4. In the **Certificates, Identifiers & Profiles** section, select the **Certificates** section to start the process of creating apps. If you just paid the $99 fee, you may see an error stating that **The selected team does not have a program membership that is eligible for this feature**.

    Don't worry – that just means that the payment hasn't been processed at Apple's end yet. Try again in about 30 minutes to an hour, and the screen should work okay.

5. We will need to set up some certificates to allow us to export to the iOS App Store. From the **Certificates** page, click on the + button on the right side of **Certificates**:

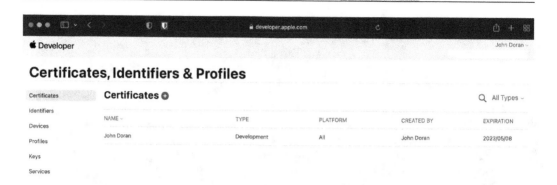

Figure 14.23 – The Certificates page

6. When the page asks what kind of certificate we need, select the **Apple Distribution** option under the **Software** section, and then click on **Continue**:

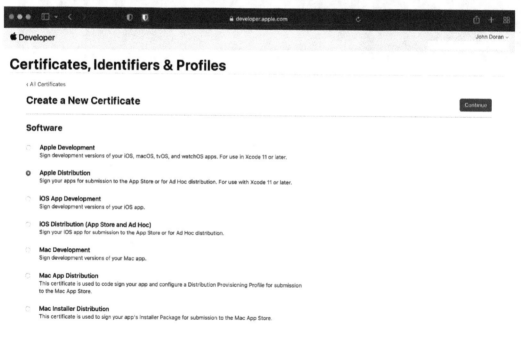

Figure 14.24 – Selecting the certificate type

You may notice that there's another type here that also says that there is an iOS distribution type as well. You might be wondering why we aren't picking that one. As of Xcode 11, this is the new type of certificate that Apple wants developers to use for devices that aim to go on the App Store.

At the time of writing, if you are only planning on developing for iOS, you can choose **iOS Distribution** instead. However, due to the possibility that Apple may discontinue it in the future, I am choosing **Apple Distribution** instead.

7.   Next, we need to create a **Certificate Signing Request (CSR)**. You'll be brought to a page that goes through the process of creating one, but, in our case, we will start off by opening the `Applications\Utilities` folder on our Mac and opening the **Keychain Access** program.

8.   From there, go to **Keychain Access | Certificate Assistant | Request a Certificate From a Certificate Authority...**:

Figure 14.25 – Requesting a certificate

9.   Once there, fill in the information with your email address in the **User Email Address** property. Then, for **Common Name**, put in a name, and leave the **CA Email Address** field blank. Then, for the **Request is** option, select **Saved to disk**:

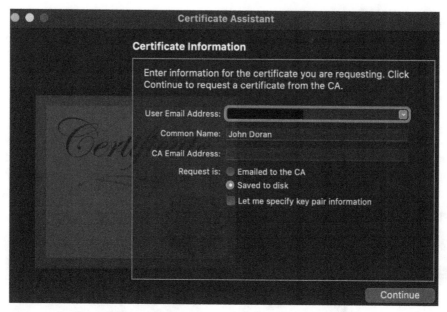

Figure 14.26 – Filling in our certificate information

4.   Then, click on the **Continue** button and select a spot to save the certificate. I personally used my desktop, but you can use any location you please, so long as you remember where it is later on:

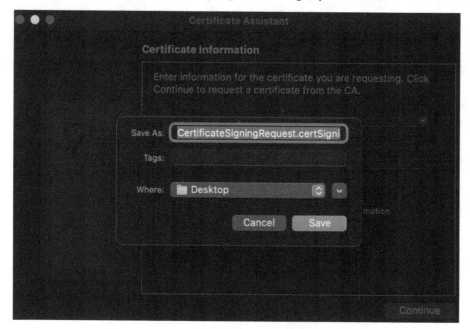

Figure 14.27 – Saving the certificate

5. Afterward, the screen will state that the request has been created on the disk. Go ahead and click on **Done**, and then return to your web browser.

6. Scroll down and then click on the **Continue** button. From there, you'll be brought to the **Generate your certificate** page. Click on the **Choose File** button and then select the file we just created. Then, click on the **Continue** button:

Figure 14.28 – Uploading the certificate

7. You'll then be brought to a screen saying that your certificate is ready. Go ahead and click on the **Download** button, and save the certificate to your disk. If using Safari, you may be asked whether you want to allow downloads; click on **Allow**:

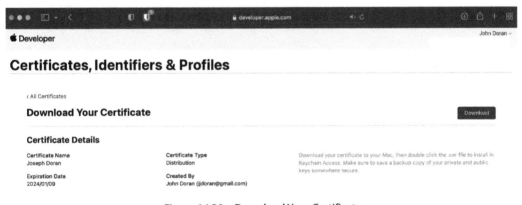

Figure 14.29 – Download Your Certificate

8. Afterward, double-click on the `.cer` file to give the data access to **Keychain**. Under **Keychain**, change the value to **login**. You'll be asked whether you want to add the certificates; go ahead and click on **Add**:

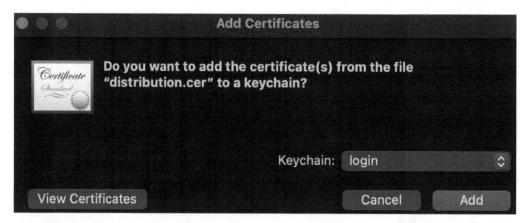

Figure 14.30 – Adding certificates to a keychain

9. The next step is to create an App ID. To do this, go to the left sidebar and click on the **Identifiers** section. I currently have some identifiers (previously referred to as App IDs) listed here already, due to Xcode opening our `Endless Roller` project, which we can customize by clicking on the **Edit** button. However, if you didn't do so earlier and have a different bundle ID than the ones listed, let's go through the details next:

Figure 14.31 – A list of identifiers

10. We can create a new ID by clicking on the + button in the top-right corner of the screen.

11. From there, select **App**, and then under **App ID Description**, put in the name of your game – in my case, I used `Endless Roller`. Then, under **App ID Suffix**, enter the bundle ID that's identical to the one that is used in Unity. In my case, it was `com.JohnPDoran. EndlessRoller`. Under **App Services**, you can select the options that want to use, but in this case, we don't need to worry about these, so we can just scroll all the way down and then click on the **Continue** button.

In this case, the bundle I mentioned previously would not work, due to there already being an ID with this specific bundle, and you need to have unique ones. With that in mind, I just went and renamed the original App ID to Endless Roller and then completed this section.

The last aspect we will need to set up here is a provisioning profile. Apple defines a provisioning profile as "a collection of digital entities that uniquely ties developers and devices to an authorized iPhone Development Team and enables a device to be used for testing." This means that it's a link between a device and the developer account that makes the project.

> **Important note**
>
> For more information on provisioning profiles, check out `https://medium.com/@alexi.schreier/wtf-is-a-provisioning-profile-on-ios-a9b65d79221f`.

12. To do this, click on the **Profiles** section on the left side of the menu. From there, click on the blue + icon to the right of **Profiles**. Under **Distribution**, select the **App Store**, and then click on **Continue**:

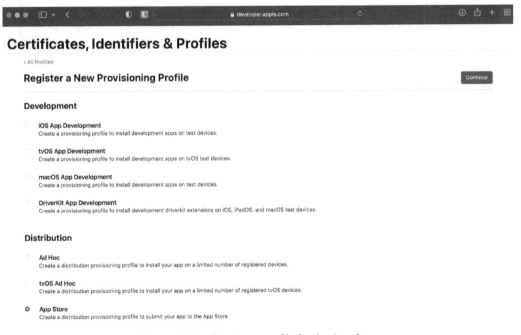

Figure 14.32 – Creating a profile for the App Store

13. From there, you'll need to select your App ID. Endless Roller may be selected; otherwise, search for it in the drop-down list and select it, and then click on **Continue**.

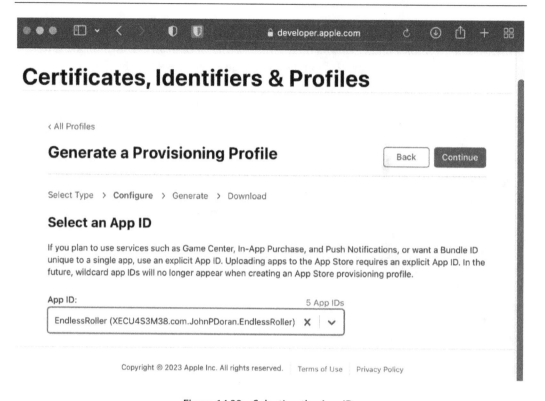

Figure 14.33 – Selecting the App ID

14. Then, select your certificate and click on **Continue**.

15. Then, select what certificate you want to use and hit **Continue**. Finally, we will need to add a profile name – I'll use Endless Roller – and then click on **Generate**:

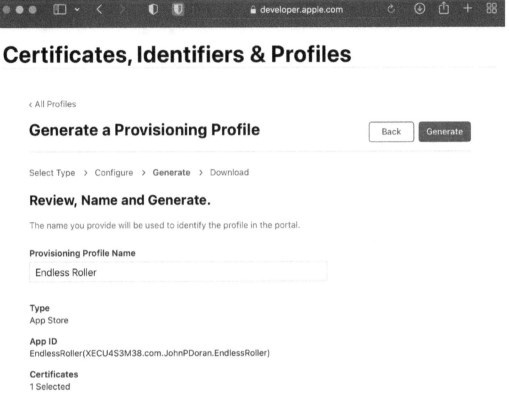

Figure 14.34 – Generating a provisioning profile

16. The button will then change to say **Download**. Go ahead and download the profile, keeping it safe, as we'll need to use it later:

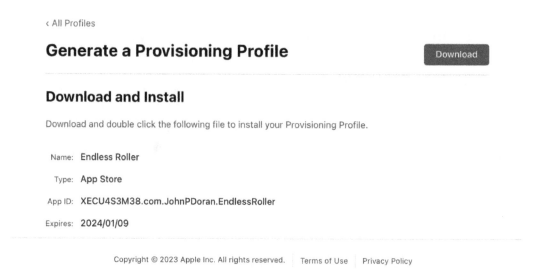

Figure 14.35 – The provisioning profile is ready

With that, our provisioning profile is ready.

Adding an app to App Store Connect

Now that we have the provisioning profile, we can actually put our app on the store. To do that, perform the following steps:

1. In your web browser, go to http://appstoreconnect.apple.com and click on the **My Apps** button:

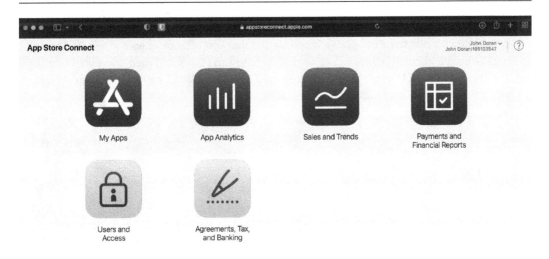

Figure 14.36 – App Store Connect

If you intend to sell your apps, you will also be required to go to the **Agreements, Tax, and Banking** section and enter your banking information.

2. From the **Apps** page, go to the top-left corner, and click on the + icon to add a new app to our profile by selecting **New App**:

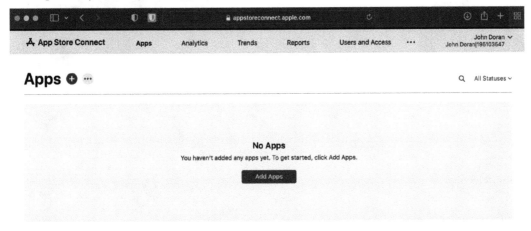

Figure 14.37 – The Apps page

3.   On this menu, select **iOS** as your platform, and insert the name of your game under **Name**. Apple requires each name to be unique, so keep in mind that you will not be able to use Endless Roller again. Under **Primary Language**, select **English (U.S.)**, and then select your bundle ID. Then, under **SKU**, enter an identifier (I used EndlessRoller). Under **User Access**, select **Full Access**. Then, click on the **Create** button:

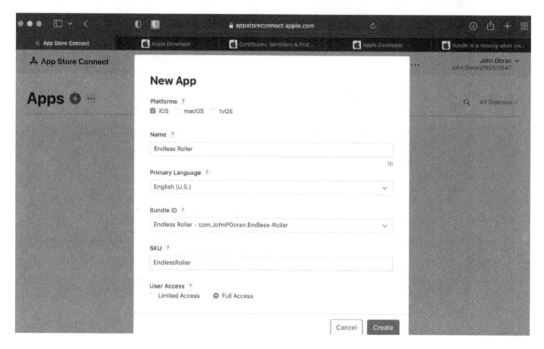

Figure 14.38 – Creating a new app

4. You'll then be brought to the **1.0 Prepare for Submission** screen. Start filling in the information for the title. Start off by filling in the **Description** textbox with the information that you used earlier for Google Play. Then, under **Keywords**, enter possible terms that people could search for in order to find your game, and under **Copyright**, go ahead and enter your name.

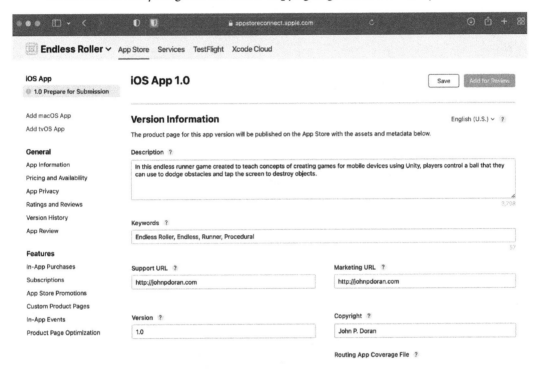

Figure 14.39 – Filling out Version Information

5. Finally, you'll need to provide some screenshots of your game to use. If you click on the **iOS Screenshot Properties** page, you'll see details on how your screenshots should be created (specifically, the size of the images). The one used in this chapter is for the iPhone 6.5" display, but you can also choose for the optional 6.7" one to support the iPhone 14 Pro:

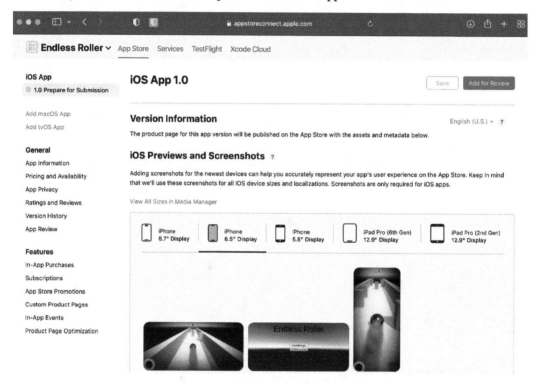

Figure 14.40 – Submitting app screenshots

6. Note that in the **Build** section, it states that you need to submit your build using one of several tools. We will do that after we finish up the remaining steps here.

7. From the **Build** section, go to the **App Information** screen. From there, change the category to **Games**, and then, under **Subcategory**, select **Casual**. Then, click on **Save**:

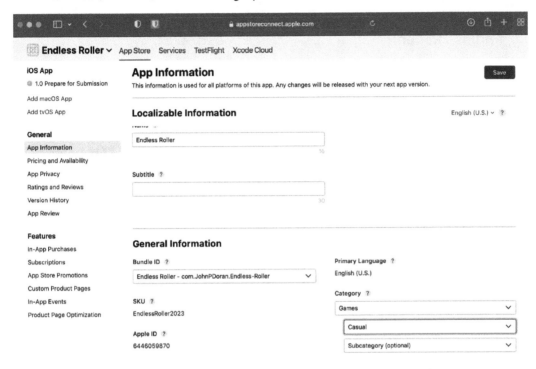

Figure 14.41 – Setting up an app category

8. Go to the **Pricing and Availability** section and select a price. In my case, I'll be using **$0.00 (Free)**, but as always, you can pick what you want. Once you've finished with the options here, click on the **Save** option:

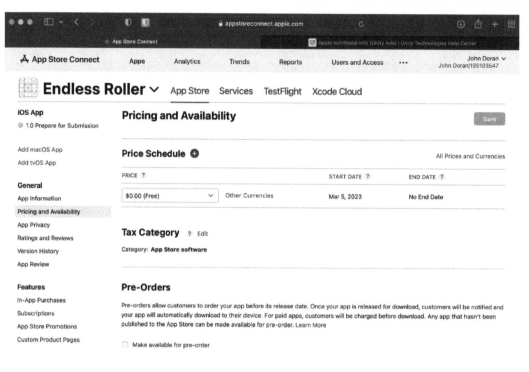

Figure 14.42 – Setting up the pricing and availability

9. Next, go to the **Privacy Policy** section. As discussed in the Google Play section, people in the past used a link that Unity themselves recommended for those using Unity Analytics and Ads (https://unity3d.com/legal/privacy-policy), but the safest option is to hire a lawyer to draft a privacy policy for your app. If you wish you create your own privacy policy, this site can help you create the materials: https://letsmakeagame.net/game-privacy-policy-generator/. In my case, I checked the **Facebook** and **Unity** options in the include links to the privacy policy of the **Third Party Services** section, and then I filled in the necessary data. Once completed, hit the **Generate** button, and you'll have the boilerplate data needed for your own privacy policy to then host.

10. Fill in the **Privacy Policy URL** section, and then click on the **Get Started** button.

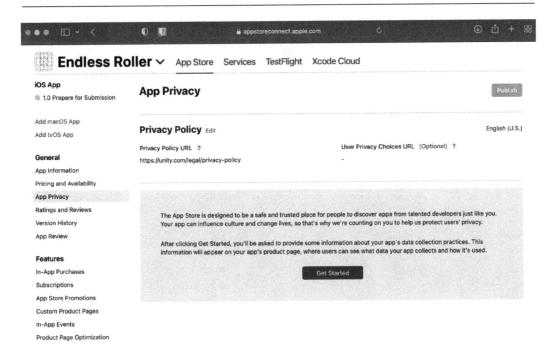

Figure 14.43 – Setting up app privacy

11. Fill out the appropriate answers, based on the types of things your app uses. In our case, since we are using Unity Ads, Analytics, and IAPs (in-app purchases), we will need to go through each of their pages and ensure that we are using all of their info. The following includes the information that I used to fill in the details at my end: `http://documentation.cloud.unity3d.com/en/collections/2654776-apple-privacy-surveys#engage-nutritional-labels`.

12. After completing that information, your **Product Page Preview** screen should look something like this:

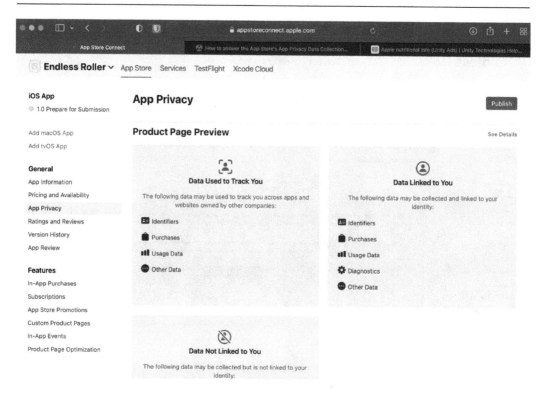

Figure 14.44 – App Privacy completed

13. Once finished, click on the **Publish** button.

14. Once all of the information is filled in, go ahead and open up Xcode again and your exported project (follow the same steps from *Chapter 2, Project Setup for Android and iOS Development*).

15. The addition of the Facebook SDK has added a number of things that we'll have to add to our project in order for it to compile on iOS. Upon switching back to the iOS platform, I got an error saying that CocoaPods failed to install correctly. With that in mind, I had to make the following changes to the project.

16. Switch back to a PC, Mac, and Linux standalone build. From your Mac desktop, open a terminal window and enter the following code – `sudo gem install cocoapods -v 1.10.2`. This will install a stable version of CocoaPods that will work with this version of Unity. Afterward, back in Unity, switch the platform back to iOS and you should see the error go away.

17. In addition, I also updated the Unity JAR resolver by going to `https://github.com/googlesamples/unity-jar-resolver` and downloading the latest release, which, in my case, was the `external-dependency-manager-1.2.175.unitypackage` file.

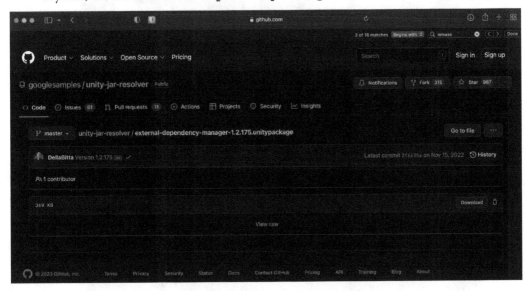

Figure 14.45 – The updated unity-jar-resolver

18. Upon opening the file and importing the files, Unity asked whether I wanted to replace the obsolete libraries, which I accepted by hitting the **Apply** button.

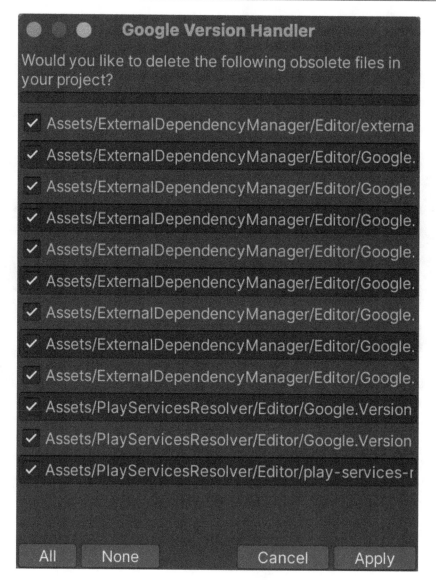

Figure 14.46 – Updating the files

19. Once updated, go to **Assets | External Dependency Manager | iOS Resolver | Settings**. Under **Cocaopods Integration**, change the value to **Xcode Project**.

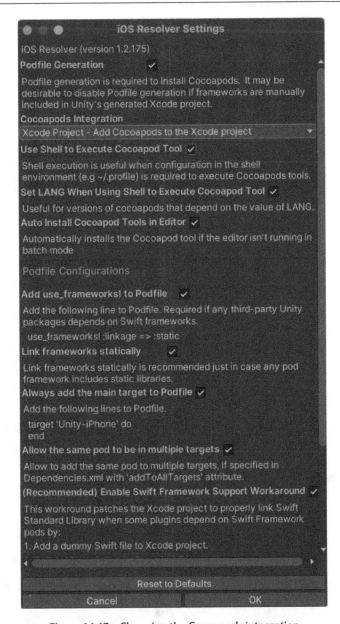

Figure 14.47 – Changing the Cocoapods integration

Using the Facebook SDK, we will no longer be able to open our project using the base project that Unity provides for us, so we will need to instead use the terminal to general a workspace file for us to use.

20. Then, after building the project, open a terminal window at the location of your project. Then, depending on your processor, you may need to enter a different command.

21. If your Mac processor uses an ARM processor (such as the M1), enter the following command – `sudo arch -x86_64 gem install ffi`.

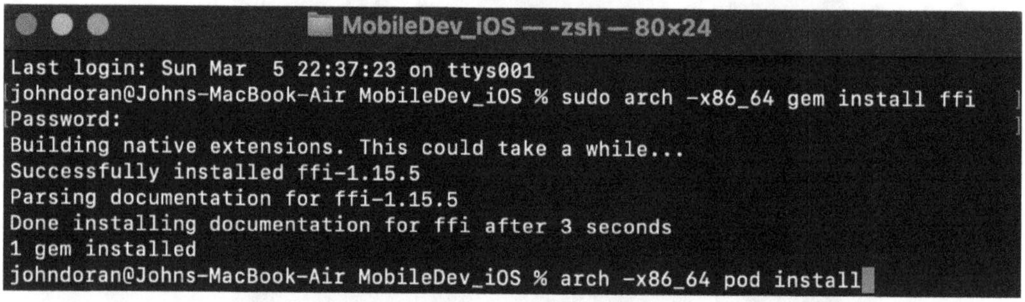

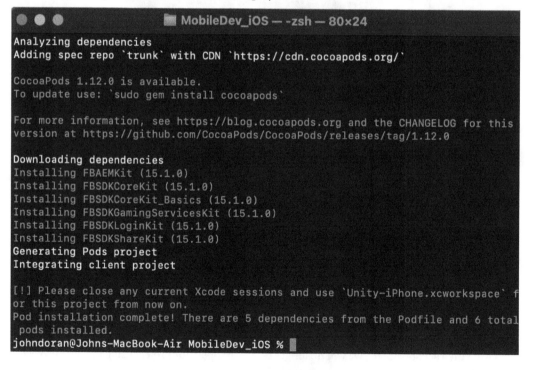

Figure 14.48 – Executing the gem installation

22. This command will only need to be used once. Once the task is completed, enter the following command – `arch -x86_64 pod install`. This command will only need to be executed every time you create a new build of the project.

Figure 14.49 – The completed gem installation

23. If your Mac processor uses an x86 processor (such as an Intel), enter the following command instead – `pod install`.

24. Once the Pod Install is successful, double-click the newly created `Unity-iPhone.xcworkspace` in your project directory to open the workspace in Xcode.

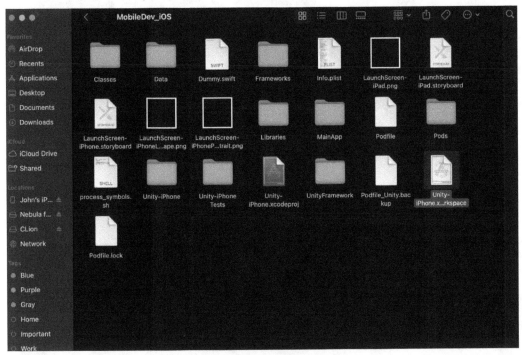

Figure 14.50 – A new workspace file

If you try to run the game now, it will give you an error about a cycle in dependencies between targets. Thankfully, we can fix that once we enter into Xcode ourselves.

25. Once in Xcode, on the far-left menu, select **Unity-iPhone project**, and then on the section to the right of that, under **TARGETS**, select the **UnityFramework** option. From the tabs that show up at the top of the screen, click on **Build Phases**. From there, you should see a series of options. Drag the **Headers** section above the **Compile Sources** section. If all goes well, it should look something like this.

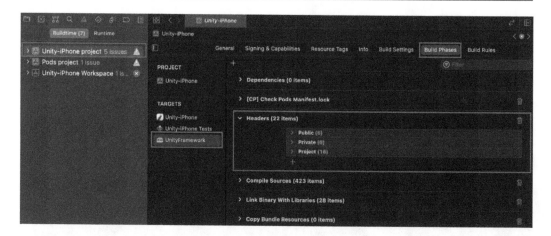

Figure 14.51 – Adjusting the Header order

26. Apple also disallows Framework files to be included, so we will need to stop them from being embedded as well. To do that, go to **Build Phases**, and under **Build Options**, change the **Always Embed Swift Standard Libraries** option to **No**.

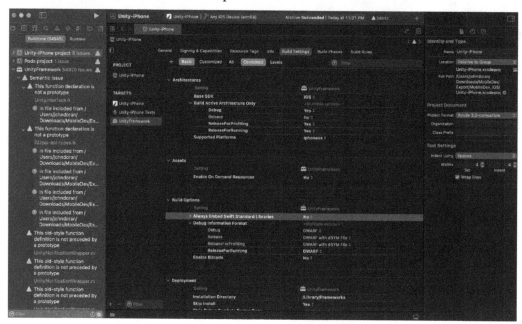

Figure 14.52 – Build Options

27. Once the project has opened in Xcode and exported successfully, go to **Product** | **Archive** and wait for it to finish:

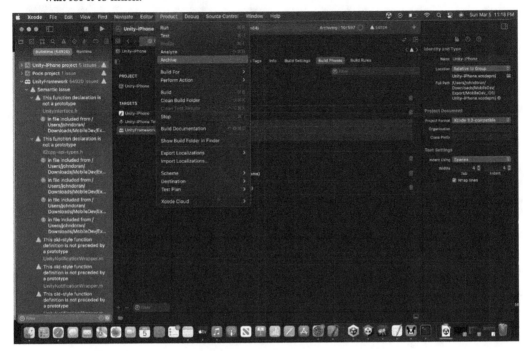

Figure 14.53 – Creating an archive

28. This generally takes a while, so wait for it to complete. You may be asked to use an access key. Go ahead and click on the **Allow** button.

29. Upon finishing, you should be brought to the following menu. Go ahead and select the **Distribute App** button to upload the project to the App Store:

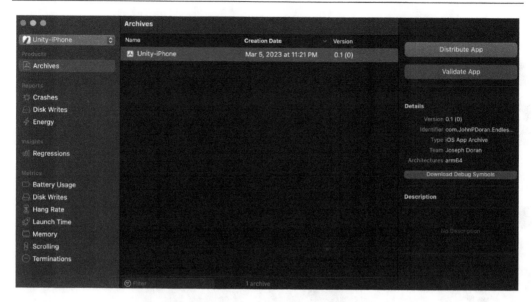

Figure 14.54 – Distributing the app archive

30. You'll be asked to select some options. In general, use the default options, and afterward, it will show you a .ipa file uploaded to the store. Before uploading, it will give you one last look at the information about each aspect of the project. Go ahead and click on the **Upload** button, and wait for it to finish:

Figure 14.55 – Reviewing the .ipa content

When your app has been uploaded, you'll see a screen like the following:

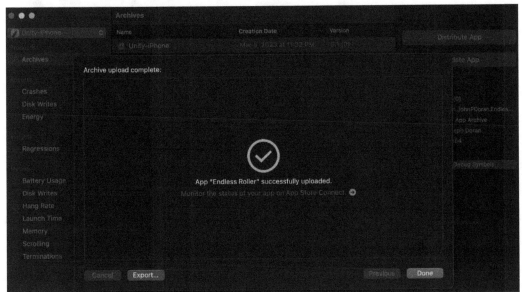

Figure 14.56 – Archive upload complete

However, this will not show up immediately on **App Store Connect**; you may have to wait for a moment (or a couple of hours) before it's updated. However, once it is ready, you'll see it under the build section we mentioned earlier.

31. Once it's uploaded, you should be able to click on the **Select a build** button before you submit your app.

32. From there, select the build we created, and then click on the **Done** button:

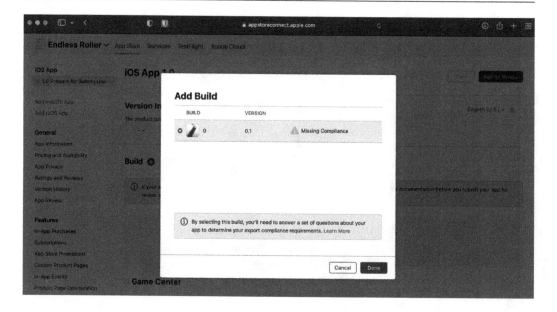

Figure 14.57 – Add Build

33. Note that there is a section that says that it is missing compliance info. Click on the **Manage** button and then enter the appropriate information, depending on what is used in your game. For instance, the use of Unity Analytics and IAPs requires `https` calls. I used standard encryption algorithms and said I wasn't going to make the app available in France.

    For more information on Unity's stance on this, you can look at `https://forum.unity.com/threads/unity-iap-and-export-compliance.742898/` and `https://forum.unity.com/threads/how-to-answer-apples-app-store-new-export-compliance-information-dialogue.1363785/`.

34. Then, click on the **Save** button. Once you're finished with everything and have double-checked all of your information, you can go ahead and click on the **Add for Review** button to wait for feedback from Apple.

Generally, it takes up to 3–4 weeks for first-time developers to receive feedback, although it can be longer or shorter, depending on seasonal demand. As you release more and more titles, it takes less time each time around. If approved, you'll receive an email that lets you know that the app is uploaded, or they may provide details of things that need to be modified before approval for placement on the store can be given.

Summary

In this chapter, you learned how to publish your games on both Google Play and the Apple iOS App Store. You learned how to put the game on Google Play by setting up the Google Play Console and, finally, how to publish your app on the store. You then learned how to put a copy of the iOS version of your game on the App Store and all of the setup involved therein.

I hope that you've enjoyed this exploration of features and that you continue to explore the possibilities of this area. In the next chapter, we will discover one of the newest additions to mobile game development – augmented reality.

15

Augmented Reality

Made popular with Niantic's *Pokemon GO* and on Snapchat filters, **Augmented Reality (AR)** is a way of blending digital elements with the real world. Specifically, it is a technology that superimposes a computer-generated image on a user's view of the real world, hence providing a composite view, meaning that both the real world and then digital elements put on top of it are displayed to the player.

In this chapter, we will explore how to set up our project to utilize AR for both Android and iOS devices and how we can customize them. This project will be a simple AR project in which the player can look at various surfaces in the game environment and spawn objects on top of them. The goal of this chapter will be to explore the basic concepts of AR and see how they can be used in a project.

This chapter will be split into several topics. It will contain a simple, step-by-step process from beginning to end. Here is the outline of our tasks:

- Setting up a project for AR
- Detecting surfaces
- Interacting with the AR environment
- Spawning objects in AR

By the end of this chapter, you will have a good understanding of AR technology and how to create a basic AR project. Whether you're a beginner or an experienced developer, this chapter will provide you with a solid foundation for further exploration and experimentation with AR which should come useful not only for mobile development but also for those looking to get experience with the same technology used in headsets from Meta as well as Apple's Vision Pro.

Technical requirements

This book utilizes Unity 2022.1.0b16 and Unity Hub 3.3.1, but the steps should work with minimal changes in future versions of the editor. If you would like to download the exact version used in this book, and there is a new version out, you can visit Unity's download archive at `https://unity3d.com/get-unity/download/archive`. You can also find the system requirements for Unity at `https://docs.unity3d.com/2022.1/Documentation/Manual/system-requirements.html` in the **Unity Editor system requirements** section. To deploy your project, you will need an Android or iOS device.

You can find the code files present in this chapter on GitHub at `https://github.com/PacktPublishing/Unity-2022-Mobile-Game-Development-3rd-Edition/tree/main/Chapter15`.

Setting up a project for AR

Before we can start adding notifications to our project, we will need to add three packages that Unity makes available to enable AR for both iOS and Android devices. In our case, we are going to be utilizing both ARCore and ARKit to create our project, and the AR Foundation package to act as an intermediary so we can use both ARCore and ARKit while using a similar connection. Since this is a brand new way to create projects, we will actually create a new Unity project to demonstrate how to use it. Please follow the steps given here:

1. To get started, open Unity Hub on your computer.

2. From startup, we'll opt to create a new project by clicking on the **New** button.

3. Next, under **Project Name** put in a name (I have chosen `Mobile AR`), and under **Templates**, make sure that **3D** is selected:

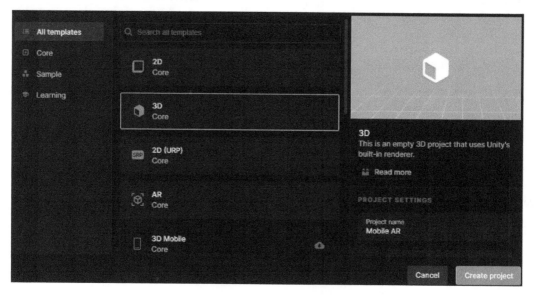

Figure 15.1 – Creating a 3D project

4. Afterward, click on **Create Project** and wait for Unity to load up.

5. From the Unity Editor, go to **Window | Package Manager**.

6. If it hasn't been set already, click on the **In Project** drop-down menu from the toolbar of the **Packages** menu and select **Unity Registry**.

7. From here, go to the search bar in the top right and type in XR. From there, you will need to select either **ARKit XR Plugin** if you want to support iOS devices or **ARCore XR Plugin** for Android, and click **Install**. Afterward, scroll down the available options until you reach **AR Foundation** and select it. Once there, click the **Install** button:

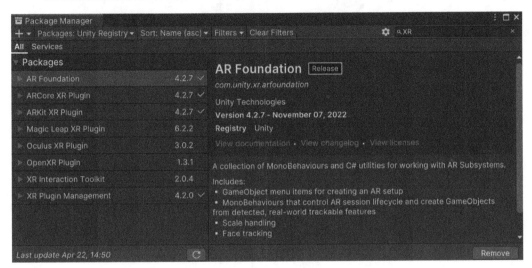

Figure 15.2 – Installing packages

We now have all of the packages we need so we can exit **Package Manager**.

> **Note**
>
> While AR Foundation does most things that you'd want to do with AR, there are a few things that are for iOS or Android only. For more information on what AR Foundation can do and what ARCore and ARKit provide individually, check out https://docs.unity3d.com/ Packages/com.unity.xr.arfoundation@5.0/manual/index.html#platform-support.

8. Next, open up the **Build Settings** menu by going to **File | Build Settings**. From there, change your platform to either **iOS** or **Android** and click on the **Switch Platform** button. Afterward, click on the **Player Settings...** option.

9. Next, complete *step 10* if you are planning on using iOS or *step 11* if you are planning on using Android, or complete both steps if you plan on using both iOS and Android.

10. If you are using iOS, make sure that, in the iOS **Platform Settings** section, the **Requires ARKit support** option is checked as well.

11. For those using Android, go to the Android **Player Settings...** and under **Other Settings**, go to **Rendering** and uncheck the **Auto Graphics API** option. Then, under the **Graphics APIs** section, select the **Vulkan** option and press the − button to remove it from the list. Then, scroll down and uncheck the **Multithreaded Rendering** option.

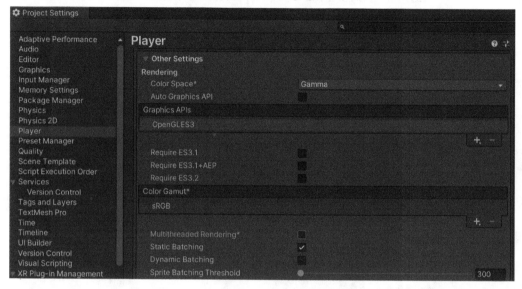

Figure 15.3 – Android Player Settings setup

12. The reason we have to disable this functionality is that, as of the time of writing, it is not compatible with ARCore. You'll also want to set **Minimum API Level** to **Android 7.0 'Nougat' (API level 24)** or higher.

When working on ARCore projects in Unity, it's recommended that you enable the ARM64 target architecture. If your app only supports the 32-bit ARMv7 architecture, it may not work properly on 64-bit devices, and it may not be available for download from the Google Play Store. This is because some 64-bit devices don't support 32-bit ARCore libraries. So, to avoid any issues, it's best to enable the ARM64 target architecture in your Unity project.

Under **Configuration**, set **Scripting Backend** to **IL2CPP**. Next, under **Target Architectures**, enable the **ARM64** option.

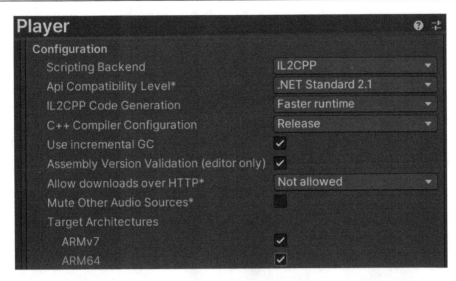

Figure 15.4 – Changing Target Architectures

13. Now, from the **Player Settings...** menu, select the **XR Plugin Management** option, and then, under **Plug-in Providers**, check the **ARCore** field, and for iOS, check the **ARKit** option.

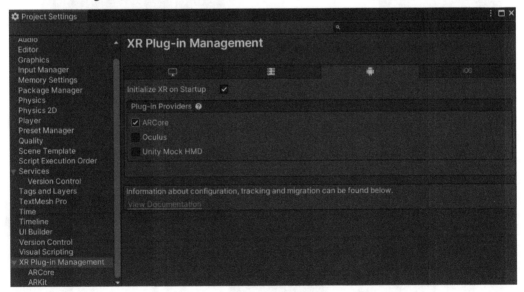

Figure 15.5 – Enabling ARCore

With that, we've taken care of all of the settings needed to support our project and have it export correctly!

Now that we have included AR Foundation, we can now create a basic scene for a VR project.

Basic setup

Since the player can be anywhere when the game starts, we can't use a camera in the traditional sense, so we will start by removing the original one. Follow the steps given here:

1. From the **Hierarchy** panel, select the **Main Camera** object and delete it by right-clicking and selecting **Delete** or pressing the *Delete* key.

    There are two key objects that we will need to create before we can start implementing our own features: **AR Session** and **AR Session Origin**.

2. Right-click in the **Hierarchy** panel and select **XR | AR Session**:

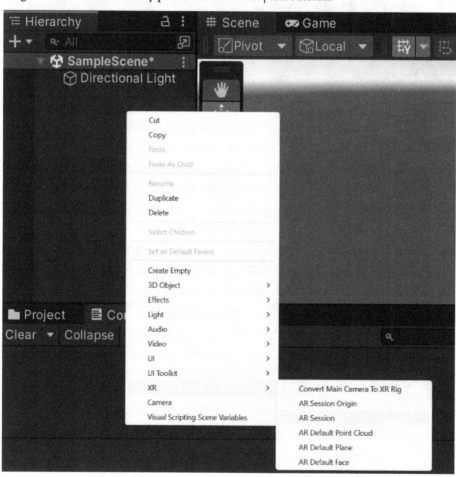

Figure 15.6 – Creating an AR session

AR Session is what controls the life cycle of any AR experience, which allows us to enable or disable AR features depending on the platform we are working on.

> **Note**
>
> **AR Session** is also responsible for telling you whether your device supports AR. For information on handling this, check out `https://docs.unity3d.com/Packages/com.unity.xr.arfoundation@4.2/manual/index.html#checking-for-device-support`.

3. Create an **AR Session Origin** object by right-clicking and selecting **XR | AR Session Origin**.

    AR Session Origin is used to scale and offset virtual content while the game itself is playing. You may notice that the object has a child, **AR Camera**, which is the camera that will follow the game as it is running.

    Before we deploy to the device to ensure everything is working correctly, let's add a cube to our scene so we can see that it is working correctly.

4. Switch to the **Scene** view if you haven't done so already. Then, from the top menu, click on **GameObject | 3D Object | Cube**:

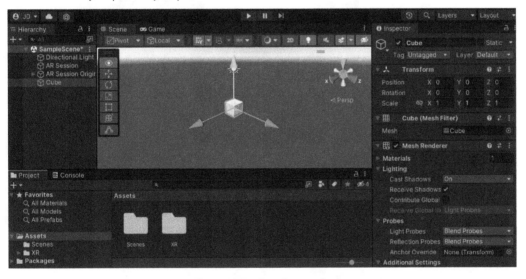

Figure 15.7 – Creating a cube

5. Now, build your project and put the game on the device in the same manner as discussed in *Chapter 2, Project Setup for Android and iOS Development*.

> **Tip**
>
> For iOS users, you may notice when you build the project, it will tell you that the project is lacking a `.xml` file. If this appears, click on the **Yes, fix and build** option when prompted.
>
> For Android users, you may need to install the Google Play Services for AR if it is not installed.

6. Upon running your project, give access to the camera if needed and open the game. Once the project shows your environment, step back as the game starts:

Figure 15.8 – Our first AR result

The reason why we have to step back to see the cube is that the position of all objects is based on the area the phone was physically at when the game started. The cube is also quite large because, at a default scale of 1,1,1, that means that it is 1 meter (or around 3.3 feet) wide on each side in relation to real-sized objects. We obviously don't want to require the user to step back upon starting the game so we will need to keep track of where usable surfaces are in our environment, which is what we will be doing next.

To detect surfaces within our real-world environment, we will need to make use of a new component, **AR Plane Manager**. This component allows us to create, remove, or update GameObjects in our scene based on the surfaces within the real-world environment. The following steps will automatically create invisible planes with colliders that we could possibly use for gameplay reasons:

1. We no longer need the original cube we created, so we can delete it from the scene by right-clicking it and selecting **Delete** or by selecting it and pressing the *Delete* key.

2. From the **Hierarchy** panel, select the **AR Session Origin** object. From there, add the **AR Plane Manager** component to it by clicking on the **Add Component** button at the bottom of the **Inspector** window and then typing in the name of the component and pressing *Enter*.

At this point, we will have surfaces being generated to our scene while being run, but for things such as debugging, it would be a good idea to visually see the planes that are being generated. So, that's what we will do next using the following steps:

1. From the top menu, go to **GameObject | XR | AR Default Plane**.

    This object has several different components that are used in creating a visual plane; of note, are the **AR Plane** and **AR Plane Mesh Visualizer** components. **AR Plane** represents a plane detected by the AR device, and **AR Plane Mesh Visualizer** is in charge of using the data from **AR Plane** to modify the **MeshFilter** and **MeshCollider** components to overlay the detected wall, and the **Line Renderer** component to display the boundaries. The **Mesh Renderer** component will draw the information displayed from these modifications.

2. From the **Project** window, create a new folder called `Prefabs`.

3. Drag and drop the **AR Default Plane** object into the `Prefabs` folder to turn it into a Prefab. If it is done correctly, you should notice the GameObject's text in the **Hierarchy** window is now blue:

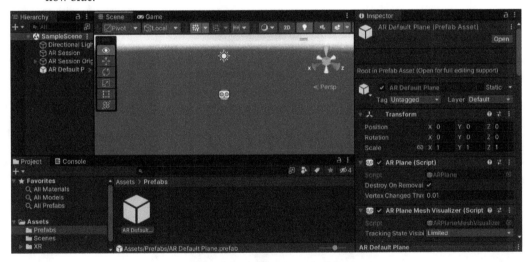

Figure 15.9 – Creating a Prefab

4. Once created, you can delete the **AR Default Plane** object in the **Hierarchy** window.

5. Select the **AR Session Origin** object. Click the **Add Component** button and add an **AR Plane Manager** component. Afterward, drag and drop the **AR Default Plane** Prefab into the **Plane Prefab** property of the **AR Plane Manager** component:

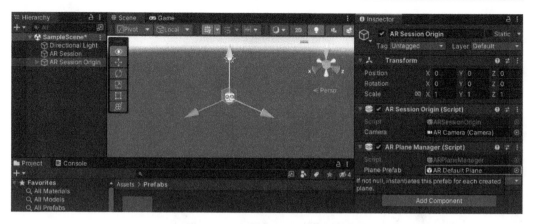

Figure 15.10 – Assigning the Plane Prefab

This will tell **Plane Manager** that, any time it detects a new plane within the scene, it should spawn a Plane Prefab and have it draw the details for it.

6.   Save your project and build your game again. Once it is running on your device, walk around your room, moving the camera as you do so:

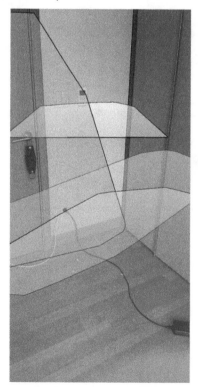

Figure 15.11 – Plane creation in AR

The longer you stay within an area with movement, the longer the phone will have to build a more realistic depiction of the surfaces in your environment.

Feel free to open the Prefab we created and modify how your planes will be visualized!

It's great that we can now see things happening in the game environment, but we currently have no way to actually interact with the world—that is what we will be looking into in the next section.

Interacting with the AR environment

One of the ways that we can have the player interact with the world is by allowing them to spawn objects within the scene to help players see where items will spawn. We can create an indicator to show where they will actually spawn to. Let's look at the steps to do just that:

1. Create a quad using **GameObject | 3D Object | Quad**.

    Quads represent a plane, the simplest type of geometry. In our case, we will use the quad as an indicator to the player where they will be spawning an object if they tap on the screen.

2. With the quad selected, go to the **Inspector** window and go to the **Transform** component and set **Position** to (0,0,0), **X Rotation** to 90, and **Scale** to (0.2,0.2,1).

    We made the quad smaller to be 20 centimeters long and rotated it so it could represent a floor better. We do not want these values to change but we will eventually want to move and rotate this object to follow our player when they move the camera. To protect this data, we can instead create a parent object for it. That way, whenever the parent moves or rotates, the child will move and rotate in the same manner.

3. Create an empty GameObject by selecting **GameObject | Create Empty**. Select the object and rename it Placement Indicator. Then, go to the **Transform** component and set **Position** to (0,0,0).

4. From the **Hierarchy** window, drag and drop the **Quad** GameObject on top of the **Placement Indicator** object to make it a child:

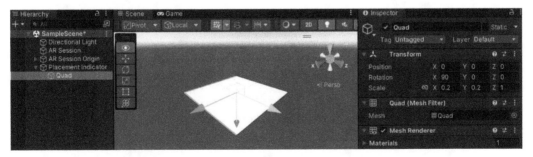

Figure 15.12 – Creating the Placement Indicator object

Now that we have an object to work with, we need some way to figure out where the player's camera is facing so we can move the object. We can do this through the use of a new component, **AR Raycast Manager**.

5. From the **Hierarchy** window, select the **AR Session Origin** object. From there, add the **AR Raycast Manager** component to it.

The **AR Raycast Manager** component exposes the ability to raycast to AR Foundation. This will allow us to perform a Raycast within the physical environment that we are in. A Raycast, also known as hit testing, allows us to create a ray, which is an invisible line that allows us to check whether there is something that collides from its point of origin and direction. This is used oftentimes in games for things such as checking whether a bullet would hit the player.

Now that we have this setup done, let's see how we can work with these components in code and see how we can use the information to place AR objects within real-world spaces using the following steps:

1. Go to the **Project** window and go back to the `Assets` folder. From there, create a new folder called `Scripts`.

2. Go inside the `Scripts` folder and create a new C# script called `PlaceARObject`.

3. At the top of the file, add the following `using` statements:

```
using UnityEngine.XR.ARFoundation; /* ARRaycastManager */
using UnityEngine.XR.ARSubsystems; /* TrackableType */
```

4. Add the following properties to the class:

```
/// <summary>
/// A reference to the Raycast Manager for being able
/// to perform raycasts
/// </summary>
ARRaycastManager raycastManager;

/// <summary>
/// A reference to the AR camera to know where to draw
/// raycasts from
/// </summary> Camera arCamera;
```

5. Then, we need to initialize the properties in the `Start` function:

```
/// <summary>
/// Start is called before the first frame update.
/// Initialize our private variables
/// </summary>
void Start()
{
    raycastManager = GameObject.FindObjectOfType
```

```
        <ARRaycastManager>();
    arCamera = GameObject.FindObjectOfType<Camera>();
}
```

6. Finally, we need to replace our `Update` function and use `LateUpdate` instead:

```
/// <summary>
/// LateUpdate is called once per frame after all
/// Update functions have been called
/// </summary>
private void LateUpdate()
{
    /* Figure out where the center of the screen is */
    var viewportCenter = new Vector2(0.5f, 0.5f);
    var screenCenter =
        arCamera.ViewportToScreenPoint(viewportCenter);

    /* Check if there is something in front of the
        center of the screen and update the placement
        indicator if needed */
    UpdateIndicator(screenCenter);
}
```

7. In the preceding snippet, we are using an `UpdateIndicator` function that currently doesn't exist, so let's add that next:

```
/// <summary>
/// Will update the placement indicator's position and
/// rotation to be on the floor of any plane surface
/// </summary>
/// <param name="screenPosition">A position in screen
/// space</param>
private void UpdateIndicator(Vector2 screenPosition)
{
    var hits = new List<ARRaycastHit>();

    raycastManager.Raycast(screenPosition,
        hits, TrackableType.Planes);

    /* If there is at least one hit position */
    if (hits.Count > 0)
    {
        // Get the pose data
        var placementPose = hits[0].pose;
```

```
var camForward = arCamera.transform.forward;

/* We want the object to be flat */
camForward.y = 0;

/* Scale the vector be have a size of 1 */
camForward = camForward.normalized;

/* Rotate to face in front of the camera */
placementPose.rotation =
    Quaternion.LookRotation(camForward);

transform.SetPositionAndRotation
    (placementPose.position,
        placementPose.rotation);
    }
}
```

8. Save the script and return to the Unity Editor. Attach the `PlaceARObject` script to the **Placement Indicator** GameObject.

9. Export your game to your device of choice and verify that it is working:

Figure 15.13 – Placement Indicator in AR

As you can see, the plane will now move and rotate so that it is always facing us! You may notice the plane has a flickery texture. This is due to the z-fighting concept we discussed previously in *Chapter 4, Resolution-Independent UI*. Basically, both objects have the same position so it's up to Unity to decide what order to draw them in. We can fix this by placing the quad slightly above the plane's position, which we will do now.

10. Update the `UpdateIndicator` function to use the following code at the end:

```
/* Rotate to face in front of the camera */
placementPose.rotation =
    Quaternion.LookRotation(camForward);

/* Move the quad slightly above the floor to
    avoid z-fighting */
var newPosition = placementPose.position;
newPosition.y += 0.001f;

transform.SetPositionAndRotation(newPosition,
    placementPose.rotation);

    }
}
```

11. Save the script and export the game again. As you can see, now the quad is placed cleanly above the given surface:

Figure 15.14 – Adjusted Placement Indicator

Now that we have an indicator of sorts, let's make it so we can actually spawn an object in AR.

Spawning objects in AR

The simplest way to spawn an object in AR would be to make it so that when the player taps on the screen, it will spawn an object where our **Placement Indicator** object is. But before we do that, we first need to make an object that we'd want to create within the scene.

Follow the steps given here:

1. Create a sphere by going to **GameObject** | **3D Object** | **Sphere**.

2. From the **Inspector** window, set **Position** to (0, 0, 0) and set **Scale** to (0.2, 0.2, 0.2).

3. Add a **Rigidbody** component to the sphere by going to **Component** | **Physics** | **Rigidbody**.

    By adding the **Rigidbody** component, we are letting Unity know that we want this object to be affected by things such as gravity and react to collision events and forces being applied to it. At this point, you could customize the object as much as you'd like, change the mesh and collider, and so on.

4. Go to the **Project** window, and open the Prefabs folder. Create a Prefab of our sphere by dragging and dropping it from the **Hierarchy** window to the **Project** window:

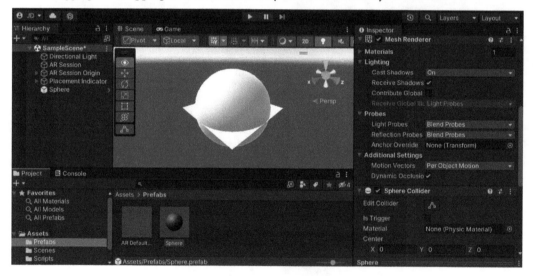

Figure 15.15 – Creating a 3D object to spawn

5. Now that the object is a Prefab, we can delete it from the **Hierarchy** window.

6. Open the PlaceARObject script and add the following property to it:

    ```
    [Tooltip("The object to spawn when the screen is tapped")]
    public GameObject objectToSpawn;
    ```

7. Then, update the `LateUpdate` function to the following:

```
/// <summary>
/// LateUpdate is called once per frame after all
/// Update functions have been called
/// </summary>
private void LateUpdate()
{
    /* Figure out where the center of the screen
       is */
    var viewportCenter = new Vector2(0.5f, 0.5f);
    var screenCenter =
        arCamera.ViewportToScreenPoint(
            viewportCenter);

    /* Check if there is something in front of the
       center of the screen and update the
       placement indicator if needed */
    UpdateIndicator(screenCenter);

    /* If we tap on the screen, spawn an object */
    if (Input.GetMouseButtonDown(0))
    {
        /* Spawn the object above the floor to see
           it fall */
        Vector3 objPos = transform.position +
            Vector3.up;

        if (objectToSpawn)
        {
            Instantiate(objectToSpawn, objPos,
                transform.rotation);
        }
    }

}
```

8. Save the script and return to the Unity Editor.

9. From the **Hierarchy** window, select the **Placement Indicator** object. From the **Inspector** window, set the **Object To Spawn** property to our **Sphere** Prefab:

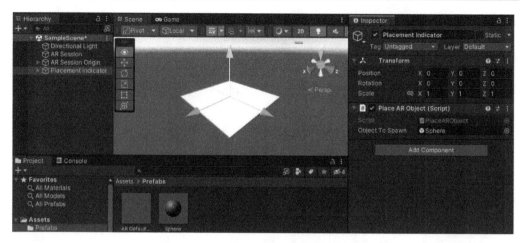

Figure 15.16 – Setting the object to spawn

10. Save your project and build it to your device, and tap the screen to have spheres spawn onto the screen:

Figure 15.17 – Objects spawning in our AR environment

As you can see, we can now spawn objects into our scene, and we can see them interact with each other correctly! Taking this further, you can create whatever type of gameplay experience you'd like!

Summary

Throughout this chapter, you have learned how to utilize Unity's AR toolsets to augment reality by adding artificial computer-generated objects into the real world. This new and growing technology is still being developed, and the skills gained from working in it will likely grow in importance in the future as things such as **Virtual Reality (VR)**, **Mixed Reality (MR)**, and other forms of **Extended Reality (XR)** become more and more commonplace.

In this chapter, you learned how to install ARKit for iOS, ARCore for Android, and AR Foundation for a multiplatform AR solution. Once installed, you learned how to set the platform settings for both iOS and Android AR development. Afterward, we did the basic setup to have Unity use its AR tools to allow users to add a simple mesh to the environment. We then built upon that to detect surfaces within the real world using the AR Plane Manager and learned how to visualize it by using the AR Default Plane object. We then learned how to interact with the AR environment using the AR Raycast Manager to detect when we hit the meshes within the real world and have objects in the computer-generated world react to it. Finally, we saw how to spawn objects in AR using this information.

> Tip
>
> In addition to AR Foundation, ARCore, and ARKit, there are several other frameworks and plugins available for adding AR to Unity apps.
>
> If your project requires specific functionalities beyond what Unity provides, alternative frameworks can offer the necessary tools or better support and performance for your specific use case. For example, Vuforia (`https://www.ptc.com/en/products/vuforia`) is known for its robust marker-based tracking, while Wikitude (`https://www.wikitude.com/download-wikitude-sdk-for-unity/`) specializes in location-based AR experiences.
>
> Ultimately, the choice of AR framework depends on factors such as platform support, required features, developer expertise, and project-specific needs. It's essential to evaluate the strengths and limitations of each framework to select the one that best aligns with your goals and requirements.

This should give you all of the information you need to start experimenting on your own and see whether you can create your own games for both mobile devices and games within an AR environment. So, go forth and use the knowledge from this book to make your games the best they can be and I look forward to playing them!

Index

www.packtpub.com

Subscribe to our online digital library for full access to over 7,000 books and videos, as well as industry leading tools to help you plan your personal development and advance your career. For more information, please visit our website.

Why subscribe?

- Spend less time learning and more time coding with practical eBooks and Videos from over 4,000 industry professionals

- Improve your learning with Skill Plans built especially for you

- Get a free eBook or video every month

- Fully searchable for easy access to vital information

- Copy and paste, print, and bookmark content

Did you know that Packt offers eBook versions of every book published, with PDF and ePub files available? You can upgrade to the eBook version at packtpub.com and as a print book customer, you are entitled to a discount on the eBook copy. Get in touch with us at customercare@packtpub.com for more details.

At www.packtpub.com, you can also read a collection of free technical articles, sign up for a range of free newsletters, and receive exclusive discounts and offers on Packt books and eBooks.

Other Books You May Enjoy

If you enjoyed this book, you may be interested in these other books by Packt:

Learning C# by Developing Games with Unity - Seventh Edition

Harrison Ferrone

ISBN: 978-1-83763-687-7

- Understanding programming fundamentals by breaking them down into their basic parts

- Comprehensive explanations with sample codes of object-oriented programming and how it applies to C#

- Follow simple steps and examples to create and implement C# scripts in Unity

- Divide your code into pluggable building blocks using interfaces, abstract classes, and class extensions

- Grasp the basics of a game design document and then move on to blocking out your level geometry, adding lighting and a simple object animation

- Create basic game mechanics such as player controllers and shooting projectiles using C#

- Become familiar with stacks, queues, exceptions, error handling, and other core C# concepts

- Learn how to handle text, XML, and JSON data to save and load your game data

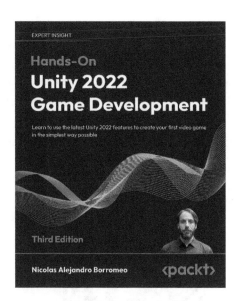

Hands-On Unity 2022 Game Development - Third Edition

Nicolas Alejandro Borromeo

ISBN: 978-1-80323-691-9

- Build a game prototype that includes gameplay, player and non-player characters, assets, animations, and more

- Set up and navigate the game engine to dive into the Unity Editor and discover unique and new features released in 2022

- Learn both C# and Visual Scripting to customize player movements, the user interface, and game physics

- Apply shaders to improve your game graphics using Shader Graph and Universal Render Pipeline (URP)

- Create win-lose conditions for the game by using design patterns such as Singleton and Event Listeners

- Implement Game AI to build a fully functional enemy capable of detecting and attacking the player

- Debug, test, optimize, and create an executable version of the game to share with your friends

Packt is searching for authors like you

If you're interested in becoming an author for Packt, please visit `authors.packtpub.com` and apply today. We have worked with thousands of developers and tech professionals, just like you, to help them share their insight with the global tech community. You can make a general application, apply for a specific hot topic that we are recruiting an author for, or submit your own idea.

Hi!

I am John P. Doran, the author of *Unity 2022 Mobile Game Development*. I sincerely hope that your experience of reading this book was enjoyable and that it proved valuable in enhancing your productivity and efficiency when developing games on mobile devices using Unity.

I kindly request you to consider leaving a review on Amazon, where you can share your thoughts on the book. Your feedback is not only crucial to me, but also to potential readers and will greatly assist.

Go to the link below or scan the QR code to leave your review:

`https://packt.link/r/180461372X`

Your review will help us to understand what's worked well in this book, and what could be improved upon for future editions, so it really is appreciated.

Best wishes,

John P. Doran

Download a free PDF copy of this book

Thanks for purchasing this book!

Do you like to read on the go but are unable to carry your print books everywhere?

Is your eBook purchase not compatible with the device of your choice?

Don't worry, now with every Packt book you get a DRM-free PDF version of that book at no cost.

Read anywhere, any place, on any device. Search, copy, and paste code from your favorite technical books directly into your application.

The perks don't stop there, you can get exclusive access to discounts, newsletters, and great free content in your inbox daily

Follow these simple steps to get the benefits:

1. Scan the QR code or visit the link below

https://packt.link/free-ebook/9781804613726

2. Submit your proof of purchase
3. That's it! We'll send your free PDF and other benefits to your email directly

Printed in the USA
CPSIA information can be obtained
at www.ICGtesting.com
LVHW071821180224
772142LV00007B/591